Representative American Speeches 2003–2004

Editors

Calvin M. Logue, Ph.D.,

Lynn M. Messina, Ph.D.,

and

Jean DeHart, Ph.D.

The Reference Shelf
Volume 76 • Number 6

The H.W. Wilson Company
2004

The Reference Shelf

The books in this series contain reprints of articles, excerpts from books, addresses on current issues, and studies of social trends in the United States and other countries. There are six separately bound numbers in each volume, all of which are usually published in the same calendar year. Numbers one through five are each devoted to a single subject, providing background information and discussion from various points of view and concluding with a subject index and comprehensive bibliography that lists books, pamphlets, and abstracts of additional articles on the subject. The final number of each volume is a collection of recent speeches, and it contains a cumulative speaker index. Books in the series may be purchased individually or on subscription.

Library of Congress has cataloged this serial title as follows:

Representative American speeches. 1937 / 38–
    New York, H. W. Wilson Co.™
        v. 21 cm.—The Reference Shelf
Annual
Indexes:
    Author index: 1937/38–1959/60, with 1959/60;
    1960/61–1969/70, with 1969/70; 1970/71–1979/80,
    with 1979/80; 1980/81–1989/90, 1990.
Editors: 1937/38–1958/59, A. C. Baird.—1959/60–1969/70, L. Thonssen.—1970/71–1979/80, W. W. Braden.—1980/81–1994/95, O. Peterson.—1995/96–1998/99, C. M. Logue and J. DeHart.—1999/2000–2002/2003, C. M. Logue and L. M. Messina.—2003/2004– , C. M. Logue, L. M. Messina, and J. DeHart.
    ISSN 0197-6923 Representative American speeches.
    1. Speeches, addresses, etc., American. 2. Speeches, addresses, etc.
    I. Baird, Albert Craig, 1883–1979 ed. II. Thonssen, Lester, 1904–
    III. Braden, Waldo Warder, 1911–1991 ed.
    IV. Peterson, Owen, 1924– ed. V. Logue, Calvin McLeod, 1935– ,
    Messina, Lynn M., and DeHart, Jean, eds. VI. Series.
PS668.B3   815.5082   38-27962
                                                                          MARC-S
Library of Congress [8503r85] rev4

Cover: U.S. senator Hillary Rodham Clinton addresses the Second Annual African American Leadership Summit on Capitol Hill on July 15, 2004. (Photo by Mark Wilson/Getty Images)

Visit H. W. Wilson's Web site: www.hwwilson.com

Printed in the United States of America

Contents

Preface vii

I. U.S. Intelligence.. 1

1) Robert Hutchings. Strategic Choices, Intelligence Challenges 3
2) Jane Harman. The Intelligence on Iraq's WMD: Looking Back to
   Look Forward 13
3) David Kay. Testimony Before the Senate Armed Services Committee
   About WMD in Iraq 20
4) Dianne Feinstein. Call for Restructuring of the Intelligence Community 25
5) James L. Pavitt. Foreign Policy Association 33
6) Thomas H. Kean and Lee H. Hamilton. Release of 9/11 Commission Report 47

II. Foreign Policy 55

1) Gary Hart. Principled Engagement: America's Role in the
   21st-Century World 57
2) Rachel Bronson. New Directions in U.S. Foreign Policy?: From Regime
   Change to Nation-Building 68
3) Hillary Rodham Clinton. New American Strategies for Security and Peace 74
4) Colin L. Powell. 2004 Annual Kennan Institute Dinner 81
5) John Kerry. Security and Strength for a New World 93
6) George W. Bush. Progress in the War on Terror............................ 100

III. The American Veteran 107

1) Harold J. "Bud" Seifert. Veterans Day 2003 109
2) Nicole Webb. Hope and Freedom.. 115
3) Jerry Barnes. Veterans Day Speech 117
4) Gale Norton. Women During the War 121
5) John D. Hopper Jr. Tuskegee Airmen Dinner.............................. 127

IV. Intellectual Property 133

1) Jack Valenti. The Moral Imperative 135
2) James V. DeLong. Privacy and Piracy 140
3) James B. Comey Jr. Mitigating the Impact of Intellectual Property Theft
   and Counterfeiting.. 148
4) Graham B. Spanier. The Digital Piracy Dilemma 153

5)   Jim Donio. Coalition of Entertainment Retail Trade Associations (CERTA) Congressional Fly-In Media Briefing 158

V. Challenges to the Environment 161

1)   Gaylord Nelson. National Press Club Luncheon 163
2)   Eileen Claussen. Tackling Climate Change: Five Keys to Success 168
3)   Dale Bosworth. Delivering Natural Resource Values: Four Threats to Our Mission... 177
4)   Pete V. Domenici. National Association of Manufacturers 184

Cumulative Speaker Index: 2000–2004 189

Index 193

Preface

When 2003 began, the United States was drawing closer to war with Iraq, as the Bush administration declared its certainty that Iraq possessed weapons of mass destruction (WMD). The administration based its contentions on intelligence reports that it considered reliable enough to justify a preemptive strike. President George W. Bush's doctrine of preemption would prove a tough sell at the United Nations, where France, Germany, Russia and other countries became outspoken critics of what they perceived as U.S. aggression. By the end of the summer of 2004, after more than 1,000 American servicemen and -women had given their lives in Iraq, the intelligence used to bring the country to war was deemed faulty; UN secretary-general Kofi Annan declared the U.S. military operation in Iraq "illegal," and a significant amount of American support for the war had eroded.

As the 2004 presidential campaign progressed, the public's attention was increasingly drawn both to Iraq and to the hearings of the bipartisan 9/11 Commission investigating the terrorist attacks of September 11, 2001. The primary question then became, whom did Americans most trust to secure the nation while bringing the Iraq conflict to a successful conclusion? President Bush continued to insist that his decisive actions against the Taliban in Afghanistan and his consistent position on Iraq made him the stronger leader; the Democratic challenger, Senator John Kerry, accused the president of misleading the nation and dragging it virtually alone into war.

According to the Bush administration, the capture of Iraqi dictator Saddam Hussein in late 2003 justified the war as a fight against tyranny and was a major step toward eliminating a potential threat to the region. Nevertheless, with no concrete evidence to support the initial justification for going to war, Hussein's possession of WMD became, in the president's 2004 State of the Union address, Hussein's possession of *plans* to develop WMD programs. Much of this shift in emphasis resulted from two factors: the failure to find any WMD on the ground in Iraq and the damaging testimony of such investigators as Dr. David Kay, who claimed "we were almost all wrong" about Iraq's military capabilities.

The two-pronged issue of intelligence gathering and interpretation became central to American discussions about national security and foreign policy, and so the first chapter of this book covers U.S. intelligence. Included here is one speech from the end of 2003, when Americans were becoming increasingly concerned about possible intelligence failures, asking whether better intelligence could have prevented the attacks on September 11, 2001, and whether the information used to justify the invasion of Iraq had been flawed or misinterpreted. The remaining speeches in this section are from 2004, including Dr.

Kay's testimony on Iraq's WMD program, and concluding with the findings of the 9/11 Commission, led by former governor Thomas Kean and former senator Lee Hamilton.

The fact that the United States used the intelligence it had gathered to plan a preemptive strike against another country was the occasion for sharp disagreement between advocates and critics both of the shape U.S. foreign policy was taking in the Bush administration and about the direction it should take in the future. Therefore, chapter 2 is devoted to this subject and includes speeches by individuals who express their concerns about a number of important issues, including the U.S. attempt at nation-building around the world, whether it is promoting or undermining the democratic principles reflected in its constitution, and how America's image has been affected by the war in Iraq. The chapter concludes with campaign speeches by the presidential incumbent and his Democratic challenger, as President Bush offers a positive view of America's war on terror while Senator Kerry presents his concerns about the way that war has been fought and his own philosophy on diplomatic and military engagement.

The speeches in chapter 3 salute the American veterans of yesterday and today, the men and women who have often been the instruments of the foreign policies practiced by their commander in chief. As the central figures in several international conflicts during the 20th century, U.S. veterans were cheered by one generation and unfairly reviled by another, and in the current conflicts in Iraq and Afghanistan, as well as in the global war on terror, they continue to demonstrate courage and self-sacrifice in the face of mounting difficulties. The speakers included here express their appreciation for the men and women who over the years have fought to defend Americans' freedom and often, as in Afghanistan and Iraq, the freedom of others.

The last two chapters in the book cover issues that have also been of great interest to Americans during 2003 and 2004: intellectual property rights and the nation's natural resources. The Internet explosion has facilitated the illegal downloading, copying, and distribution of copyrighted materials such as music and movies, prompting calls for action by lawyers, businessmen, and officials at universities, where students are sometimes the worst offenders. The individuals whose speeches are included in chapter 4 discuss the moral and legal ramifications of music and video piracy. Chapter 5 includes speeches by current and former U.S. government officials for whom conserving the country's natural resources is also a moral obligation and who seek to foster greater public interest in an area of life that so many of their compatriots take for granted.

We would like to thank all of the speakers who graciously granted us permission to reprint their speeches here. We would also like to express our gratitude to Jennifer Peloso, Norris Smith, Rich Stein, and Eugene F. Miller for their invaluable assistance in producing this book.

December 2004

I. U.S. Intelligence

Strategic Choices, Intelligence Challenges

Robert Hutchings

Chair, National Intelligence Council, 2002– ; born Bainbridge, MD, July 1946; B.S. in naval science, U.S. Naval Academy, 1969; M.A. in government, College of William and Mary, 1974; Ph.D. in government, University of Virginia, 1979; U.S. Naval officer, 1969–75; deputy director, Radio Free Europe, 1979–85; assistant national intelligence officer for Europe, 1986–89; national security council director for European affairs, 1989–92; special assistant to the secretary of state with rank of ambassador, 1992–93; fellow and director of international studies, the Woodrow Wilson International Center for Scholars, 1993–96; assistant dean of the Woodrow Wilson School of Public and International Affairs, Princeton University, 1997–2002; author, including American Diplomacy and the End of the Cold War *(1997) and* At the End of the American Century *(1998); a director of the Atlantic Council of the United States and of the Foundation for a Civil Society; awarded the Order of Merit of the Republic of Poland, 1999.*

Editors' introduction: With the nation on alert against terrorist attacks and the conflict in Iraq continuing, citizens, members of professional organizations, and U.S. government leaders debated how to restructure U.S. intelligence for the challenges of the post-9/11 world. Returning to Princeton University, from which he was on a public-service leave of absence, Mr. Hutchings explained to some 200 students, faculty, journalists, and community representatives convened at the Woodrow Wilson School of Public and International Affairs the "new set of challenges and demands on the U.S. Intelligence Community." The speech was followed by an exchange over dinner with invited faculty and students, focusing particularly on the ethical dimensions of public policy. The National Intelligence Council engages in midterm and long-term strategic thinking about intelligence issues. Founded at Princeton University in 1930, the Woodrow Wilson School emphasizes experiential, policy-oriented research and learning in its graduate program.

Robert Hutchings's speech: It is wonderful to be back, resuming the dialogue we had when I was teaching here a year ago, only this time in my governmental capacity. Let me offer a broad-gauged look at the kind of challenges we face as a country and how these will affect the work of intelligence. This will be

Delivered on December 1, 2003, at 4:30 P.M., Robertson Auditorium, Princeton, NJ. Reprinted with permission of Robert Hutchings.

mostly from a U.S. perspective, but I hope these thoughts have wider relevance.

For those who don't know, the National Intelligence Council, or NIC, is a center of strategic thinking that reports to the director of Central Intelligence in his capacity as head of the Intelligence Community as a whole. The NIC consists of a chairman and vice chairman and 12 National Intelligence officers—who include former ambassadors, senior academics, retired generals, and senior intelligence officers—as well as their deputies and various support staff. We participate in policy deliberations at the highest levels and provide analyses of key foreign policy issues for the President and other senior policy makers. My own role is to manage the overall effort as well as represent the Intelligence Community in principals' and deputies' committee meetings of the President's National Security Council.

I should acknowledge that the NIC was also the producer of the now famous National Intelligence Estimate on Iraq's weapons of mass destruction programs. I will come back to that NIE in a few minutes, but I will speak more broadly first.

We are the government's foreign policy think tank; at least, that's the way I conceive of our role. We have both the mandate and capacity to think strategically and over the horizon, and we are better placed to do so than any other part of government. Much of our work is dominated by current issues, especially the situation in Iraq. But we have a responsibility to maintain a longer-term perspective as well. And I would say that we have a particular obligation to do so at this particular juncture in history.

A World in Flux

My starting point is that we are facing a more fluid and complicated set of international alignments than anything we have seen since the formation of the Western alliance system in 1949. (Such a statement would not have been accurate during the 1990s, however. Throughout the decade the elements holding together the international system were stronger than those pulling it apart.) I would attribute the current flux to three chief factors:

1. First, it is a commonplace but nonetheless true that with the end of the Cold War and the collapse of the Soviet empire we lost the galvanizing element that held together that system.

   • The bipolar world of the Cold War has been replaced by a unipolar global system—to which the world is still adjusting.

   • And because the Cold War ended peacefully—not with a bang but a whimper—we may not fully have appreciated how dramatic a transformation this was.

2. Second, 9/11 was a turning point. Because those attacks were directed at the United States and carried out on American soil,

we were uniquely affected. Our friends and allies offered sympathy and support, of course, but they did not and do not feel the same sense of urgency that we do, so the international consensus of the previous era has eroded.

It is a politically useful rallying cry to say that countries are either with us or against us, but it is more likely that some countries will be with us on some of the issues some of the time.

3. Third, the breakdown of consensus over Iraq reflected a fundamental restructuring of the international system.

I would add that it wasn't just because of this particular incident: that would be too simplistic an historical judgment. If the clash hadn't occurred over Iraq, it would have occurred over something else.

These trends will also be affected by the plans for a changed U.S. military posture around the world—announced by the White House last week—which will loosen our ties with some traditional allies and expand them with others.

So we are facing major flux in all the areas of the world that we have traditionally considered vital:

• The greater Middle East is obviously in tremendous flux, and U.S. involvement there will be more direct and intense than ever before. Looking out 15–20 years, it is hard to imagine this region staying much the same.

• East Asia is also on the brink of major change, as China continues to move toward greater economic openness and political flux. The key question is whether that political system is sufficiently elastic, and its leaders sufficiently imaginative, to accommodate continued rapid economic growth and the social pressures it will bring.

And on the Korean peninsula, a unification scenario cannot be far off, with all the uncertainties that entails.

• The U.S.-European relationship, too, has already changed from a single transatlantic security community to an alliance a la carte. And, again, this is not the consequence of particular personalities or policies but of a deeper structural change in the relationship. These changes were building up throughout the 1990s, but they were largely obscured by the sugarcoated rhetoric of undiminished transatlantic solidarity. Iraq brought them into full view.

The Challenge of Unipolarity

An underlying aspect of this structural change relates to the challenge of a unipolar international system. I see that you are holding a conference on this subject later this week. We at the National Intelligence Council did so as well, engaging a group of IR theorists in a series of three conferences (which included Tom Christensen) last spring and summer. The report of that group, prepared by John Ikenberry, is on our Web site.

The core issue has to do with what we might call the problem of American power—not just the *use* of American power (whether we are using it wisely or unwisely), but the very fact of *having* such unrivaled power. We are in an unusual, perhaps unique, period in international politics in which one country dominates so thoroughly. And this creates new challenges for American policy:

- It is harder to maintain alliances, because other countries lack the capacity to be full partners.

- It may prompt other states to make common cause against us—as France, Germany, and Russia did earlier this year—in an effort to constrain American power.

- It can create resentment on the part of others and foster anti-Americanism.

- And it may tempt *us* to take on more than we can handle, simply because there is nothing to stop us from doing so. As Ikenberry and Co. argued, unipolarity selects for unilateralism. (In this regard, it is worth noting that unilateralism did not begin with the Bush administration. The same charge was leveled at the Clinton administration, in which I also served.)

Challenges Facing the Intelligence Community

All of this adds up to a new set of challenges and demands on the U.S. Intelligence Community. Let me highlight just a few of them.

1. Strategic Surprise

During the Cold War, there was very little that we didn't know about the Soviet Union—at least within the universe of things we needed to know. There was a defined threat, which focused our collection and analysis. We even knew the Warsaw Pact's battle plan.

After the Cuban missile crisis, there was an increasing recognition on both sides that a certain amount of transparency was stabilizing. Each side allowed the other a degree of unfettered intelligence collection, in order to reduce the danger of miscalculation and misunderstanding.

It is worth noting that the role of intelligence in keeping the Cold War from turning hot is one of the neglected stories of the last half-century.

Needless to say, that degree of maturity doesn't exist among our present-day adversaries—some of which do not even occupy a defined territory.

And unlike the single massive threat of the Cold War, we must now worry about threats emanating from almost anywhere. A recent RAND project on "red-teaming the terrorist threat"—an effort to imagine what targets international terrorists would go after next—came up with dozens of scenarios, each of them plausible.

2. Denial and Deception

The threats we worry about most come from adversaries who are practiced in denial and deception—that is, from closed, authoritarian systems that deny access to their weapons program and develop elaborate programs to deceive outside weapons inspectors as to what their activities really signify.

We obviously faced this with respect to the Iraqi regime, which built D&D into its entire WMD program—and refined its D&D capacities over by a dozen years of international scrutiny.

In the NIE on Iraq WMD—about which I will say more shortly—we were aiming at a very difficult target. Every Iraqi program had "dual-use" built in that provided a plausible cover story: this was the game of hide-and-seek that Iraq had been playing with UN inspectors since 1991.

The threats we worry about most come from adversaries who are practiced in denial and deception.

And we are facing a similar situation now in North Korea. I wish that those who are second-guessing the Intelligence Community's assessments of Iraq's WMD program would look at a current issue like North Korea's nuclear program and appreciate how hard it is. We are applying the most sophisticated technical systems and best interpretive and analytic capabilities—and still can't be sure. This isn't an intelligence "failure" in the making; this is just the way it is.

In the Q&A someone is likely to ask why the U.S. invaded Iraq but not North Korea, which already has nuclear weapons and arguably poses a greater threat. So let me launch a preemptive rhetorical strike: What makes you think North Korea has nuclear weapons? How do you know? That "knowledge" is in fact a judgment—one based on solid evidence and sound reasoning, but still a judgment, based on imperfect information.

3. Smaller, More Mobile Targets

We have gone from an era in which we were looking for large things in more or less fixed locations—armored divisions, missile silos, etc.—to one in which we are looking for small things on the move.

This is true in the war against terrorism and in counter-proliferation efforts, and it is also true of our support to war fighters.

During Operation Iraqi Freedom, we needed to direct special operations units to individual buildings in which a key leader was known to have arrived an hour before—and then to tell them which door to enter.

This requires ever more sophisticated technical means as well as improved human intelligence—and synergistic use of all the sources of intelligence from overhead imagery to communications intercepts.

Now and in the future, intelligence and military operations are going to be fused, from the battlefield to the national level. There was a remarkable, unprecedented level of military-intelligence cooperation in Afghanistan and in Iraq.

During Operation Iraqi Freedom, we held three teleconferences daily with Centcom. This was real-time information-sharing calling for quick turn-around assessments, coordinated among all elements of the Intelligence Community.

Obviously, this level of direct support to war-fighters stretches the Intelligence Community thin for other tasks. Even as we speak, there is a very difficult tradeoff between assets devoted to the difficult security situation—which obviously takes priority—and those assigned to the Iraqi Survey Group that is searching for weapons of mass destruction.

The doctrine of preemption imposes an extraordinarily high standard on the Intelligence Community.

Analytically, we are looking at such issues as the scope and evolution of the jihad, the actions of neighboring countries, and the workings of the black arms market, as well as issues related to political and economic reconstruction.

4. The Burden of Preemption

The doctrine of preemption imposes an extraordinarily high standard on the Intelligence Community. U.S. intelligence will be measured by whether a case has been made that justifies and legitimates intervention.

We will be asked not merely to indict, but also to convict—and, through our covert action possibilities, to prosecute as well. These functions obviously go well beyond what the Intelligence Community traditionally has been called on to perform. Those putting together the Iraqi WMD estimate never conceived of their task as one of making a case for intervention. Intelligence is policy neutral. We do not propose, we do not oppose any particular course of action.

Moreover, candidates for "preemption" tend to be the hardest targets. Intelligence judgments about them will be just that—*judgments*, based on evidence that will rarely be conclusive or incontrovertible.

5. Public Scrutiny: The Iraqi WMD Estimate

That brings me to the Iraqi WMD estimate and the extraordinary public scrutiny it has engendered. My deputy, Stuart Cohen, wrote a superb editorial in Friday's *Washington Post*, so I won't try to recapitulate all his arguments. Besides, he is a true expert on the subject, having served on the first UN inspection team in Iraq a decade ago.

But let me offer a few additional points about that NIE, which has spawned a cottage industry of misinformation:

- First, the judgments of that estimate were honestly arrived at. The estimate was published before I arrived, but I know the four National Intelligence Officers who put it together.

  One is a Mormon bishop and one of the world's leading experts on nuclear programs. Another is a Ph.D. physicist from CalTech and head of the Denial and Deception board for the entire Intelligence Community. A third is retired Army general and graduate of West Point and with an M.P.A. from the Kennedy School. The fourth is a politics Ph.D. from Princeton and author of perhaps the best book on international terrorism.

  Three of them were appointed NIOs during the Clinton administration. The fourth goes back long before—all the way back to Carter, I believe. They are not "political," and they are absolutely incorruptible. If anyone ever told them to alter their judgments for political reasons, their response would be to dig in their heels even harder.

- Second, the debate a year ago was never about intelligence. I took part in many such discussions right here in this auditorium as well as in other venues, and the debates were not about intelligence but about policy. There was broad agreement, within governments and outside, about Iraq's WMD programs—based on UNSCOM and UNMOVIC, foreign intelligence, and U.S. government assessments made over three administrations.

  I was just in Europe a few weeks ago and reconfirmed that the British, French, and Germans all held the same basic judgments that we did.

- Third, there was a powerful body of evidence on programs and a compelling basis for judging that they had weapons. The fixation is now on the weapons, but the programs—the capacity of a regime that had actually used CW on 10 separate occasions to weaponize large quantities on short notice—were arguably just as worrying.

- Fourth, as to the weapons themselves, the amounts of CW we estimated Iraq to have had would fit in a backyard swimming pool or, at the upper limit of our estimate, in a small warehouse. A tremendously lethal arsenal of BW could of course be much smaller. And this in a country the size of California.

- Fifth, as David Kay, head of the Iraqi Survey Group, has pointed out, there were ample opportunities before, during, and after the war to hide or destroy evidence as well as weapons. We may never know definitively what Iraq had at the time the war began.

Conclusion: The Challenge of Global Coverage

Meanwhile, the preoccupation with retrospection on that NIE is taking a toll. One of our challenges in the NIC—one of my principal challenges—is to keep our focus on the larger strategic issues before us even as Iraq dominates the agenda.

Let me conclude, as I began, with some broad observations about the intelligence challenges of the early 21st century. (Or, as one M.P.A. applicant wrote in his public policy paper, the challenges "for the next millennium and beyond." Now there was a young man with a vision!)

The threats and issues we now face are dispersed and global, and they grow out of complex cultural roots.

As I argued at the beginning, we are likely to see major change in the Greater Middle East, in East Asia, and in the transatlantic relationship. And we are simultaneously waging a global struggle against terrorism, which can take us into countries and regions traditionally low on our list of priorities. It is an exciting time to be in government, but also a demanding one.

The threats and issues we now face are dispersed and global, and they grow out of complex cultural roots. This means that both the breadth and the depth of our coverage has to be correspondingly greater. New analysts being brought in will help enormously but cannot entirely fill that gap, particularly given the priority that must be attached to Iraq, terrorism, and WMD programs.

Let me mention a few ways in which we are trying to meet these new strategic challenges. Within the NIC, we have just created a new NIO account to deal with transnational threats, including terrorism—not to duplicate the work of the many organizations dealing with day-to-day counterterrorist work, but to look over the horizon at broader trends that day-to-day operators may miss.

- For example, we know that failed states can offer safe havens for terrorists. But which states will fail, and which of those will in fact be attractive sites for terrorists?

- Also, we need to monitor global trends in political Islam—not all of which are associated with terrorism, let me hasten to add.

- What about other sources of global terrorism? Will Leftist terrorism, which virtually disappeared from Europe after the disbanding of the Red Brigades and the Bader-Meinhof gang, make a comeback? Will class-based terrorism make a revival in Latin America?

On these and many other issues, we must look outside government to find the expertise on which we must draw. Here the NIC can play a critical bridging role between outside experts and policy makers. Having spent a career wandering between these two worlds, I see this as one of the principal roles I can play.

In addition to calling on outside experts to review all of our estimates, we maintain regular contracts with hundreds of academics and other experts.

As I mentioned, earlier this year, we engaged a group of international relations theorists in a series of three conferences to examine strategic responses to American preeminence—how other countries are reacting to U.S. power. We reconvened just last week with a deeper look at East Asia and will follow up with looks at other regions over the coming year.

We also convened a group of leading thinkers from five continents to explore anti-Americanism around the world. It's a delicate subject to be batting around in Washington, so I'm still trying to figure out how best to present their findings to my counterparts on the policy side!

Finally, we just launched an ambitious, year-long project called NIC 2020, which will explore the forces that will shape the world of 2020 through a series of dialogues and conferences with experts from around the world. For our inaugural conference, we invited 25 experts from a wide variety of backgrounds to join us in a broad-gauged exploration of key trends.

- These included prominent "futurists"—the longtime head of Shell's scenarios project, the head of the UN's millennium project, and the director of RAND's center for the study of the future.

- And Princeton's own Harold James gave the keynote address, offering lessons from prior periods of "globalization."

- Beyond that, we had experts on biotechnology, information technology, demography, ethnicity, demography, and energy, as well as more traditional regional specialists.

Later on we will be organizing conferences on five continents, and drawing on experts from academia, business, governments, foundations, and the scientific community, so that this effort will be truly global and interdisciplinary. We will commission local partners to convene these affairs and help set them up, but then we will get out of the way so that regional experts may speak for themselves in identifying key "drivers" of change and a range of future scenarios.

As the 2020 project unfolds, we will be posting discussion papers, conference reports, and other material on our unclassified website, so I encourage you to follow the project as it unfolds over the coming year.

It may seem somewhat self-indulgent to engage in such futurology, but I see this as integral to our work. If we are entering a period of major flux in the international system, as I believe we are, it is important to take a longer-term strategic review.

We are accustomed to seeing linear change, but sometimes change is logarithmic: it builds up gradually, with nothing much seeming to happen, but then major change occurs suddenly and unexpectedly. The collapse of the Soviet empire is one example. The growing pressures on China may also produce a sudden, dramatic transformation that cannot be understood by linear analysis.

As I used to say in class, linear analysis will get you a much changed caterpillar, but it won't get you a butterfly. For that you need a leap of imagination. I'm hoping that the 2020 project will help us make that leap, not to predict the world of 2020—that is clearly beyond our capacity—but to prepare for the kinds of changes that may lie ahead.

Thanks for your attention. I look forward to your questions and comments.

The Intelligence on Iraq's WMD: Looking Back to Look Forward

Jane Harman

U.S. representative (D), 36th California District, 1992– ; born Queens, NY, June 28, 1945; B.A. in government, Smith College, 1966; J.D., Harvard University Law School, 1969; White House aide; legislative aide; director, secretary, outside general counsel, Human International Industries; counsel, Jones, Day, Reavis and Pogue; director and general counsel, Harman International Industries; chief counsel and staff director, U.S. Senate Judiciary Subcommitte on Constitutional Rights, 1975–77; deputy secretary to the cabinet, the White House, 1977–78; special counsel, Department of Defense, 1979; Regent's professor, University of California, Los Angeles, 1999; ranking Democrat, House Permanent Select Committee on Intelligence; Select House Committee on Homeland Security; Los Angeles County Technology Committee; board, Planned Parenthood of Los Angeles; founder and member, South Bay Alliance for Choice; steering committee, Women's Policy, Inc.

Editors' introduction: President George W. Bush in part attempted to justify going to war with Iraq with intelligence reports claiming that Iraq had weapons of mass destruction (WMD). When those findings proved to be faulty, critics questioned the efficiency and reliability of the U.S. Intelligence Community. While Representative Harman recognized that "there were good reasons to support regime change in Iraq," she told a Los Angeles World Affairs Council luncheon that "a clearer picture of the true nature of the intelligence information could have led to more policy options—more time for diplomacy to work." The World Affairs Council promotes a better understanding of current world events by hosting prominent speakers, who address its members in person.

Jane Harman's speech: In four days, the president will deliver his annual State of the Union address before both houses of Congress, his cabinet, the Ambassadorial Corps, the Supreme Court, and a worldwide television audience.

Almost one year ago, on January 28th, 2003, the President devoted one-third of his State of the Union address to what he described as "a serious and mounting threat to our country" posed by Iraq's possession of weapons of mass destruction. He spoke, in those famous 16 words, about efforts by Iraq to secure enriched uranium from Africa. He talked about aluminum tubes "suitable for nuclear weapons production." He described stockpiles of chemical and biological weapons and said, "We know that Iraq, in the late 1990s, had several mobile biological weapons labs."

One week later, on February 5th, Secretary of State Colin Powell, with Director of Central Intelligence George Tenet sitting behind his right shoulder, used charts and photographs to elaborate on the administration's WMD case. "These are not assertions," Powell said, "these are facts corroborated by many sources." Among Powell's claims were:

- That "we know, we know from sources that a missile brigade outside Baghdad was dispersing rocket launchers and warheads containing biological warfare agent to various locations."

- That "there can be no doubt that Saddam Hussein has biological weapons and the capability to rapidly produce more, many more."

- That photos showed "active chemical munitions bunkers" with "sure signs that the bunkers are storing chemical munitions."

Powell has subsequently said that he spent days personally assessing the intelligence. He included only information he felt was fully supported by the analysis. Hence, no mention of enriched uranium from Africa, no claim that Al Qaeda was involved in 9-11.

The effect was powerful. Veteran columnist for the *Washington Post* Mary McGrory, known for liberal views and Kennedy connections, wrote an op-ed the following day entitled "I Am Persuaded." Members of Congress, like me, believed the intelligence case. We voted for the resolution on Iraq to urge UN action but to authorize military force if diplomacy failed. We felt confident we had made the wise choice.

But as the evidence pours in . . .

- Our Intelligence Committee's review of the prewar intelligence;

- David Kay's interim report on the failure to find WMD in Iraq;

- An impressive study by the Carnegie Endowment for International Peace;

- The President's Foreign Intelligence Advisory Board's critique;

- Thoughtful commentaries like that of Ken Pollack in this month's *Atlantic Monthly*;

- And investigative reporting including a lengthy front page story by Barton Gellman of the *Washington Post* on January 7,

. . . we are finding out that Powell and other policymakers were wrong. British intelligence was wrong. And those of us who believed the intelligence were wrong. Indeed, I doubt there would be discussions of David Kay's possible departure if the Iraq Survey Group were on the verge of uncovering large stockpiles of weapons or an advanced nuclear weapons program.

Let me be clear. There were good reasons to support regime change in Iraq—which was the policy of the Clinton administration and was supported by an overwhelming vote in Congress in 1998. It is also true that Iraq violated 16 UN resolutions by failing to prove it had dismantled its WMD and continuing efforts to deceive UN inspectors.

But if 9/11 was a failure to connect the dots, it appears that the Intelligence Community, in the case of Iraq's WMD, connected the dots to the wrong conclusions. If our intelligence products had been better, I believe many policymakers, including me, would have had a far clearer picture of the sketchiness of our sources on Iraq's WMD programs, and our lack of certainty about Iraq's chemical, biological and nuclear capabilities.

A far clearer picture of the true nature of the intelligence information could have led to more policy options—more time for diplomacy to work, and more time to build international support for military action, which was likely inevitable given the ruthless, deluded characters of Saddam and his sons.

> *It appears that the Intelligence Community, in the case of Iraq's WMD, connected the dots to the wrong conclusions.*

With more time, there would have been a greater ability to learn the lessons for the postwar from five prior nation-building efforts in the last decade—more time to prepare a careful strategy and build an effective budget for the real costs of winning the peace.

Finally, if we had known the threat from Iraq was less urgent, we could have continued to focus more heavily on the threat from Osama Bin Laden and Al Qaeda. Instead, we diverted attention and resources to a war in Iraq in the midst of our hunt for the true villains of September 11.

The October 2002 NIE on Iraq's WMD Programs

The Intelligence Community communicates its judgments to senior officials in many ways—in verbal briefings, in short memos, and in longer reports. The cornerstone document on Iraq's WMD before the war was the National Intelligence Estimate published in October 2002. NIEs are the most carefully written, methodically coordinated products of the intelligence agencies.

Having studied the 19 volumes of source materials that went into the 2002 National Intelligence Estimate on Iraq, and having read that NIE carefully, my conclusion is it was a significantly flawed document.

While the Intelligence Community has portrayed that NIE as consistent with judgments throughout the 1990s, in fact, it included at least two important new statements: First, that Baghdad possessed chemical and biological weapons; and second, that Baghdad was reconstituting its nuclear weapons program. These were centerpieces of the NIE and of the case for war and it appears likely that both were wrong.

Recently, I met with the senior analysts who wrote the October 2002 NIE. Describing their mindset at the time, they believed the decision to go to war had already been made. They wrote as if they were advising the military commanders on the likely status of Iraq's weapons as they prepared for a war. It was a mindset that, according to the analysts, focused on "making the case" and "making the tough calls." They felt they had to come down on one side or the other—did Saddam have chemical and biological weapons or didn't he? Would he use them on our troops?

I think the Intelligence Community misunderstood its audience and its role. Let's remember that this NIE was requested by Congress—by my colleague Senator Bob Graham, then head of the Senate Intelligence Committee—in order to inform members' decisions about the timing and need for military action. It was published a few days before the key vote in the Senate to authorize the use of force. This is a very different audience—and purpose—than the military commander preparing to fight.

Almost 12 years ago, DCI Robert Gates, a Republican who served in the first Bush administration, set out standards to keep political or personal bias out of analysis. Gates said it is not the analyst's job to make the tough calls. Their job is to describe as accurately as possible what is known, "make explicit what is not known, and clearly distinguish between fact, inference, and judgment."[1]

Gates insisted that dissenting views receive prominence: "We must not dismiss alternatives or exaggerate our certainty under the guise of making the 'tough calls.' We are analysts, not umpires, and the game does not depend on our providing a single judgment."

In testimony before our Committee last fall, former Deputy Secretary of Defense and CSIS President John Hamre underscored another of Gates's warnings: to protect against "groupthink," an institutional mindset that fails to challenge arguments which take on the patina of "truth."

A troubling example of groupthink, as we are coming to learn, was the unquestioned assumption that the failure to prove that Saddam Hussein destroyed weapons of mass destruction after 1991 was proof that they still existed. That tautology infected intelligence reporting around the world and was the centerpiece of Colin Powell's UN address.

Let me add that policymakers—including members of Congress—have a duty to ask tough questions, to probe the information being presented to them. We also have a duty to portray that information publicly as accurately as we can.

The Intelligence Community in a State of Denial

Four months ago, Republican Committee Chairman Porter Goss and I sent a bipartisan letter to the DCI outlining shortcomings we had identified in prewar intelligence. Subsequently, questions have also been raised by the Senate Intelligence Committee, which, like our Committee, plans to issue a report. We said that collection had not provided sufficient insights into an admittedly very tough intelligence target. In addition, the departure of the UN weapons inspectors from Iraq in 1998 ended the world community's best window into what Iraq was doing. Analysis overstated the intelligence and failed clearly to present alternative hypotheses or contrary information, such as claims that Iraq had destroyed weapons, or that its WMD programs were hollowed out by deception, corruption and deceit among players in the regime. The Chairman and I have yet to receive a serious substantive response to our letter.

I believe that unanswered questions regarding U.S. intelligence have left the nation in a precarious position and endanger our ability to understand and deal with threats posed over three administrations since the end of the Cold War.

> *Unanswered questions regarding U.S. intelligence have left the nation in a precarious position.*

Last month, the *Los Angeles Times* ran a detailed piece casting doubt on the Intelligence Community's judgments about North Korea's nuclear program. A recent *Washington Post* piece suggested that China is also skeptical of the assessment that North Korea has a uranium enrichment program in part because of questions regarding the credibility of U.S. intelligence in Iraq. Several days ago, the North Koreans claimed their own statements had been exaggerated. Our Intelligence Community has been vocal about the North Korea threat: how good are its assessments?

Libya's recent decision to abandon its WMD programs provides the Intelligence Community with another chance to compare its assessments with the truth on the ground. These should be viewed as opportunities for lessons learned rather than a time to circle the wagons.

Policymakers, too, should be learning lessons from the Iraq and Libya experiences to improve strategies to combat WMD proliferation. Libya seems to have recognized that relinquishing WMD is a surer path to security than possessing WMD. Sanctions and patient diplomacy—backed by the threat of military force—appear to have worked. Patience was something notably lacking in the administration's approach to building a coalition for Iraq.

The Imperative of Intelligence Community Reform

Why does all this matter? I often say it is important to look back in order to look forward. The lessons of our prewar intelligence on Iraq must inform and shape the Intelligence Community over coming years.

Leadership. There is no reform as important as ensuring that the right leadership sets the right tone. It is essential to have a work environment that welcomes constructive criticism and opportunities for lessons learned.

Leadership also requires the power and institutional structures necessary to get the job done and be held accountable. We ought to be thinking seriously about reorganizing the Intelligence Community and creating a Director of National Intelligence, a cabinet position with strong statutory and budget authority, to run it.

This idea has long had bipartisan support. Former National Security Advisor Brent Scowcroft has recommended it, and the bicameral Joint Congressional Inquiry on 9-11, on which I served, endorsed it. The current structure is a mess. The director of Central Intelligence only has direct authority over the CIA. The bulk of the community's technical signals and imagery collection efforts are in agencies that report to the secretary of defense. The FBI is part of the Justice Department. And Congress recently reorganized 22 agencies into a mammoth Department of Homeland Security that is both an important new customer of intelligence and contains its own intelligence function.

Collaboration. We also need to build stronger collaborative capabilities to take on the new threats. The new Terrorist Threat Integration Center, a joint venture of intelligence agencies to fuse intelligence analysis, and the new Terrorist Screening Center to strengthen watchlisting, are potential bright spots in devising new capabilities.

More traditional targets, such as proliferation of weapons of mass destruction, also require greater collaboration across the Intelligence Community. Technical experts and regional experts must work hand-in-glove. And we will never effectively penetrate and understand foreign targets without greater emphasis on language skills and a more diverse workforce.

"Virtual reorganization." A DNI may be far off. Meanwhile, several distinguished groups, such as the Markle Foundation Task Force, have identified important steps that could be taken toward a "virtual reorganization," using today's business models and information technology tools. Make it easier for analysts in different agencies to find each other and compare notes in real time. Facilitate the capability to "surge" and create "task forces" by changing personnel policies and providing virtual workspaces. Move from a "need to know" culture to a "need to share" culture. Create career incentives for community assignments. All of these steps could significantly enhance intelligence capabilities.

For another model, we should look at how the Defense Department has been transformed by the Goldwater-Nichols Act of 1986 and the "jointness" that it instilled across fiefdoms. If blue, green, and khaki can be made "purple," the many elements of the Intelligence Community should be able to work more cohesively. We should examine ways to apply the model of combatant commanders to intelligence missions, for example. Goldwater-Nichols sorted out the Defense Department's capabilities. It assigned the Services to "organize, train, and equip" forces, and assigned the various commands called CINCs to run operations. Similarly, the Intelligence Community might focus the directors of agencies like NSA on organizing, training, and equipping intelligence forces, while stronger community CINCs are established to manage joint operations against specific targets.

Laws. Finally, the new missions and new threats require an appropriately strong and effective legal framework to guide them. That framework must recognize, as the Founding Fathers did, that security and liberty are mutually reinforcing. To remain strong, we need both.

Conclusion

The U.S. military is stretched dangerously thin, relationships with key allies are seriously strained, and the costs of war and homeland security are contributing to a budget deficit which has broken all previous records. In these circumstances, the Intelligence Community's responsibilities are staggering. There is no margin of error and no room left for surprises in the coming year and, if there's one thing we can count on, it's surprises.

The good news is the quality and courage of the professionals in the Intelligence Community who work so tirelessly to keep us safe and to protect our national interests. I've met and thanked hundreds of them all around the world. They put the country ahead of their own safety and comfort, and deserve our gratitude and our respect.

They clearly share our desire for the best intelligence possible. To get it, things must change, starting with the Intelligence Community's acknowledgement of deficiencies in the prewar intelligence on Iraq.

Quite frankly, this willingness to learn lessons should start at the top. The president should lead the effort to improve his intelligence on weapons of mass destruction and terrorism. I urge him in his State of the Union address next Tuesday to acknowledge the problems and outline specific steps to fix them.

Chiseled on the main entrance to the CIA are the words "And ye shall know the truth and the truth shall make you free." Freedom depends on accurate, timely, and actionable intelligence. It is the point of the spear in the war on terrorism. We must do better.

Notes:

1. Robert Gates, "Guarding Against Politicization," *Studies in Intelligence* 36, no. 5 (1992).

Testimony Before the Senate Armed Services Committee About WMD in Iraq

David Kay

Senior fellow, Potomac Institute for Policy Studies, with a concentration on counterterrorism and weapons proliferation, 2004– ; bachelor's degree, University of Texas; master's in international affairs and Ph.D., Columbia University; 15 years of international management experience with international organizations and trade associations, including the International Atomic Energy Agency (IAEA); extensive business experience in Asia, the Middle East, and Europe; Defense Science Board, U.S. State Department's Advisory Commission on International Organizations, the Rockefeller Foundation's Advisory Group on Conflicts in International Relations, and the U.S. Delegation to the UN General Assembly; analyst, NBC and MSNBC; articles in New York Times, Washington Post, Christian Science Monitor, Washington Quarterly, *and* New Republic; *IAEA's Distinguished Service Award; U.S. Secretary of State's Commendation.*

Editors' introduction: Based in part on inaccurate intelligence information that Iraq had stockpiled weapons of mass destruction (WMD), in 2003, President George W. Bush led the United States to war against Iraq. In June 2003, a month after President Bush had announced the official end of the "combat operations," the director of the Central Intelligence Agency appointed Dr. Kay to head a search for WMD. By January 2004, Dr. Kay had concluded there had been no such stockpiles, and he resigned his position. Congress began hearings on the U.S. intelligence about the existence of WMD in Iraq. In testifying before the U.S. Senate Armed Services Committee, Dr. Kay stated that "we were almost all wrong, and I certainly include myself here." The problem was in "the information that had been collected."

David Kay's testimony: As you know and we discussed, I do not have a written statement. This hearing came about very quickly. I do have a few preliminary comments, but I suspect you're more interested in asking questions, and I'll be happy to respond to those questions to the best of my ability.

I would like to open by saying that the talent, dedication and bravery of the staff of the [Iraq Survey Group] that was my privilege to direct is unparalleled and the country owes a great debt of gratitude to the men and women who have served over there and continue to serve doing that.

Delivered on January 28, 2004, at Washington, DC. Reprinted with permission of David Kay.

A great deal has been accomplished by the team, and I do think . . . it important that it goes on and it is allowed to reach its full conclusion. In fact, I really believe it ought to be better resourced and totally focused on WMD; that is important to do it.

But I also believe that it is time to begin the fundamental analysis of how we got here, what led us here and what we need to do in order to ensure that we are equipped with the best possible intelligence as we face these issues in the future.

Let me begin by saying, we were almost all wrong, and I certainly include myself here.

Sen. [Edward] Kennedy knows very directly. Senator Kennedy and I talked on several occasions prior to the war that my view was that the best evidence that I had seen was that Iraq indeed had weapons of mass destruction.

I would also point out that many governments that chose not to support this war—certainly, the French president, [Jacques] Chirac, as I recall in April of last year, referred to Iraq's possession of WMD.

The Germans certainly—the intelligence service believed that there were WMD.

It turns out that we were all wrong, probably, in my judgment, and that is most disturbing.

We're also in a period in which we've had intelligence surprises in the proliferation area that go the other way. The case of Iran, a nuclear program that the Iranians admit was 18 years on, that we underestimated. And, in fact, we didn't discover it. It was discovered by a group of Iranian dissidents outside the country who pointed the international community at the location.

The Libyan program recently discovered was far more extensive than was assessed prior to that.

There's a long record here of being wrong. There's a good reason for it. There are probably multiple reasons. Certainly proliferation is a hard thing to track, particularly in countries that deny easy and free access and don't have free and open societies.

In my judgment, based on the work that has been done to this point of the Iraq Survey Group, and in fact, that I reported to you in October, Iraq was in clear violation of the terms of [UN] Resolution 1441.

Resolution 1441 required that Iraq report all of its activities—one last chance to come clean about what it had.

We have discovered hundreds of cases, based on both documents, physical evidence and the testimony of Iraqis, of activities that were prohibited under the initial UN Resolution 687 and that should have been reported under 1441, with Iraqi testimony that not only did they not tell the UN about this, they were instructed not to do it and they hid material.

I think the aim—and certainly the aim of what I've tried to do since leaving—is not political and certainly not a witch hunt at individuals. It's to try to direct our attention at what I believe is a fundamental fault analysis that we must now examine.

> *The world that we were finding was not the world that they had thought existed.*

And let me take one of the explanations most commonly given: Analysts were pressured to reach conclusions that would fit the political agenda of one or another administration. I deeply think that is a wrong explanation.

As leader of the effort of the Iraqi Survey Group, I spent most of my days not out in the field leading inspections. It's typically what you do at that level. I was trying to motivate, direct, find strategies.

In the course of doing that, I had innumerable analysts who came to me in apology that the world that we were finding was not the world that they had thought existed and that they had estimated. Reality on the ground differed in advance.

And never—not in a single case—was the explanation, "I was pressured to do this." The explanation was very often, "The limited data we had led one to reasonably conclude this. I now see that there's another explanation for it."

And each case was different, but the conversations were sufficiently in depth and our relationship was sufficiently frank that I'm convinced that, at least to the analysts I dealt with, I did not come across a single one that felt it had been, in the military term, "inappropriate command influence" that led them to take that position.

It was not that. It was the honest difficulty based on the intelligence that had—the information that had been collected that led the analysts to that conclusion.

And you know, almost in a perverse way, I wish it had been undue influence because we know how to correct that.

We get rid of the people who, in fact, were exercising that.

The fact that it wasn't tells me that we've got a much more fundamental problem of understanding what went wrong, and we've got to figure out what was there. And that's what I call fundamental fault analysis.

And like I say, I think we've got other cases other than Iraq. I do not think the problem of global proliferation of weapons technology of mass destruction is going to go away, and that's why I think it is an urgent issue.

And let me really wrap up here with just a brief summary of what I think we are now facing in Iraq. I regret to say that I think at the end of the work of the [Iraq Survey Group] there's still going to be an unresolvable ambiguity about what happened.

A lot of that traces to the failure on April 9 to establish immediately physical security in Iraq—the unparalleled looting and destruction, a lot of which was directly intentional, designed by the security services to cover the tracks of the Iraq WMD program and their other programs as well, a lot of which was what we simply called Ali Baba looting. "It had been the regime's. The regime is gone. I'm going to go take the gold toilet fixtures and everything else imaginable."

I've seen looting around the world and thought I knew the best looters in the world. The Iraqis excel at that.

The result is—document destruction—we're really not going to be able to prove beyond a truth the negatives and some of the positive conclusions that we're going to come to. There will be always unresolved ambiguity here.

But I do think the survey group—and I think Charlie Duelfer is a great leader. I have the utmost confidence in Charles. I think you will get as full an answer as you can possibly get.

And let me just conclude by my own personal tribute, both to the president and to [CIA Director] George Tenet, for having the courage to select me to do this, and my successor, Charlie Duelfer, as well.

Both of us are known for probably at times a regrettable streak of independence. I came not from within the administration, and it was clear and clear in our discussions and no one asked otherwise that I would lead this the way I thought best and I would speak the truth as we found it. I have had absolutely no pressure prior, during the course of the work at the [Iraq Survey Group], or after I left to do anything otherwise.

I think that shows a level of maturity and understanding that I think bodes well for getting to the bottom of this. But it is really up to you and your staff, on behalf of the American people, to take on that challenge. It's not something that anyone from the outside can do. So I look forward to these hearings and other hearings at how you will get to the conclusions.

I do believe we have to understand why reality turned out to be different than expectations and estimates. But you have more public service—certainly many of you—than I have ever had, and you recognize that this is not unusual.

I told Sen. [John] Warner [chairman of the Senate Armed Services Committee] earlier that I've been drawn back as a result of a recent film of reminding me of something. At the time of the Cuban missile crisis, the combined estimate was unanimity in the intelligence service that there were no Soviet warheads in Cuba at the time of the missile crisis.

Fortunately, President Kennedy and [then-Attorney General] Robert Kennedy disagreed with the estimate and chose a course of action less ambitious and aggressive than recommended by their advisers.

But the most important thing about that story, which is not often told, is that as a result after the Cuban missile crisis, immediate steps were taken to correct our inability to collect on the movement of nuclear material out of the Soviet Union to other places.

So that by the end of the Johnson administration, the Intelligence Community had a capability to do what it had not been able to do at the time of the Cuban missile crisis.

I think you face a similar responsibility in ensuring that the community is able to do a better job in the future than it has done in the past.

Call for Restructuring of the Intelligence Community

Dianne Feinstein

U.S. senator (D), California, 1992– ; born June 22, 1933, San Francisco, CA; B.A. in history, Stanford University, 1955; appointee, Women's Parole Board, 1960; San Francisco Board of Supervisors, 1970–78, and president, 1970–71, 1974–75, 1978; first woman mayor, San Francisco, 1978–88; Democratic nominee for governor, California, 1990; first woman senator from California; first woman member of Senate Judiciary Committee; Appropriations Committee; Energy and Natural Resources Committee; Select Committee on Intelligence; Rules and Administration Committee; Inter-American Dialogue, 1988– ; Director, Bank of California, 1988–89; Japan Society of Northern California, 1988–89; San Francisco Education Fund, 1988–89; cochair, Democratic Senatorial Campaign Committee, Women's Council.

Editors' introduction: Because many leaders and citizens questioned the credibility of intelligence employed by the Bush administration to justify the war against Iraq, they took steps to correct the mistakes in judgment. In a speech on the U.S. Senate floor, Senator Feinstein called on the Senate to approve legislation, which she introduced in both the 107th and 108th Congresses, that would restructure the Intelligence Community through the creation of a Director of National Intelligence. She also advocated the creation of an independent commission to examine the quality and use of prewar intelligence.

Dianne Feinstein's speech: I thank the chairman of the Intelligence Committee for his remarks. I think he well and ably set out the structure of what we are doing. I also thank Senator Lott for his remarks, particularly the remarks that said we should work together. That has been one of the problems. I want to go into that.

But before I do, I would like particularly to thank the Senator from Florida, the former chairman of the Senate Select Committee on Intelligence, for his three speeches. I had the privilege of previewing these. I think he delivered them eloquently and forcefully. I want him to know I very much appreciate his careful scholarship and his reasoned approach, which mark not only his remarks here but also his tenure as chairman of the Intelligence Committee. He has presided over what continues to be one of the most difficult chapters in the history of our Intelligence Community.

Delivered on February 5, 2004, at Washington DC.

Senator Lott has just said, with considerable spark, that we should work together. I could not agree more. Except I am told there has been limited participation by Democratic staff in the investigation, the report of which we will receive this afternoon. This necessarily, then, creates a problem because the two staffs have not fully worked side by side.

Second, the committee has been prevented from examining the use of intelligence by policymakers. This I believe is a real problem. Our own resolution sets out that we should be able to examine the use of intelligence by policymakers and administration officials. To a great extent this is the reason we are here today creating an independent commission which will have more authority than the elected officials of this government have.

I learned this morning that the independent commission that is functioning today has access to the president's daily intelligence briefs. The Intelligence Committee of the Senate does not have access to the president's daily intelligence briefs, nor have we had, to the best of my knowledge, through this investigation.

I was very pleased to see that over the past weekend the president has apparently reversed course, accepting the recommendations from Dr. Kay, from members of the Senate, and from a host of experts to the effect that only a full and outside investigation will be able to be both credible and acceptable to the world at large.

I did not believe so before. I voted against the Corzine resolution when it came up before. I changed my mind because if we, the elected representatives, are not permitted to look into the use of intelligence as provided by S. Res. 400, and it has to be an outside committee that will have that right, so be it. But I find it to be really idiosyncratic, because I believe the full power should be vested in the officials of our government, of which the Senate plays a very major role, not necessarily always an independent committee, as it appears to be happening.

Such a commission, though, will be able to remove some of the partisanship that has infected this issue and, I hope, provide a reasoned, careful, and credible assessment. I am concerned that the president has let it be known he intends to appoint all of the members of the commission and carry this out through Executive order. This I believe will adversely affect the commission's independence.

Let me give you an example. Many believe the handling of the National Commission on Terrorist Attacks on the United States— that is a Commission now functioning—headed by Gov. Thomas Kean and Congressman Lee Hamilton, is a case in point. There have been many reports that chronic delays in providing documents and foot dragging in arranging interviews have frustrated the efforts of this commission to complete its work within the timeline the White House insisted upon.

The commission is asking for an extension of time and Senators McCain and Lieberman have introduced legislation to do so. I understand the president yesterday agreed to extend this timetable to July 26 of this year. I strongly believe the commission should be given whatever time it needs to complete its examination and we, in fact, should pass the McCain-Lieberman bill.

Nevertheless, it is my hope that a commission, whether it is created by Executive order or by statute, will be able to answer four questions.

The first is: Were the prewar intelligence assessments of the dangers posed by Saddam Hussein's regime wrong? This is not as simple a question as it seems, for in the months prior to the invasion of Iraq these assessments had two separate, equally important parts. The first is whether Iraq had the capability to place the United States in such danger as to warrant the unprecedented step of a unilateral preemptive invasion of another sovereign nation. Just two days ago Secretary Powell, asked if he would have recommended an invasion knowing Iraq had no prohibited weapons, replied: "I don't know because it was the stockpile that presented the final little piece that made it more of a real and present danger and threat to the region and to the world." He added: "The absence of a stockpile changes the political calculus; it changes the answer you get."

Were the prewar intelligence assessments of the dangers posed by Saddam Hussein's regime wrong?

Second, was such a threat imminent or was it grave and growing? Critical to this debate during the summer and fall of 2002 was the immediacy of the threat which supported the argument that we needed to attack quickly, could not wait to bring traditional allies aboard or to try other options short of invasion.

The second question is whether the intelligence assessments were bad as well as wrong. This requires a fine distinction between an intelligence assessment that is wrong, and one that is bad. Intelligence assessments are often wrong, for by their nature they are an assessment of the probability that a future event will take place. But wrong does not always mean bad. Sometimes an intelligence assessment follows the right logic and fairly assesses the amount, credibility and meaning of collected data, and still is wrong. What the independent commission needs to do is to separate these two different, but related, issues.

The third question is to determine—if the intelligence assessment was both bad and wrong—to what degree and why?

Did the Intelligence Community negligently depart from accepted standards of professional competence in performing its collection and analytic tasks?

Was the Intelligence Community subject to pressures, personal or structural, which caused it to reach a wrong result through bad analysis?

Were the ordinary internal procedures by which intelligence is subject to peer review properly carried out?

A commission must delve deeply into the mechanisms of intelligence analysis to reach these answers.

The fourth and final question is whether the intelligence assessments reached by the Intelligence Community, whether right or wrong, good or bad, were fairly represented to the Congress and to the American people. Did administration officials speaking in open and closed session to members of Congress accurately represent the intelligence product that they were relying upon? Were public statements, speeches, and press releases, fair and accurate? This is the cauldron boiling below the surface.

This final question is particularly grave, because it touches upon the constitutionally critical link between the executive and legislative branches. The founders knew what they were doing when they developed a shared responsibility for warmaking—only Congress can declare war, with the president, as commander in chief, conducting it—and the need is vital for members of Congress to have fairly presented, timely, and accurate intelligence when they consider whether to invest the president with the authority as commander in chief to put American lives, as well as those of innocent civilians, at risk.

My vote, in particular, was based largely on intelligence, and statements about that intelligence, related to Saddam's certain possession of chemical and biological weapons and the probability or likelihood that he had both weaponized and deployed them. Also, the fact that he had violated the UN missile restrictions and possessed a delivery system for a chemical or biological warhead, and could deliver that warhead 600 miles, threatening other Middle Eastern nations or perhaps, from offshore, the United States.

There were many statements made by the administration that when combined with the intelligence created an overwhelming case, I think particularly for me and for many others. I don't think there would have been 77 votes in the Senate to authorize use of force had these statements not be made.

Let me give just five examples of such statements:

Secretary of State Powell, on September 8, 2002, said on *Fox News Sunday*: "There is no doubt that he has chemical weapons stocks." He also said: "With respect to biological weapons, we are confident that he has some stocks of those weapons, and he is probably continuing to try to develop more."

President Bush, on September 12, 2002, said in his address to the UN General Assembly: "Right now, Iraq is expanding and improving facilities that were used for the production of biological weapons."

President Bush, in his October 7, 2002, address also said: "We know that the regime has produced thousands of tons of chemical agents, including mustard gas, sarin nerve gas, and VX nerve gas."

Secretary Powell, again in his February 5, 2003, address to the UN Security Council, said: "Our conservative estimate is that Iraq today has a stockpile of between 100 and 500 tons of chemical weapons agent. That is enough agent to fill 16,000 battlefield rockets. Even the low end of 100 tons of agent would enable Saddam Hussein to cause mass casualties across more than 100 square miles of territory, an area nearly five times the size of Manhattan . . . when will we see the rest of the submerged iceberg? Saddam Hussein has chemical weapons. Saddam Hussein has used such weapons. And Saddam Hussein has no compunction about using them again, against his neighbors and against his own people."

What a strong statement—a statement that has to backed up with almost certain facts. President Bush said, on October 2, 2002, in Cincinnati: "Facing clear evidence of peril, we cannot wait for the final proof, the smoking gun that may come in the form of a mushroom cloud."

I remember hearing this speech, which made a deep impression upon me. The President of the United States said this. Members of the Intelligence Committee are looking at intelligence. When combined with the president's statements, the statements of the secretary of state and the statements of the vice president, how can you not believe them? That is why this committee's investigation into the use of intelligence which we have been prohibited from entering into is so important that we do. We are the official people's representatives on this Committee on Intelligence, and to cut us out from one part of an investigation that our own resolutions say we should look at, I think, is unconscionable.

When all of this is combined with the intelligence provided to Congress, the aerial photographs of what was believed to be chemical weapons plants, and the National Intelligence Estimate of October 2002, this information created an overwhelming belief that there was an imminent threat to our nation, and a dominant majority of the Senate of the United States voted for the resolution authorizing the use of force.

You can imagine my surprise that after more than 1,500 sites— top priority sites—have been searched and millions of dollars spent on Dr. Kay's special investigation, no weapons have been found. And Dr. Kay submits to us that he does not believe any will be found.

So the reality of what has been learned in Iraq versus the intelligence presented to us causes enormous concern.

Again, I truly believe that had it not been for the strength of the intelligence and statements made to Congress, including the Senate Select Committee on Intelligence, a vote for regime change alone, without the belief of an imminent threat, would not have had the majority it did, may well not have passed, and if it did, most likely would have passed with a bare majority.

These statements and the intelligence upon which they were based now appear to be unsupported by the available evidence, and have been contradicted by Dr. Kay's findings. A commission must look closely at these and other similar statements.

Even as the commission moves forward, I believe Congress should undertake two related tasks. The first is to carefully review the implications of the President's so-called preemption doctrine. I have strongly criticized this policy since its inception. Although clearly the United States will always retain the right to defend itself in specific circumstances from a real, imminent threat, preemption as a doctrine departs from core American values. We must be strong in defense but not allow this country to become an aggressive nation of conquest.

I also believe the doctrine runs counter to 50 years of bipartisan American foreign policy, which is based on the belief that international law, multilateral agreements, and diplomacy are also effective means to promote and to protect American security.

Finally, and on a more fundamental and practical level, the doctrine requires a faith in the perfectibility of intelligence analysis that is simply not attainable. Preemption inherently requires us to be right every time on the nature and imminence of threats.

Unfortunately, as every senior intelligence official I have spoken to tells me, intelligence is rarely going to be that accurate, for the

---

The preemptive concept bets everything on one roll of the dice and we had better be right every time.

---

very reason I have mentioned earlier—it is, at its heart, probability analysis.

This past weekend, Dr. Kay spoke to this issue, saying, and I quote, "If you cannot rely on good, accurate intelligence that is credible to the American people and to others abroad, you certainly can't have a policy of preemption."

The preemptive concept bets everything on one roll of the dice and we had better be right every time.

I spoke about this when the doctrine was announced and offered the hypothetical of a preemptive attack based on intelligence that was wrong, that results in destruction and death, and undermines American credibility and our position around the world. The hypothetical, so far, at least, is true in Iraq.

I hope the president and his advisers will reconsider the ill-advised adoption of preemption in light of what we have already learned from its first exercise.

The second thing the Congress should do, and do now, is begin the process of restructuring the Intelligence Community and begin by taking a single, critical step: Pass legislation creating a Director of National Intelligence and change from the current situation where a single man is both head of the entire Intelligence Community—with its 15 departments and agencies—and the head of the Central Intelligence Agency. It is an impossible job with insufficient authority.

I have introduced legislation that would accomplish this in both the 107th and 108th Congresses. Each time I stood on this floor to urge its passage and each time I expressed my belief that the current structure could result in a colossal intelligence failure.

In June of 2002, I said: "This legislation creates the Director of National Intelligence to lead a true Intelligence Community and to coordinate our intelligence and antiterrorism efforts and help assure the sort of communication problems that prevented the various elements of our Intelligence Community from working together effectively before September 11 never happen again."

I fear it has happened again. Once more, I stand in the Senate to urge the passage of the legislation.

It has to be pointed out that our present intelligence structure for the most part is based on a post–World War II, Cold War environment. It is not suited for the new challenges of asymmetric threats and non-state entities, as well as quite possibly from states also involved in terrorism. We have a Soviet-era Intelligence Community in a post-Soviet world.

We need to have a Director of National Intelligence now more than ever and we should not wait any longer for the results of

---

We need to have a Director of National Intelligence now more than ever.

---

another commission. I remind my colleagues that creating a Director of National Intelligence was the very first recommendation of the bipartisan joint inquiry into the attacks on September 11, a recommendation contained in a report signed by every member of the Intelligence Committees of the Senate and the House. Senator Graham spoke earlier about this provision and I agree with his explanation of the pressing need for the change.

Such a position, if created today, would provide substantial improvement in the function and quite possibly the restructuring of the more than one dozen agencies and departments. It would give one person, appointed by the president for a 10-year term, the statutory authority to determine strategies across the board, to set priorities, and to assign staff and dollars across departments and agencies.

It is my understanding the Senate Select Committee on Intelligence will take up this legislation in 2004, I am told, in April. It is my hope that working together we can include this legislation as part of the Intelligence Authorization Act for fiscal year 2005 and make it law this Spring.

As I have said earlier, the so-called bipartisan investigation by the Senate Select Committee on Intelligence has had little effective participation by Democratic senators, or their staffs. In fact, in many ways had the Intelligence Committee been able to carry out its responsibilities, as set for in Senate Resolution 400, much of the debate on the floor on this issue would be unnecessary. Nonetheless, I look forward to this afternoon when the report will be made available to committee members.

I deeply believe that the Senate Select Committee on Intelligence should turn its attention to its core responsibilities—conducting vigorous oversight of the Intelligence Community, and carefully considering legislation to make necessary changes. To that end I urge Chairman Roberts to take up legislation restructuring the Intelligence Community, including, but not limited to, my bill to create a Director of National Intelligence, hold comprehensive hearings on these proposals, and report out legislation in time for inclusion in this year's Intelligence Authorization bill.

As I have said earlier, my vote in favor of the Resolution to Authorize the Use of Force in Iraq was perhaps the most difficult, and consequential, vote of my career. It was a decision based on hours of intelligence briefings from administration and intelligence officials, plus the classified and unclassified versions of the National Intelligence Estimates. My decision was in part based on my trust that this intelligence was the best our nation's intelligence services could offer, untainted by bias, and fairly presented.

It was a decision made because I was convinced that the threat from Iraq was not only grave but imminent.

Because of my vote, and the votes of the 76 other Senators who voted for the Resolution, our troops are stuck in Iraq, under fire, and taking casualties. Our armed forces are stretched thin; we have antagonized our enemies and alienated many of [our] closest allies.

In the post-9/11 world, a world where we confront asymmetric threats every day, intelligence plays a key role informing the policy-making process. The administration bears primary responsibility for our intelligence apparatus—ensuring that it works well, is honest, and is properly focused. The administration is also responsible for honestly and fairly presenting the results of the intelligence process to the Congress, informing, for instance our vote on the Resolution to Authorize Force.

I now fear that the threat was not imminent, that there were other policy options, short of war, that would have effectively met the threat posed by Saddam Hussein.

And that is why a full investigation of the prewar intelligence is so critical.

Foreign Policy Association

James L. Pavitt

Deputy director for operations, Central Intelligence Agency (CIA), 1999–2004; B.A. in history, Phi Beta Kappa, University of Missouri; National Defense Education Act Fellow, Clark University; intelligence officer, U.S. Army, 1969–71; legislative assistant, House of Representatives, 1971–73; at CIA from 1973, serving in Europe, Asia, and at CIA headquarters, Langley, Virginia; special assistant to deputy director for operations; director for intelligence programs, National Security Council, 1990; special assistant to the president for national security affairs, 1992; deputy director for operations, CIA's Nonproliferation Center; began counterproliferation division, 1995; associate deputy director for operations, 1997–99.

Editors' introduction: With the conflict in Iraq continuing, government officials and citizens debated the causes and consequences of the fighting through a variety of forums, including Congressional hearings, 24-hour cable news channels, and the 2004 presidential election campaigns. In a rare speech, responding to criticism of the U.S. Intelligence Community's gathering of information about President Saddam Hussein's intentions prior to the war, Deputy Director Pavitt told the Foreign Policy Association that "now is not the time for radical reorganization of the Intelligence Community, for creating a new structure." While "proud of the . . . heroes" working in the Intelligence Community," Mr. Pavitt reminded that, "Even with all that we have learned from 9/11, from the war on terrorism . . . there will be failures." The Foreign Policy Association, founded in 1918, provides independent publications, programs, and forums to increase Americans' awareness of and foster popular participation in matters relating to foreign policy. Mr. Pavitt had announced his intention to resign from the CIA prior to this speech, soon after CIA Director George Tenet's resignation was made public.

James L. Pavitt's speech: Thank you very much. It is a privilege to be here this evening. In the tradition of the men charged with keeping America's most sensitive secrets, I rarely speak in public. But I decided it was important to come to this city and speak to this audience, to speak openly about the Directorate of Operations—the clandestine service—the most secret, yet, least understood part of the Central Intelligence Agency.

I would like to borrow the words of an Englishman from another time who—better than any spy novel—captured the spirit and ethos of the clandestine service:

Delivered on June 21, 2004, at 5:30 P.M., University Club, College Hall, New York City.

From time to time, God causes men to be born who have a lust to go abroad at the risk of their lives and discover news—today it may be far off things, tomorrow, of some hidden mountain, and the next day of some nearby men who have done a foolishness against the state. These souls are very few; and of these few, not more than ten are of the best.

For the most secret part of the U.S. Intelligence Community, there has been far too much buzz over the past few years on what it is we do. My officers have been described as gun-slinging cowboys on the one hand and, risk-averse on the other and, worse yet, just plain incompetent. In the media there has been a lot of talk—some complimentary, a great deal critical, but most of the commentary is from sources who are far from informed. It seems a lot of people with very short careers in the clandestine service or, more often, people at the periphery of the intelligence profession consider themselves qualified pundits. The title "intelligence expert" is one all of us see with increasing regularity on television these days. Yet, for all the experts and all the expert opinion, I fear the American people don't get much real insight into my business from these "experts."

So I thought it perhaps worth your time to hear from me—the man who runs America's spy service. I will retire in August after 31 years of service at CIA. Despite a long tradition of silence, a tradition of allowing the wildest statements about my business to go unanswered, I feel both compelled and obligated as the leader of the clandestine service to set the record straight about America's spy service.

But first, let me tell you a little more about what I won't tell you. I will not divulge the names of officers, I will not divulge ongoing operations, I will do nothing to compromise information which is vital to our national security. But I will provide some insider details. I will offer some real insight into the operations and the people who make up the clandestine service—one of America's best, but least known, and least appreciated national treasures. Hopefully, you will get some appreciation of the men and women who fill the ranks of the clandestine service. These are truly extraordinary Americans doing extraordinary things—who work in silence on the front lines of the intelligence war.

My good friend George Tenet often says he has the greatest job in the world: I beg to differ—I think as Deputy Director for Operations, I do. Every morning, I am briefed on an astounding array of incredible secret operations, agent meetings, recruitments of new agents, placement of technical devices, captures of terrorists, near misses and harrowing escapes clandestine service officers have carried out in the past 24 hours. Not a day goes by in which I am not astounded by the imagination, the creativity, and the bravery the men and women of the Directorate use to keep our nation safe and collect human intelligence of incalculable value.

These have been particularly challenging times for America and for our nation's spy service. We are now nearly three years beyond the devastation of September 11—a day that indelibly scarred this city and this nation. Like Pearl Harbor—the event which led to the creation of America's intelligence services—9/11 redefined us, refocused us, and made our mission all the more critical. It changed what we do and how we do it forever.

We are no strangers to criticism, and the events of the past few years have generated a great deal of it. Some is very thoughtful, and we welcome that.

We have learned, adjusted and grown from thoughtful and honest critique. We are better for many changes made, and we are more able. But some of the criticism is unwarranted and frankly, ill-informed—for example, the charges that the CIA has lost its status as the gold standard in intelligence or that our officers are unwilling to go to the hardest, most dangerous places. I can tell you that is simply not true!

Shallow uninformed criticism provides precious little insight into what America's clandestine service is all about. What human intel-

---

Shallow uninformed criticism provides precious little insight into what America's clandestine service is all about.

---

ligence is and what it is not. Let me do that for you tonight.

For all the critique, for all the rhetoric about failure, no one has ever asked me to stop recruiting spies and stop producing human intelligence reports. Indeed, the demand grows and customers at every level want more.

Many of those who criticize us for not having enough spies, enough agents on Iraq, on terrorism, on North Korea, on Iran, do not have the first idea of what a spy, an agent really is. An agent—a human being with access to vital, secret information who agrees to give this information to us—is not a simply attainable commodity. Contrary to popular fiction, they cannot simply be bought—indeed, some of the very best agents have never taken a dime. They are human beings—carefully cultivated, developed, and brought to a relationship based on a level of trust that transcends any simple business arrangement.

Among the trendy sound bites on intelligence is the clamor for "connecting the dots," for sharing sensitive operational information with analysts and other consumers of intelligence so they have all the dots connected, so that nothing whatsoever is overlooked.

I fully support information sharing. Information sharing is essential—the information from our sources and the "product" of our operations is meant to be used—to inform our top policymakers and to enable law enforcement officials to thwart terrorist attacks. We risk agents and officers every day to collect that data.

But that sharing does not eliminate our sacred duty to protect our sources and methods. We always balance expanded access to information with smart compartmentation and what we call the "need-to-know" principle.

I know the spy business and the people who conduct it better than most, and I am here tonight to give you a bit of an insider's view. As the DDO, I know better than anyone the men and women who spend their days recruiting spies and stealing secrets. I know their commitment, their integrity, their desire to serve, their sense of duty and patriotism and their willingness to make tremendous personal sacrifices for the national good.

The officers of the clandestine service work in the most dangerous and most demanding places in the world. Places like Qandahar, Afghanistan—where Al Qaeda and the Taliban target our personnel for assassination. Places like Moscow—the heart of our number one global competitor, working under the toughest, most pervasive surveillance in the world. Places like Bogota, where narcoterrorists conduct assassinations in broad daylight. Places like Baghdad where our officers are constantly under attack from an enemy bent on their deaths—where we lose to hostile fire armored vehicles at the rate of one a week. In times that demand heroes, America is fortunate to have these heroes serving on the front lines.

Let me tell you more about my officers:

The officer abroad who spent more than 20 hours on the streets to collect critical intelligence, meeting an agent for whom the consequences of exposure would be certain death.

The officer in Iraq who dealt with a nervous, jumpy intelligence volunteer who promised and delivered the location of Uday and Qusay Hussein.

The officer in Afghanistan who, wounded in an Al Qaeda firefight, turned his vehicle into the line of fire to protect his Afghan and American partners—and gave his life to ensure his colleagues could return home.

The officer abroad who ventures into the toughest immigrant neighborhoods—where the local police think twice about going—to scour the Islamic community for a penetration of a terrorist cell, an Al Qaeda fundraiser, someone who can provide a critical piece of intelligence.

The officer who posed as a foreigner to gain access to the inner circle of a major terrorist facilitator in one of the toughest, most dangerous areas in South Asia.

A young paramilitary officer, recently married, with a young child who has spent more time in Afghanistan and Iraq since 9/11 than with his family and whose only proviso when asked to travel into the toughest of environments was, "Tell me where I can be of the most service."

Sometimes the officers themselves speak most eloquently about what they do and what the job means. This from a first-tour officer injured in a firefight that took the lives of his military partners last fall while hunting terrorists in Afghanistan: "What the best training cannot prepare you for is what it feels like to be shot, what it feels like to see a friend in significant pain, what it feels like to have your weapon jam under fire. . . . I have to admit, I was feeling sorry for myself, but it was the thought of my family and friends that kept me level headed and focused on surviving. I continue to be committed to our profession because I believe in our mission."

Organizations often show their true colors—indeed as some have put it—their cultures—in the worst of times. In February 2003, we faced such a period with the tragic loss of a young first tour officer who was killed in Afghanistan in a terrible training accident. My Chief of Station in Kabul wrote me a note shortly thereafter, which, I believe, captures the spirit and ethos of the clandestine service. I quote from his note: "One thing we cannot do, and every single officer here shares this view, is back away from the job at hand, and that necessarily means accepting attendant risks. . . . It is dangerous here, in Kabul, at the bases, all around. To a man, the attitude remains, if not me, who then?"

I've spent some time now discussing how the clandestine service is taking on the challenges of the present. Now I'd like to provide some history. Let's go back to the darkest days of the Cold War— the mid-1970s, when the Soviet Union and the United States seemed close to the nuclear confrontation we all dreaded during those dark days. In Moscow, our small station was under incredible, close surveillance—our officers were constantly watched and followed, tracked by trained dogs and technical devices. It was the toughest operating environment imaginable. Through the lens of the past 13 years, it is hard to remember the Soviet Union for the evil, repressive, society it was; in many ways, it was the model for the "republic of fear" Saddam created in Iraq.

In mid-1977, a small furtive man, hiding near the official gas station reserved for foreign diplomats, approached an official he believed to be an American and passed him a note, quickly, carefully, under the noses of surveillance. He was disgusted with the Soviet regime, quietly worshipped America from afar, and believed he was in a position to help.

Adolf Tolkachev—a senior research scientist in the Russian military aerospace program—did more than just help. The operation at which he was at the very center ensured us air superiority at a critical juncture of the Cold War. The intelligence he provided from

1977 to 1985 saved the U.S. taxpayers literally billions of dollars in research and development fees on look-down/shoot-down radar, aeronautics design, and early stealth technology.

Working in secret—in the basement of his office complex, in the toilets of the Lenin Library, risking his life at every turn—Tolkachev silently fought one of the greatest battles of the Cold War. Passing literally thousands of documents that were nothing short of pure gold.

Tolkachev never left Russia throughout the operation. As someone who held the highest level clearances, he was denied the privilege of foreign travel. Our officers went to tremendous lengths to elude and escape surveillance to meet him in the dead of night or early morning, quickly passing film and documents. Tolkachev, fighting his solo battle, was glad for the rare moments of contact with his allies.

In the end, Tolkachev was caught—and paid the ultimate price for his service—death in the basement of the notorious Lubyanka prison in Moscow. Oleg Penkovsky may have been the spy who "saved the world" during the Cuban missile crisis—but in the secret archives of the Cold War, Adolf Tolkachev and our officers who worked with him were heroes in one of the decisive battles in the Cold War.

These accounts describe the clandestine service I know. It is a national treasure that only a few people have the privilege to serve.

These rare, extraordinary men and women, who go abroad to the world's toughest places, understand the high stakes of their work and they are willing to take the necessary risks. They accept that, in the secret world, success is unheralded and failure is trumpeted. Yet they continue their difficult, demanding work, in silent service to our country.

Let me say it again: They are a national treasure.

As the result of exceptional leadership within the Agency and a new appreciation of the value of human intelligence by our nation's leaders, we are in a much stronger position today than we were a decade ago. As you know from recent press articles, we embarked on a wholesale rebuilding of the clandestine service in the late 1990s. We have made tremendous strides but still have work to do.

The fact is, despite strong protests from within my agency, the clandestine service was left to wither during most of the '90s. As part of the so-called "peace dividend" after the Cold War ended, too many in Washington believed that intelligence was no longer needed and our operations officer corps could shrink without consequence.

And shrink it did. We trained roughly two dozen new officers in 1995. Even as our missions were expanding and changing, the number of intelligence positions throughout the Government, especially overseas, dropped by almost a quarter in the mid-'90s. At CIA, recruitment of both operations officers and analysts came to a virtual halt.

Compare that with today: Our recruiting and training efforts are unprecedented. And interest in CIA from talented men and women from all over this country is at an all-time high.

We get 2,200 resumes a week from some of America's best and brightest. Not only young college graduates, but also experienced professionals: retired military and law enforcement officers, linguists, scientists, lawyers, engineers, doctors.

Today, the average clandestine service trainee classes number significantly higher and we aim to double the number of new officers in two years. Recruits spend a full year learning every aspect of our tradecraft, from how to detect surveillance, to the fine art of recruitment and agent handling to armed defense in extreme situations.

In the last five years, the clandestine service has grown 30 percent. And we plan to grow it another 30 percent in the next five years. But as good as our recruiting and training is, it can't buy experience, and it will take time for our skilled new graduates to become the seasoned pros we need them to be.

The world we face today, the challenges we face are far more dangerous and require as great if not a greater commitment than those associated with the Cold War. We face a global enemy in the terrorists bent on our destruction, the challenge of providing force protection for nearly a quarter million U.S. troops in Iraq, Afghanistan, the Balkans, the Korean Peninsula, preventing the proliferation of weapons of mass destruction, dealing with regional challenges such as Iran, North Korea, Russia, and China.

The fight against Al Qaeda and the hate-filled extremist movement it fuels across the globe is an intelligence war—as much as if not more than any conflict in our nation's history. We will not prevail against this agile and determined enemy without creative, vibrant, and expanded human intelligence capabilities.

The CIA has known this for years. The opening shots in the war on terrorism were fired well before 11 September 2001. The Directorate's Counterterrorist Center will mark its 20th anniversary in 2006. Even in our leanest years—the 1990s, when Congress was cutting our funding—we were ensuring sustained resources to counterterrorism, not as much as we needed to meet the gathering threat, but as much as we could given our limited resources.

Well before 11 September 2001 we understood the important connection between domestic and international terrorism. We were working side by side with the FBI and other law enforcement agencies to counter the threat. The partnership was real.

Well before 11 September 2001, we were fighting Al Qaeda and disrupting its activities. We unraveled terrorist plots that aimed to murder innocents and shatter peace. Plans for attacks in the U.S., Jordan, and Israel around the millennium were thwarted. Others still were quashed in the fall of 2000, and again in the summer of 2001.

Well before 11 September 2001, we told the public and we told the Congress and the executive branch that terrorists threatened our nation.

Well before 11 September 2001, we knew Al Qaeda was planning something bigger than we had seen, something terrible. All the while, we at CIA were loudly sounding the alarm and constantly seeking more resources to counter this threat. The bombings of our embassies in Africa and the USS *Cole* were not enough. The chatter we picked up in early summer 2001 was not enough to provide us specific information about the attack.

The tragedy of September 11th changed everything. The Intelligence Community, at long last, received the funding and the tools it needed to fight the war on terrorism—at the cost of 3,000 innocent souls.

People still ask me if I think we could have stopped the horror of that day—if we had, in fact, connected all the dots before us. There are some who have placed the blame on a handful of individual officers for not ensuring the FBI watch listed two of the hijackers. It is a question my officers have asked themselves, have tormented themselves with, for it is only human to wonder "what if?"

Although we can speculate endlessly, given what we had that day, I sadly conclude that the answer is no. Short of cracking Osama bin Laden's impenetrable inner circle, sealing our borders and recognizing box cutters as potential weapons, we could not have stopped those planes from hitting the World Trade Center, the Pentagon and that field in Pennsylvania. In a chilling interview on Al Jazeera, bin Laden himself bragged that not even all of the hijackers knew the full extent of their mission that day.

We did not foil the evil of September 11. We failed to stop this horror. Indeed, not only did we fail, much of our national security apparatus failed as well to protect the American people. But we did not allow the horror to prevent us from fighting back—right from the start. Ignoring the order to evacuate CIA headquarters, many of my CTC officers stayed to take charge of the intelligence counterattack. Many officers from other parts of the DO volunteered to stay on— many for several days without break. One senior officer who had retired from the government on the 11th was driving to his retirement home, literally swung his car around on the road when he heard of the attacks, drove back in the gates, revoked his retirement, and went right back to work.

In less than two weeks, CIA paramilitary officers were on the ground in Afghanistan, working with old friends in familiar places, in the traditions of their OSS forefathers, preparing the way for the eventual military campaign that deposed the Taliban and deprived bin Laden and his lieutenants of a sanctuary in which to plan future attacks.

Destroying terrorism and those who have attacked us is the primary mission of my officers, not only in Pakistan and Afghanistan, but worldwide. A worldwide threat requires a worldwide response.

And our efforts have had significant impact on our enemies. We've captured or killed nearly two-thirds of known Al Qaeda top leadership. Khalid Shaykh Muhammed, Khalid bin Attash, Abu Zubaydah Hambali, Abu Musab al Baluchi, and a host of others are in custody.

None of this—none of this—would be possible without human intelligence: My operations officers, the agents they recruit and the partnerships they build with foreign intelligence services all serve the counterterrorist mission. Satellite photos and communications intercepts can get you only so far. It is the human source that so often delivers the final piece of a puzzle. Human intelligence from the spies the clandestine service recruits resulted in many of the captures. A human source gave us the critical piece of intelligence to conduct the operation leading to the capture of the architect of 9/11, the Al Qaeda mastermind Khalid Shaykh Muhammed; a human source provided us the trail to Hambali, Al Qaeda's ringleader for a second wave of terror attacks on America; and it is human intelligence that will eventually help us bring Osama bin Ladin to justice, or justice to him.

Destroying terrorism and those who have attacked us is the primary mission of my officers.

Let me be clear: The threat from Al Qaeda remains. Let me be even clearer: as sure as I am of anything, I am sure all of us here are sitting in the cross hairs. Al Qaeda has unambiguous plans to hit the homeland again, and New York City, I am certain, remains a prime target. Human intelligence will play a critical role in preventing future attacks, but I can't offer you guarantees—and I wouldn't trust anyone who does.

Let me move away from terrorism for a moment to another issue challenging America and its spy service.

From the task of collecting intelligence before the war in Iraq to the current task of supporting the new republic's first breaths of freedom, the clandestine service has been fully engaged in Iraq.

I am often asked why Iraq was so hard.

Simply put, Iraq under Saddam was the republic of fear. If you were suspected of or caught assisting his adversaries, your family was tortured and you were shot. Indeed, it was no secret to Iraqis that getting caught working with us meant the end for them and their families.

As I mentioned at the outset, some of our critics have been on the mark regarding Iraq. Indeed, as some critics have claimed, during the prewar period, we did not have many Iraqi sources. We certainly did not have enough! Until we put people on the ground in northern Iraq, we had less than a handful. As I mentioned before, the operating environment was tremendously prohibitive and developing the necessary trust with those Iraqis who had access was extraordinarily difficult in light of the risks they faced. Once on the ground, however, our officers recruited literally dozens of agents—some of whom paid the ultimate price for their allegiance to us—who were determined to help all Iraqis win their freedom.

Did we get access to the heart of Saddam's weapons programs? No. In those final months, did we get closer to the inner circle of the military and political process? Absolutely! And in that compressed period of a few months, we collected intelligence our own military deemed of vital importance.

CIA officers first played pathfinder roles, moving well ahead of the combat lines, obtaining critical intelligence that informed battlefield planners. Then, when U.S. troops launched on March 19, 2003, my officers were right there with them.

And well before Saddam's statue was toppled in Baghdad, our officers, their equipment, and communications gear flew into the capital under hostile fire. We needed to be there—to provide crucial intelligence to the advancing combat forces.

Today, as Iraq transitions from tyranny to self-determination, Baghdad is home to the largest CIA station since the Vietnam war. I am extremely proud of our performance in Iraq, and of our role in liberating its people from decades of repression.

The missions the clandestine service takes on for America are not all fast-breaking. Many take years or longer. Human intelligence led the way to one of the most significant counter-proliferation successes in years: Libya's renunciation of weapons of mass destruction last December.

As the result of a patient, decade-long operation involving million-dollar recruitment pitches, covert entries, ballet-like sophistication, and a level of patience we are often accused of not possessing, the clandestine service exposed the network of Pakistani scientist A. Q. Khan. Khan was the source of nuclear materials in Libya, Iran, and North Korea and the potential source to non-state actors. Working with British intelligence, we surprised Libya's leaders with the depth of our knowledge about its weapons programs. We pressed them on the right questions, exposed inconsistencies and convinced the Libyans that holding back was counterproductive.

In the end, Colonel Qadhafi had no option but to abandon his WMD programs and accept international inspections. Nice work by any high standard!

None of this comes easily. Espionage is not James Bond or Jason Bourne or any of the hundreds of other fictional spies who occupy the world of novels and movies. Human intelligence demands a balance of delicacy, poise, timing, and understanding of human beings. It relies on an operations officer getting to know an agent or potential agent as well as he or she knows a member of his or her family. The officer must learn the motivations, emotions, loyalties, vulnerabilities, and limits that drive this most unique of human beings. It requires professional detachment that allows the officer to see the truth from the half-truth, the nuance of fact, the coloration of bias. It is no wonder why human intelligence is, as I told you, more art than science.

It has been well established that the Intelligence Community, including the clandestine service, did not have the resources it required before the 9/11 attacks. Most of you are aware of the traumatic resource reductions we received throughout the decade of the '90s, cuts made in the wake of the supposed post–Cold War "peace dividend," the reluctance of Congress and the nation's leadership to sustain the clandestine service so that we could answer the alarm we had been sounding about Al Qaeda's threat to America. These cuts, the lack of funding, left America's spy service weakened and America vulnerable. As I said before, 9/11 changed all that—the Congress provided a tremendous influx of counterterrorism funding in the wake of 9/11 and Iraq focused funding prior to the war in Iraq.

> ## *Now is not the time for radical reorganization of the Intelligence Community.*

The tremendous resources devoted to the war on terrorism and the effort in Iraq have made a difference; the influx of funding has helped. But it has helped us catch up in a race in which we had been allowed to fall too far behind. Frankly speaking, the men and women of the clandestine service have been in a flat-out sprint since 9/11. The increased funding has helped us to grow our capability in the global war on terrorism and support our troops in Iraq. But we will need longer-term, strategic funds to win the race around the globe. For the sake of America's security, for our future, we need sustained congressional and executive commitment to grow and nurture a clandestine service worthy of this country and the challenges we face.

In my opinion, now is not the time for radical reorganization of the Intelligence Community, for creating a new structure, a different framework in the hope of always getting it right and always connecting the dots. Some have said my retirement and George Tenet's resignation create the "perfect storm" for radical restructuring in the Intelligence Community. Let me remind you that in the book and the movie *The Perfect Storm*, the ship sank and the crew drowned.

I would argue against change for the sake or appearance of change particularly in these politically charged times and at a time of great terrorist threat. No one really seeks a perfect storm. The aftermath of 9/11 brought about tremendous change in the way we do business; but change for its own sake is dead wrong. I believe thoughtful empowerment of the DCI and sustained executive and congressional commitment to improve our nation's intelligence capabilities will serve our nation well.

No amount of intelligence funding, no amount of threat integration, no amount of rebuilding the Intelligence Community, as some have called for, will or can guarantee perfect results.

At its very best, human intelligence is an inexact art, and while we may be able to find and connect many of the dots, I would be lying to you if I said we can connect them all. I would be suspect of anyone offering quick solutions or quick answers through hasty reorganization and centralization.

Even with all that we have learned from 9/11, from the war on terrorism—as good as we've become, there will be failures. Perfection is impossible in a profession devoted to the complexities and unknowns of the world.

You already know what I worry about—another attack by terrorists on the homeland—indeed this is what I lose sleep over. But I also worry that racing to change risks many things to include our nation and the clandestine service. The clandestine service provides the American public with no balance sheet, no scorecard at the end of the year tallying victories and losses. Our failures—real or perceived—are the stuff of headlines—our successes are largely unheralded. Therefore, I hope I have expanded your understanding of what we do.

As we search for ways to improve our intelligence capability, we as a nation must take care not to dismiss or undo the magnificent gains of human intelligence. There is far more at stake than an organization's pride. Our challenges remain daunting, our responsibility enormous.

I fear that we are being pushed into a "mistake-free zone," and only bad can come of that. Fear of failure creates caution—in people and in organizations. One of the bedrocks of my business is a willingness to take risks—calculated risks that withstand legal scrutiny—but risks that are inherent to all we do. Mistakes and failure come with the territory as well—we will always strive for perfection with the understanding it is unattainable.

As my friend and former director Richard Helms put it, "Secret intelligence has never been for the fainthearted." In my business, you simply have to accept the real probability of failure, learn from your shortcomings and do better. Those afraid to make mistakes will never be bold or creative enough to solve the problems our nation faces. This business is not for everyone.

Imagine for a moment what would have happened if the CIA, during the height of the Cold War, had abandoned its effort to send the first spy satellite into space. The program was called Corona and it failed 12 times over two and a half years. Finally, in August 1960, it launched, orbited, and sent back to America the first overhead photos of the Soviet Union. The vast amounts of intelligence it gathered quickly overtook all we had gained from the U-2 spy program.

Indeed, some of our best officers have learned from their mistakes. In the previous century, a junior intelligence officer in Switzerland received word on Sunday evening that a disturbed Russian sought to speak to an American official. Not wanting to spoil his weekend tennis outing, our officer told the duty officer to direct the disturbed Russian to return the next day—Monday—during duty hours. Unfortunately, Vladimir Lenin chose not to return to the mission. Allen Dulles, our longest-serving DCI, was the junior intelligence officer. He recovered admirably from this early stumble and learned a lesson he imparted to future generations of operations officers.

Today, a willingness to think creatively and to take risks is arguably more important than ever. Our enemies in the war on terror seek our destruction. They have been weakened but not beaten. And there will be more deadly attacks.

And there is an important analogy.

Al Qaeda succeeded, with terrible human toll, on 11 September. Many times before, and many times after that horrid day in 2001, the terrorists failed and intelligence succeeded. Too often that is forgotten in the endless rush to assign blame.

- Seventy terrorists were brought to justice before 9/11, and hundreds after.

- The millenium plot, which targeted us among others, was disrupted with dozens of terrorists apprehended.

- The Ramadan plot in the Gulf was foiled.

- We stopped attacks against the U.S. in Yemen and Saudi Arabia.

- We disrupted attacks against the U.S. military in Europe and a U.S. embassy in a European capital.

- A major arrest deterred plans to kidnap Americans in three countries and carry out hijackings overseas.

We must be agile and aggressive in our response to this shrewd and single-minded foe.

We are and will continue to be.

As George Tenet once put it, "In times like these, the need for heroes is compelling." If you remember nothing else I have said tonight, remember this: There is no shortage of heroes in the company I keep.

- From the South Asian Muslim woman who became a U.S. citizen and is now—in her words—"living the American dream" by serving in the clandestine service;

- to the Arabic-speaking former operations officer who returned to us on September 12th, 2001, after leaving us for the private sector, because he decided there was no more important calling;

- from the Chief of Station targeted for assassination in South America;

- to the memory of Mike Spann—the first American hero to fall in Afghanistan fighting the Taliban and Al Qaeda.

I am tremendously proud of the people—the heroes—I have led for the last five years. They are heroes for whom there are no parades, no public accolades, and rare acknowledgment of their deeds. They are a living national treasure. They have earned your adulation and they need your support.

Release of 9/11 Commission Report

Thomas H. Kean and Lee H. Hamilton

Thomas H. Kean, president, Drew University, 1990– , and chair, National Commission on Terrorist Attacks Upon the United States (known as the 9/11 Commission), 2003–2004; born Livingston, NJ, April 21, 1935; B.A., Princeton University, and M.A., Columbia University Teachers College; member (R), New Jersey Assembly, 1968–77, rising to the positions of majority leader, minority leader, and speaker; governor of New Jersey, 1982–90; as governor, served on the president's Education Policy Advisory Committee and as chair of the Education Commission of the States and of the National Governor's Association Task Force on Teaching; while president of Drew University, has headed the U.S. delegation to the UN Conference on Youth in Thailand, served as vice chair of the U.S. delegation to the World Conference on Women in Beijing, and on the president's Initiative on Race; more than 25 honorary degrees and numerous awards from environmental and educational organizations; author, Politics of Inclusion *(1988).*

Lee H. Hamilton, president and director, Woodrow Wilson International Center for Scholars, 1999– , and vice chair, 9/11 Commission, 2003–2004; born Daytona Beach, FL, April 20, 1931; B.A., DePauw University, 1952; studied at Goethe University, Frankfurt, Germany, 1952–53; J.D., Indiana University School of Law, 1956; practiced law, Chicago, IL, and Columbus, IN; U.S. representative (D), Indiana's Ninth District, 1965–99; chair and ranking member of the House Committee on International Relations; chair, vice chair, and member, Joint Economic Committee; chair: Permanent Select Committee on Intelligence, Joint Committee on the Organization of Congress, October Surprise Task Force, and Select Committee to Investigate Covert Arms Transactions with Iran; member: House Standards of Official Conduct Committee and the U.S. Department of Homeland Security Advisory Council; author (with Jordan Tama), A Creative Tension: The Foreign Policy Roles of the President and Congress *(2003);* How Congress Works and Why You Should Care *(2004); American Political Science Association Hubert H. Humphrey Award and American Bar Association CEELI Award, both in 1998; Paul H. Nitze Award for Distinguished Authority on National Security Affairs, 1999.*

Editors' introduction: The 9/11 Commission was created by Congressional legislation and authorized by President George W. Bush in late 2002 to prepare a full, complete, and bipartisan account of the circumstances surrounding the September 11, 2001, terrorist attacks, including preparedness for and the immediate response to the attacks. The Commission was also to provide recommendations to guard against future attacks. In addition to Chair Kean and Vice Chair Hamilton, Richard Ben-Veniste, Fred

Delivered on July 22, 2004, at Washington, DC.

F. Fielding, Jamie S. Gorelick, Slade Gorton, Bob Kerrey, John F. Lehman, Timothy J. Roemer, and James R. Thompson served on the Commission. Concerned that "the United States government was simply not active enough in combating the terrorist threat before 9/11," Kean and Hamilton in their public statement accompanying release of the Commission's final report recommended as a remedy a new "global strategy . . . a different way of organizing our government."

Thomas H. Kean and Lee H. Hamilton's speech: Good morning. Today, we present this Report and these recommendations to the President of the United States, the United States Congress, and the American people. This report represents the unanimous conclusion of the National Commission on Terrorist Attacks upon the United States.

On September 11, 2001, 19 men armed with knives, box cutters, mace and pepper spray penetrated the defenses of the most powerful nation in the world. They inflicted unbearable trauma on our people, and turned the international order upside down.

We ask each of you to remember how you felt that day—the grief, the enormous sense of loss. We also came together that day as a nation—young and old, rich and poor, Republicans and Democrats. We all had a deep sense of hurt. We also had a deep sense of purpose. We knew what we had to do, as a nation, to respond. And we did.

But on that September day we were unprepared. We did not grasp the magnitude of a threat that had been gathering over time. As we detail in our report, this was a failure of policy, management, capability, and—above all—a failure of imagination.

Findings

We recognize that we have the benefit of hindsight. And, since the plotters were flexible and resourceful, we cannot know whether any single step or series of steps would have defeated them. What we can say with confidence is that none of the measures adopted by the U.S. government before 9/11 disturbed or even delayed the progress of the Al Qaeda plot.

There were several unexploited opportunities.

- Our government did not watchlist future hijackers Hazmi and Mihdhar before they arrived in the United States, or take adequate steps to find them once they were here.

- Our government did not link the arrest of Zacarias Moussaoui, described as interested in flight training for the purpose of using an airplane in a terrorist act, to the heightened indications of attack.

- Our government did not discover false statements on visa applications, or recognize passports manipulated in a fraudulent manner.

- Our government did not expand no-fly lists to include names from terrorist watchlists, or require airline passengers to be more thoroughly screened.

These examples make up part of a broader national security picture, where the government failed to protect the American people. The United States government was simply not active enough in combating the terrorist threat before 9/11.

- Our diplomacy and foreign policy failed to extricate bin Laden from his Afghan sanctuary.

- Our military forces and covert action capabilities did not have the options on the table to defeat Al Qaeda or kill or capture bin Laden and his chief lieutenants.

- Our intelligence and law-enforcement agencies did not manage or share information, or effectively follow leads, to keep pace with a nimble enemy.

- Our border, immigration, and aviation security agencies were not integrated into the counterterrorism effort; and

- Much of our response on the day of 9/11 was improvised and ineffective, even as extraordinary individual acts of heroism saved countless lives.

Our failure took place over many years and administrations. There is no single individual who is responsible for this failure. Yet individuals and institutions are not absolved of responsibility. Any person in a senior position within our government during this time bears some element of responsibility for the government's actions.

It is not our purpose to assign blame. As we said at the outset, we look back so that we can look forward. Our goal is to prevent future attacks.

Every expert with whom we spoke told us that an attack of even greater magnitude is now possible—and even probable. We do not have the luxury of time. We must prepare and we must act.

The Al Qaeda network and its affiliates are sophisticated, patient, disciplined, and lethal. Osama bin Ladin built an infrastructure and organization that was able to attract, train, and use recruits against ever more ambitious targets. He rallied new zealots with each demonstration of Al Qaeda's capability. His message and hate-filled ideology have instructed and inspired untold recruits and imitators. He and Al Qaeda:

- despise America and its policies;

- exploit political grievances and hopelessness within the Arab and Islamic world;

- indoctrinate the disaffected and pervert one of the world's great religions; and

- seek creative methods to kill Americans in limitless numbers, including the use of chemical, biological and nuclear weapons.

Put simply, the United States is presented with one of the great security challenges in our history. We have struck blows against the terrorists since 9/11. We have prevented attacks on the homeland. We believe we are safer today than we were on 9/11—but we are not safe.

> *We believe we are safer today than we were on 9/11—but we are not safe.*

Because Al Qaeda represents an ideology—not a finite group of people—we should not expect the danger to recede for years to come. No matter whom we kill or capture—including Osama bin Ladin—there will still be those who plot against us. Bin Ladin has inspired affiliates and imitators. The societies they prey on are vulnerable; the terrorist ideology is potent; and the means for inflicting harm are readily available. We cannot let our guard down.

Recommendations—A Global Strategy

This Commission does not have all the answers. But we have thought about **what to do**—a global strategy—and **how to do it**—a different way of organizing our government. But, based on our thorough review of the government's performance, and our examination of the enemy, we recommend the following elements for a counterterrorism strategy.

This strategy must be balanced. It must integrate all the elements of national power: diplomacy, intelligence, covert action, law enforcement, economic policy, foreign aid, homeland defense, and military strength. There is no silver bullet or decisive blow that can defeat Islamist terrorism. It will take unity of effort and sustained and effective use of every tool at our disposal:

- We need to play offense: kill or capture terrorists; deny them sanctuaries; and disrupt their ability to move money and people around the globe.

- We need to ensure that key countries like Afghanistan, Pakistan, and Saudi Arabia are stable, capable, and resolute in opposing terrorism.

- We need to sustain a coalition of nations that cooperates bilaterally and multilaterally with us in the counterterrorism mission. We need a better dialogue between the West and the Islamic world. We also highlight the need to restrict and roll back the proliferation of the world's most dangerous weapons.

- We need to put forth an agenda of opportunity—economic, educational, and political—so that young people in the Arab and Islamic world have peaceful and productive avenues for expression and hope.

- We need to join the battle of ideas within the Islamic world: communicating hope instead of despair, progress in place of persecution, life instead of death. This message should be matched by policies that encourage and support the majority of Muslims who share these goals.

- At home, we need to set clear priorities for the protection of our infrastructure, and the security of our transportation. Resources should be allocated based upon those priorities, and standards of preparedness should be set. The private sector and local governments should play an important part of this process.

- We need secure borders, with heightened and uniform standards of identification for those entering and exiting the country; and an immigration system able to be efficient, allowing good people in while keeping terrorists out.

- If, God forbid, there is another attack, we must be ready to respond. We must educate the public, train and equip our first responders, and anticipate countless scenarios.

Recommendations—Organizing Government

We recommend significant changes in the organization of the government. We know that the quality of the people is more important than the quality of the wiring diagrams. Good people can overcome bad structures. They should not have to.

Day and night, dedicated public servants are waging the struggle to combat terrorists and protect the homeland. We need to ensure that our government maximizes their efforts through information sharing, coordinated effort, and clear authority.

A critical theme that emerged throughout our inquiry was the difficulty of answering the question: Who is in charge? Who ensures that agencies pool resources, avoid duplication, and plan jointly? Who oversees the massive integration and unity of effort necessary to keep America safe? Too often the answer is: "no one." Thus we are recommending:

- A National Counterterrorism Center. We need unity of effort on counterterrorism. We should create a National Counterterrorism Center (NCTC) to unify all counterterrorism intelligence and operations across the foreign-domestic divide in one organization. Right now, these efforts are too diffuse across the government. They need to be unified.

- A National Intelligence Director. We need unity of effort in the Intelligence Community. We need a much stronger head of the Intelligence Community, and an Intelligence Community that organizes itself to do joint work in national mission centers. We need reforms of the kind the military had two decades ago. We need a "Goldwater-Nichols" reform for the Intelligence Community. The Intelligence Community needs a shift in mindset and organization, so that intelligence agencies operate under the principle of joint command, with information-sharing as the norm.

- Reform in the Congress. We need unity of effort in the Congress. Right now, authority and responsibility are too diffuse. The Intelligence Committees do not have enough power to perform their oversight work effectively. Oversight for Homeland Security is splintered among too many Committees. We need much stronger committees performing oversight of intelligence. We need a single committee in each chamber providing oversight of the Department of Homeland Security.

- Reform in the FBI. We need a stronger national security workforce within the FBI. We do not support the creation of a new domestic intelligence agency. What the FBI needs is a specialized and integrated national security workforce, consisting of agents, analysts, linguists, and surveillance specialists. These specialists need to be recruited, trained, rewarded, and retained to ensure the development of an institutional culture with deep expertise in intelligence and national security.

- Changes in Information Sharing. We need unity of effort in information sharing. The U.S. government has access to a vast amount of information. But it has a weak system for processing and using that information. "Need to share" must replace "need to know."

- Transitions. We need a better process for transitions involving national security officials, so that this nation does not lower its guard every four or eight years.

These, and other, recommendations are spelled out in great detail in our report. We have made a limited number of recommendations, focusing on the areas we believe most critical.

We are acutely sensitive to the need to vigorously protect our liberties as we guard our security. We endorse many of the actions taken in the wake of 9/11 to facilitate government action and information sharing. But we stress that these measures need to be accompanied by a commitment to our open society and the principle of review—safeguards that are built into the process, and vigorous oversight. We must, after all is said and done, preserve the liberties that we are fighting for.

Concluding Thoughts

Before we close, we offer a few more thoughts. We approached our task with a deep respect for the place of September 11th in our nation's history. Some have compared the shock we felt to Pearl Harbor, others to the Kennedy assassination. There are no comparisons. This was a moment unique in our long history.

As every four years in this democracy, we are in the midst of a presidential campaign. Our two great parties will disagree, and that is right and proper. But at the same time we must unite to make our country safer. Republicans and Democrats must unite in this cause.

The American people must be prepared for a long and difficult struggle. We face a determined enemy who sees this as a war of attrition—indeed, as an epochal struggle. We expect further attacks. Against such an enemy, there can be no complacency. This is the challenge of our generation. As Americans we must step forward to accept that challenge.

We have reviewed 2.5 million pages of documents, and interviewed over 1,200 individuals—including experts and officials, past and present.

Our work has been assisted by a superb staff. Each one of these professionals has provided dedication and expertise that has exceeded our highest expectations.

We also had the high honor of working with an extraordinary group of Commissioners. Each has shown skill, determination, and collegiality.

We close by thanking the families who lost loved ones on 9/11. You demanded the creation of this Commission. You have encouraged us every step of the way as partners, and as witnesses. From your grief, we have drawn strength. We are determined to do everything possible to prevent other families from suffering your tragedy.

On that beautiful September day, we felt deep hurt, but we believed and acted as one nation. We united as Americans have always united in the face of a common foe. Five Republicans and five Democrats have come together today with that same unity of purpose.

We file no additional views. We have no dissents. We have each decided that we will play no active role in the fall presidential campaign. We will, instead, work together in support of the recommendations in this report. We believe that in acting together, we can make a difference. We can make our nation safer and more secure.

We would be happy to take your questions.

II. Foreign Policy

Principled Engagement: America's Role in the 21st-Century World

Gary Hart

Author, lecturer, teacher, scholar, and attorney; born Ottawa, KS, November 28, 1936; graduate, Bethany Nazarene College (OK), 1958; graduate, Yale Divinity School, 1961; LLB, Yale University Law School, 1964; Ph.D., Oxford University, 2001; appellate attorney, U.S. Department of Justice, 1964–65; special assistant, U.S. Department of the Interior, 1965–67; senior counsel, Coudert Brothers law firm, Denver, CO, 1967–70 and 1972–74; managed Senator George McGovern's presidential campaign, 1970–72; U.S. senator (D), Colorado, 1975–87, serving on the Select Committee to Investigate the Intelligence Agencies of the U.S. Government (Church Committee); ran for the Democratic Party's nomination for president, 1984; cochair, Hart-Rudman Commission on National Security/21st Century, 1998; author, The Patriot: An Exhortation to Liberate America from the Barbarians *(1996),* The Minuteman: Restoring an Army of the People *(1998), and* Restoration of the Republic: The Jeffersonian Ideal in 21st-Century America *(2002).*

Editors' introduction: On September 19, 2002, President Bush proposed to Congress a resolution that authorized him "to use all means that he determines appropriate, including force, in order to enforce the United Nations Security Council Resolutions" in Iraq, prompting debate among private citizens and government officials about what future direction U.S. foreign policy should take. Maintaining that the Bush administration had abandoned "America's principles," former U.S. senator Gary Hart advised members of a forum sponsored by the World Affairs Council and the Council on Foreign Relations that, "if we want to lead the world, we must stay engaged in and ahead of the world in a way that respects the people of the world." The World Affairs Council, whose members include schools, public institutions, businesses, and interested individuals, promotes greater understanding of global affairs. The Council on Foreign Relations is an independent, national membership organization and a nonpartisan center for scholars dedicated to producing and disseminating ideas that provide a better understanding of the world and the foreign policy choices facing the United States and other governments.

Gary Hart's speech: We are now more than a decade beyond the Cold War and as yet our political leadership has failed to provide a comprehensive sense of America's role in the post–Cold War, early

Delivered on February 10, 2003, at San Francisco, CA. Reprinted with permission of Gary Hart.

21st-century world. For almost half a century our central organizing principle, upon which both a foreign policy and defense policy were built, was "containment of communism." The world in which we now live defies the simplicity and predictability such a doctrine offered. And even containment of communism left unanswered the question of how to achieve that goal, a question that often divided our country deeply, not least between those advocating the use of power to promote our interests and those advocating adherence to human rights as defining of our values.

But rather than presenting a new foundation and framework to define America's role in the world, our current administration has embarked on a dangerous effort to apply power without relationship to America's principles. Its doctrine seems to be that we are powerful enough to do as we wish, and those not with us are against us. A world divided between pro- and anti-Americans is not a world in which we will hope to be secure.

> *Our current administration has embarked on a dangerous effort to apply power without relationship to America's principles.*

Moreover, the administration's preoccupation with military superiority erodes our greatest strength—the admiration the world has for the American character. We drive the world's prosperity. We are the champions of the ideal of democracy. We are the world's greatest source of optimism, energy, and hope. Global citizens by the hundreds of millions say that they disagree with the United States government but like the American people. To compromise that goodwill through belligerence is to squander our greatest resource.

In direct contrast to a policy featuring force, and to replace a decaying Cold War–era debate between interests and values, today I would like to propose a foreign policy based upon principle, indeed a set of principles upon which I believe America should base its relations with the peoples of the world in this new century, principles representing the best traditions and beliefs of the American people.

These principles flow from the distinctive nation that we are. Historically, we are a revolutionary nation that has been at its best when it applied its revolutionary character of innovation and adaptability to the challenges of changing times. Given our revolutionary heritage, we should welcome, not resist, innovation and experimentation by other nations rather than be seen as reactionary and antagonistic to change. And, constitutionally, we are a democratic republic whose government powers are checked and balanced by a written Constitution.

As a democracy, we are committed to free elections, freedom of assembly, petition, and the press, and most of all freedom of speech. And we believe all people are created equal with equal right to participate in their own self-governance.

As a republic, we believe American citizenship bears certain duties, that we earn our rights by performance of those duties, that republics are subject to corruption and that corruption must be vigi-

lantly resisted, that there are an identifiable common good and
national interest, and that, most of all, in this Republic the people—not elites or powerful interests—are sovereign.

When we act outside these definitions of our character, for example when we exhibit the characteristics of an imperial power, a
hegemon, or a global constable, or when we resort to manipulation,
deceit, or intrigue in our dealings with other nations, we become
some other kind of nation than who we truly are. And when we do
so, we always pay a price. Indeed, we diminish our authority as a
world leader when we abandon our ideals or violate our principles.

Based upon our principles, American foreign policy must arise
from a new grand strategy for the United States in the 21st-cen-
tury world. A new world is upon us. It is characterized by globalization, or the internationalization of finance and commerce, by the
information revolution and the digital divide, by the erosion of traditional nation-state sovereignty, and by the changing nature of
conflict and violence.

Our new grand strategy will emerge from the answers to these
questions:

- First, what are our larger purposes? What are we seeking to
  achieve?

- Second, what resources—economic, political, and military—do
  we possess?

- Third, how do we intend to apply those resources to achieve our
  large purposes?

In answer to the first question, what are we seeking to achieve,
let me suggest the following:

- We wish to maintain friendly relations with all nations of good
  will through open trade and honest diplomacy;

- We also wish to foster a stable world community characterized
  by opportunity and human rights for the greatest number and a
  minimum of violence;

- We should seek to subdue destructive forces and prevent proliferation of the weapons they use;

- We should promote stewardship over and generational accountability for our collective natural environment, the oasis in
  boundless space upon which we all depend;

- We must seek to organize a new security environment to defeat
  forces of state disintegration and non-state terrorism and preserve the well-being and security of Americans at home and
  abroad;

- And, we must actively engage in the world community without
  unnecessary entanglement in ancient quarrels and grievances.

A grand strategy for America—applying our resources to these large purposes—has yet to be produced. But the world and its troubles will not wait. As a major element in achieving that strategy, I believe our foreign policy—how America conducts itself in the family of nations—must be based upon principles and that those principles must be shaped by our democratic values and our republican form of government. In achieving these large purposes, here are the principles that I believe should guide our conduct in the world:

- First, **our alliances**, both old and new, should be characterized by equality of status, common interests, and greater shared responsibilities, and participation in these alliances should not require compromise of our principles;

- Second, we must **resist imperial designs** by others without seeking empire for ourselves;

- Third, our **economic strength**, arguably our greatest strength, should be used to help create opportunity and open societies for those nations left behind;

- Fourth, our **military power** should be used only to defend our nation, protect our justifiable interests, fulfill our alliance commitments, and prevent imminent attack.

- Fifth, with our allies we must seek to **prevent the failure of states** or, if they fail, seek to manage their peaceful restructuring;

- Sixth, we should **encourage democracy**—especially among regional powers—including forms of democratic government possibly different in design and structure from our own;

- Seventh, we should adopt **a new definition of security** in an age where the nature of conflict is rapidly evolving;

- And, eighth, we must explore new areas where **international cooperation** may relieve disproportionate burdens on U.S. economic and military resources.

Now let me revisit these principles in more concrete terms.

America's alliances must be based on more than common enemies and must increasingly require more equitable sharing of the burden of creating stability. Throughout the Cold War our practice of expediency was based on the belief that the enemy of our enemy was our friend. It led us, for example, to support a corrupt and repressive regime in Iran until the shah fell and then to support an even more dangerous regime in Baghdad in a war against Iranian militants who dethroned the shah. If that policy of expediency ever served our larger purposes, it no longer does so. And, further, it is against our principles.

Today, as we muster for war against Iraq, we are forming alliances with countries like Yemen, whose head of state, Ali Abdullah Salleh, is busily importing Scud missiles from North Korea, is trading weapons throughout the region, is someone who sided with Iraq in the last Gulf war, and is refusing to let us investigate militant groups believed to harbor Al Qaeda cells in his country. He exhibits none of the qualities that define democratic leaders. Yet, he is our new best friend for one simple reason—he will let us use his territory for military purposes. Is there a price to be paid after the dogs of war are chained? Absolutely—both in compromise of our principles and in the substantial cash we are undoubtedly paying him.

And nowhere is that price more evident than in Iraq itself, which we willingly supplied with dozens of biological and chemical warfare agents in the 1980s. After the first Persian Gulf War, UN arms inspectors found quantities of chemicals and missile parts with names like Union Carbide and Honeywell on them. A recent news report states:

> The story of America's involvement with Saddam Hussein in the years before his attack on Kuwait—which includes large-scale intelligence sharing, supply of cluster bombs through a Chilean front company, and facilitating Iraq's acquisition of chemical and biological precursors—is a typical example of the underside of U.S. foreign policy. It is a world in which deals can be struck with dictators, human rights violations sometimes overlooked, and accommodations made with arms proliferators, all on the principle that "the enemy of our enemy is our friend."

That is indeed a foreign policy principle. It just happens not to be an American one.

While resisting the sacrifice of principle to expediency, we must also make our respectable alliances more relevant to the new age. Now our most important alliances, such as NATO, must be built upon equitable partnership shares of both benefits and burdens. NATO was formed to contain communism behind the Iron Curtain and it now seeks a new and more relevant purpose. That purpose may well evolve into a peacemaking commitment on the borders of Europe, such as in the Balkans, and entail the development of special-purpose forces to carry out that mission. We must redefine the common interests that cause us to continue to ally. If NATO is to accept a peacemaking role, areas of vital interest, command structures, and relative contributions must all be spelled out in advance of a crisis.

We should consider, for example, creation of a NATO intervention force with the mission of keeping the sea lanes of communication open, of protecting the flow of oil supplies, of dealing with any force that might want to block international commerce or exact some tribute for the open usage of any of the world's critical maritime straits. Over the years, this mission could then transition into a full-blown international peacemaking force.

This is but an illustration of further ways in which 20th-century alliances need to be more relevant in the 21st century.

As a matter of additional principle, the United States must not seek empire in the Middle East or elsewhere. According to published reports, senior officials in our current government propose, quietly, that we create a permanent U.S. military presence in a defeated Iraq to intimidate Iran and Syria, buffer Israel, and replace Saudi oil with Iraqi oil. Any such grandiose notion of playing hegemon in the greater Middle East region is folly and a prescription for disaster. Its political and financial costs are unknown and probably unknowable. This secret dream of empire represents hunger for power at its worst and is contrary to America's traditional principles. This is the kind of aggressive and arrogant post–Cold War thinking the American people must steadfastly resist.

Since the president has not seen fit to tell us what our larger purposes are in the region, suspicions legitimately arise when rumors of empire drift through the salons of Washington. Will we assume responsibility to reconstruct Iraq, referee its bitter ethnic quarrels, bear the cost for rebuilding a nation of 22 million, and place thousands of American service personnel in jeopardy for an untold num-

---

The American people deserve to be told the truth about their nation's policies and the obligations in lives and treasure those policies require.

---

ber of years? Or will we simply retreat from the rubble and let Iraq devolve into a sinkhole of tribal violence on CNN? The American people deserve to be told the truth about their nation's policies and the obligations in lives and treasure those policies require.

In **using our economic strength** to offer opportunity and hope in the less developed world, we can start with refugee camps and non-functional economies where well over a billion people live on less than a dollar a day. Though we can't, by ourselves, alleviate all their suffering, we can help create international institutions that can by bolstering infrastructure construction—particularly water resources development, micro-loans for the financing of shelter and income creation, assault on diseases such as AIDS and malaria, universal global literacy, and agricultural development sufficient to provide an adequate level of nutrition.

Traditional "top down" foreign aid must be replaced by new grassroots methods of creating economic opportunity. And we must make a new priority of addressing the needs of women in the developing world. Through such avenues as education, micro-lending, agricultural technology, and property rights, empowerment of women—especially mothers—improves children's health, education, and nutrition and lifts the conditions of society at large.

We must also enlist corporate America in the struggle for global economic opportunity. Though our businesses have been forces for global progress, we must insist that our companies set humane standards against child and slave labor, uphold worker rights, and eliminate environmental damage in the developing world. American corporations, representing American interests, should be as good citizens abroad as they are at home, for corporate America as well as the U.S. government is judged by its behavior, and we Americans are all judged by the behavior of both.

Finally, if we truly want our economic power to win the world to our cause, we must open our markets to the products of the world's poorest people. Protection against these products hurts American consumers and foreign workers and sets back the march of democracy. We must continue to be global leaders in expanding world trade.

American military power must be used judiciously and prudently, even more so now that we are the dominant military power on earth by several orders of magnitude. We now spend more each year on our military establishment than at least the next five

---

Our forces must be used primarily to protect our legitimate security interests and those of our allies.

---

major powers, including China, Russia, and the U.K., combined.

Our forces must be used primarily to protect our legitimate security interests and those of our allies. When they are used, certain standards must be clearly stated and met. We must define our political and military objectives, and our political goals must be tangible, obtainable, and stated in concrete terms. The American people must support the use of our forces in any sustained military operation and must be fully cognizant of the proposed levels of military force and the potential costs, including in human lives. Our military forces should be committed only after diplomatic, political, and other means of conflict resolution have been exhausted and after local forces are determined to be insufficient to resolve the conflict. We must be clear on how we intend to achieve our objective and what strategies, tactics, and doctrines we mean to employ. And command structures must be clearly defined and our plan of operation must be simple and achievable in its execution.

Given the openness of the administration's intentions in Iraq and the region, there are few if any security reasons why the American people—to whom the American military belongs—cannot be better satisfied that these conditions have been met. The principle at stake here is openness and honesty with the American people whose sons and daughters fight our wars.

We must **prevent or prepare for** state failure. Yugoslavia is an instance where we and our allies did not do so and hundreds of thousands of people suffered from that neglect. Like Yugoslavia, Iraq, Jordan, and other nations in the Middle East are artificial concoctions thrown together to satisfy European ambitions and competitions following World War I. We must now be prepared to manage their restructuring if the seams fail, especially in Iraq. The penalty for unwillingness or inability to anticipate state failure is harsh.

Iraq stands as the most immediate example of the threatened problem of a vanquished state. The United Nations has estimated as many as 10 million Iraqis, including 2 million refugees and homeless, will be at risk for disease and hunger following an American invasion. Early talk of an American military proconsul running the country conjures up images of warring Kurd, Shia, and Sunni factions laying siege to the American emperor's palace. But postwar Iraq does not stand alone. Congo and Nigeria, and even potentially Pakistan, represent immediate examples of state failure whose humanitarian consequences are staggering and, therefore, geopolitical.

Whether the U.S. likes it or not, this burden—the human costs of war—must be calculated and born when we invade a country or when a state fails. Whether it is called "nation building" or something else, the United States must enlist the greater democratic world in anticipating the collective burden of supporting fragile states or restructuring those that fail or that we cause to fail.

Russia, China, and India are key nations in their regions and are becoming so in the greater world. The success of democratic evolution in these nations will be crucial to regional and world stability. Both because of their size and their importance in their respective regions, the U.S. Commission on National Security / 21st Century gave as one of its most important recommendations "to assist the integration of key major powers, especially China, Russia, and India, into the mainstream of the emerging international system." And we should encourage greater regional leadership roles for each. Democracy in Russia is still taking root and has yet to develop in China, and its failure to develop in either giant nation would have profound implications for the United States and the world.

North Korea offers a particularly vivid example where China should be called upon to lead in regional isolation of, and collective negotiation with, a nation that endangers East Asian security more than it does ours. If we are unable to convince states neighboring outlaw nations that their interests are at stake in isolating and resolving threats such as North Korea, then we are in for a long century. The threat of North Korea also underscores my first principle that alliances should be properly formed. North Korea received much of its recent nuclear technology from Pakistan, our ally in Afghanistan. True allies do not let their immediate self-interest endanger their partners.

Only recently prominent conservative voices were heard advocating military confrontation with China. The implications of that policy are difficult to imagine. Rather, our belief in the therapy of capitalism should lead us to encourage forces of democracy in China and its emergence as a stabilizing force in the region.

> *Multilateral peacemaking will be an increasing global requirement.*

Likewise, Russia can and should become a major Western nation and a major oil exporter, in partnership with Western production companies, to replace unstable supplies in the Persian Gulf and reduce OPEC's leverage on the United States. Further, Russia must become a stable partner in the Western economic and political world—including membership in NATO—as soon as possible. And India's vast technological potential can energize a regional information revolution and help position it as an economic and political leader in the region.

An additional principle is that our **concept of security** must evolve even as the nature of conflict evolves. As an advocate of military reform for the past 20 years, I now believe it is time to apply reform principles to American diplomacy—needed are new strategies, new doctrines, and new ways of structuring relationships. Security will be achievable only if we deny the basic resources of money, weapons, sanctuary, and recruits to new forces of violence—mafias, pirates, most of all terrorists, and other "non-state actors." New kinds of threats will require new kinds of resistance—paramilitary and special forces especially trained and equipped to deal with quasi-criminal forms of warfare.

Security will increasingly be defined as opportunity for economic growth, stability of communities and cultures, adaptability of disparate countries to the new age of information and globalization, and possibly even evolution of new forms of democratic government. More expansive definitions of security will require more expansive means of achieving them—means of diplomacy, of economic growth, and of dispersed investment more immediately beneficial to dispossessed people than to already wealthy elites.

Finally, the nature of sovereignty will change in the 21st century under the pressure of globalization, and events may require selective **delegation of sovereignty** to international organizations newly designed to make the peace where violence erupts, to regulate weapons production and proliferation, or to regulate currency and financial markets to prevent imminent collapse. Care must be taken not to abrogate traditional nation-state sovereignty unnecessarily or lightly. But events may provide no alternative but to create new, carefully constructed international regimes to prevent collapse or chaos.

Multilateral peacemaking will be an increasing global require-ment. Peacemaking requires offensively trained and equipped forces—multilateral because no single nation, including the sole superpower, could or should possess or wish to possess the capability to police the world, and offensive because peace-keeping forces cannot keep the peace where none exists.

> *Our policies must with-stand the therapy of sunlight.*

Additionally, the time may come—and soon—when international institutions are required to coordinate the stabilization of markets and currencies, secure finan-cial structures, and regulate international commerce. Globalization will increasingly require coordination of macroeconomic, antitrust, banking and securities regulation, and even tax policies. To these add such human policies as the environment and public health. Other collaborative tasks may be undertaken by new regional enti-ties and even coalitions of the willing.

And there will be increasing occasions in which we must pool our sovereignty to implement programs of peace-keeping, nation-build-ing, third world development, counter-proliferation of weapons, and standards of justice. The more we ignore the imperatives of this new reality, the more we hoard our sovereignty, the more isolated we will become, the more we will be tempted to resort to our own force, and the less sovereignty we will have left to protect. *If we want to lead the world, we must stay engaged in and ahead of the world in a way that respects the people of the world.*

These principles proposed here are offered for the purpose of pro-viding a framework in which policy can be made. They are designed to help us think differently about how we should act on the world stage. And they are meant as a caution against how we should not act.

We should not emulate European *realpolitik* traditions and prac-tices associated with European statesmen of old. We are not a peo-ple who see the world principally in terms of the exercise of power, though its exercise is necessary when required for security and sta-bility. Neither American political party, nor any ideology, should possess or seek to possess the franchise on the exercise of American power.

We should not hide our policies from our own people or from the world at large. In the long run, and increasingly in the short run, there are few if any secrets. Our policies must withstand the ther-apy of sunlight. In almost every case, except the most important security secrets, if we are afraid to disclose our practices or inten-tions, it usually means we will be ashamed of them when they are ultimately exposed.

We should not behave differently to others, including the most humble nations, than we would have them behave towards us. Our dealings must not only be transparent, they must also be fair and just. This is true all the more so since we now stand constantly examined in the court of international opinion and we do not have the excuse of combating communism to rationalize our misdeeds. Even our resistance to terrorism must not become a new excuse to shortcut our principles, bully our neighbors and allies, and act as the new empire-builders.

In the closing decades of the Cold War we oscillated between a policy of "values"—human rights—and a policy of "interests"—power and its applications. We should not separate our values from our power or our power from our values. A truly great power exercises that power humanely, judiciously, and fairly to all. Power exercised for its own sake, or for the sake of a selfish or expedient interest, is ultimately self-defeating.

As a successor to the central organizing principle of containment of communism, I am instead offering the framework for a foreign policy based on democratic principles—a policy that is resolute but is also one the American people can be proud of.

Our duties as republicans and our freedoms as democrats are the source of our principles, both for ourselves and for other peoples in the world. We can only achieve a new kind of security in a new century by constant resort to these principles. And we can only preserve our status as leaders through a new grand strategy that recognizes that our small planet increasingly requires both enlightened and principled engagement in our common interest.

Perhaps most importantly, all Americans must now become engaged in America's conduct in the world. Our foreign policy, our relations with the peoples of the world, is no longer the province of so-called experts. The forces of globalization, the spread of American commercial and cultural influence, the internationalization of the Internet, the immediacy of travel, the rise of a global environmental common, all now require the engagement of the American people. We must not let our role in the world be dictated by ideologues with their special biases and agendas, by militarists who long for the clarity of Cold War confrontation, by think-tank theorists who grind their academic axes, or by Americans who too often find it hard to distinguish their loyalties to their original homelands from their loyalties to America and its national interests.

As war is too important to leave to the generals, so, in the 21st century, is foreign policy too important to be left to specialized elites and interests. In the 21st century, the veil separating the foreign policy priesthood from the people must be removed. We, the people, must insist that our nation's finest principles characterize our dealings with our global neighbors. In this new age, our policy toward the world must be the policy of the American people—a policy that reflects our belief in our freedom, a policy that shows our desire to be friends and helpful neighbors, a policy that makes us proud of our heritage when we meet our foreign neighbors abroad and when we greet them here at home, and most of all a policy that leaves a legacy to our children that makes them proud of us.

New Directions in U.S. Foreign Policy?

From Regime Change to Nation-Building

Rachel Bronson

Senior fellow and director, Middle East Studies, Council on Foreign Relations, 1999– ; born New York City, 1969; B.A. in diplomatic history, University of Pennsylvania, 1990; M.A., 1992, and Ph.D., 1997, in political science, Columbia University; fellow, Center for Science and International Affairs, Harvard University, 1994–96; senior fellow for international security affairs, Center for Strategic and International Studies, 1997–99; consultant to the Center for Naval Analyses, 1999–2001; consultant to NBC News, 2003– ; articles, "When Soldiers Become Cops," Foreign Affairs, 2002; "Reconstructing the Middle East?" Brown Journal of World Affairs, 2003; other articles in New York Times, Los Angeles Times, and International Herald Tribune; codirector, Guiding Principles for U.S. Post-Conflict Policy in Iraq, Council on Foreign Relations, 2003; testified before the 9/11 Commission and Congress's Joint Economic Committee on the Reconstruction of Iraq, 2003; several doctoral fellowships, including those in Arabic language and studies and in international affairs; Carnegie Corporation, Carnegie Scholar recipient, 2003–2005.

Editors' introduction: In the midst of Operation Iraqi Freedom, citizens, elected officials, and members of professional organizations were gripped with questions about U.S. policies in Iraq and in America's future relations with other nations. Aware that the United States "still has part of this war" in Iraq "in front of us," Dr. Rachel Bronson told members of the Asia Society that a primary goal now must be to "establish . . . law and order." The Asia Society, a nonpartisan educational organization, is dedicated to fostering an understanding of Asia and communication between Americans and the peoples of the more than 30 countries in Asia and the Pacific. Dr. Bronson addressed some 70 journalists, UN representatives, interested public, and Asia Society members attending a Town Hall meeting.

Rachel Bronson's speech: Thank you for the opportunity to speak with you tonight about whether post-conflict reconstruction and nation-building constitute a new mandate for American foreign policy. At this moment in time, I can think of no issue that is more central to American foreign policy and planning. Let me foreshadow for you my answer. Yes we must get serious about post-conflict recon-

Delivered on April 10, 2003, at 6:00 P.M., New York City. Reprinted with permission of Rachel Bronson.

struction as an inherent part of American foreign policy. Reconstruction is tricky. It requires significant planning, it is very dangerous, and it is hard to develop an effective measure of success. Unfortunately, we tend to leave it to the last minute. In Bosnia, we dropped reconstruction on the UN one week before the war ended. In Iraq I don't believe we've ever laid out a practical road map for how we would move from the chaos of the conflict to the heady goals promised by the administration for the post-conflict period.

I watch the pictures of Saddam's statues crashing to the ground with nervous optimism. I am optimistic, because it is hard not to be. We have removed a tyrant that has thwarted the United Nations for over a decade, a dictator who has been intent on maintaining a weapons of mass destruction program that has cost his country billions of foregone assets. A tyrant that has used such weapons against his people and neighbors. The sanctions that were put in place were seen to be an alternative to war, but under Saddam's leadership they had become a war by other means. People who argued that this was not a just war, never seemed to consider that it was an unjust peace. Saddam's leadership radicalized the neighborhood around him, and contributed to growing anti-Americanism. It is hard to imagine anything worse.

I watch the pictures of Saddam's statues crashing to the ground with nervous optimism.

But I am nervous. Nervous because we still have part of this war in front of us. Significant pockets of resistance exist. We still don't know where the WMD are. While we've apparently reduced the regime's ability to deploy it in an organized manner, we still don't know where it is. For those of us who believe there's a lot of it out there to be found, and I think only a few believe of us otherwise, we cannot rest easy until it accounted for.

But I am nervous for another reason. We are finishing phase one of this two-part project: the first part being the fighting, the second part being the fixing. Even if we successfully complete the military campaign, winning the peace remains before us. We have hardly put the same kind of debate, planning and fight into phase two as we did in phase one. We hear from Washington and particularly Defense Secretary Rumsfeld that planning for "the day after" was just "not knowable," but the scenario we confront today was hardly unimaginable. In fact, in a report that I codirected at the Council on Foreign Relations in December, this was exactly the scenario we envisioned.

We simply do not have the luxury of getting this wrong. We have, in my mind, over-promised Iraq and the Middle East on what we are intent on doing. Part of this war for the administration has been creating a better political order that will be contagious enough to blow winds of change through other countries. If we don't win the peace, much more is at stake than just Iraq.

We are now entering into the phase of reconstruction, or nation-building, or whatever one wants to call it. And what I would like to suggest to you is that the fundamental responsibility upon us, and indeed the fundamental aspect of nation-building, is "policing and pacifying." That is, establishing law and order. I am not saying this just because it is today's headlines. This has been a lesson learned from all previous conflicts. The pictures of looters on the street are not unexpected. We have seen these pictures after every major conflict. We saw them after Desert Storm I, but more directly we saw them in Haiti and the Balkans and to a lesser extent Afghanistan (for reasons I will get to). In fact in Germany in 1945, law and order was considered such a high priority that we turned our soldiers into a constabulary force. We actually gave them new doctrine, and changed their uniforms and tasked them with policing the peace. Germany's success wasn't just about Marshall aid and an amenable culture. We prevented our war-weary soldiers from coming home and made them police Germany, then work alongside Germans doing the dirty work, and only when the Germans were really up to it, did we leave.

What makes me nervous is that this president campaigned against nation-building, and specifically this aspect of it. During the Presidential campaign he said specifically that he didn't expect our troops to be used for "what's called nation-building." Later, three months after September 11th at a speech to the Citadel, he said again that "some thought our military would be used overseas—not to win wars, but mainly to police and pacify, to control crowds and contain ethnic conflict." They were wrong. But if our soldiers aren't going to police and pacify, who will?

Let me suggest to you some lessons from the past:

From the Balkans

From the Balkans we learned that a serious up-front commitment to law and order is necessary to building a functioning economy, a free and fair political system and a healthy civil society—goals that many inside the administration espouse for Iraq. In the Balkans, democracy and economic initiatives were prioritized over the establishment of basic law and order. The result was black markets, corruption, drug lords, and the return to power of the scions of the old system. Such outcomes would be disastrous to American interests in the strategic heartland of the Middle East.

Stability requires military police, constabulary forces, civil police and judicial teams of lawyers, judges, and correction officers. These institutions, which help to provide security within a state, were not immediately established in Kosovo or Bosnia, making it virtually impossible to establish the conditions for long-term stability. Since the conflict ended, law and order remains fragile in Bosnia. The initial rush to set up elections compromised the ability of the international community to combat organized crime, ethnic rivalries, and extremists who rejected the notion of a new democratic society. Premature U.S. withdrawal deadlines encouraged extremists, gang-sters, and shady politicians to hunker down and wait for the international community to leave. The powerful alliances between ethnic nationalist politicians and organized criminal groups were not aggressively pursued which significantly undermined collec-tive and personal security. Seven years later, crime is still high and has prevented significant economic growth. Courts and pris-ons do not function properly, and institutionalized corruption is rearing its ugly head.

In both Bosnia and Kosovo, America and its allies were compelled to undertake a significant number of unconventional tasks to ensure law and order. Among their assignments were:

- border patrols
- around-the-clock protection of mosques, churches, and other religious sites
- checkpoint operations
- criminal investigations
- judiciary support
- monitoring and verification of elections
- refugee/IDP return, escorting children to school
- riot control
- de-mining
- humanitarian aid distribution
- policing
- rebuilding infrastructure such as bridges, roads, schools, and hospitals
- arrest and prosecution of war criminals
- the establishment of indigenous institutions, such as separate military and police forces and reliable penal systems.

There is every reason to believe that these same tasks will need to be fulfilled in the postwar reconstruction of Iraq.

The Balkans experience also suggests that the United States des-perately needs international assistance to promote stability abroad. Italy's Carabinieri, France's Gendarmerie, and Spain's Guardia Civil are better suited for the tasks that straddle the blurry security line between war and peace. Such forces were used in Bosnia and often relieved American military forces of duties including escorting refugees, protecting airports, crowd control, and guard duties. United Nations civil police also assisted with ref-ugee return, humanitarian relief, and training local police units.

Even with European cooperation, much of the law and order responsibility fell to American forces. The international support required in the Balkans suggests a real need for the administra-tion to overcome the international divisions that now exist as a result of the pre-war Iraq debate. It will serve American interests to build support for reconstruction in general, but law and order responsibilities in particular.

From Afghanistan

The problem is that because the administration was reluctant to commit American troops to Afghanistan, initial efforts were limited to Kabul. An Amnesty International report from March 2003 highlights that outside Kabul, Afghan police officers have not been paid in four months and there continues to be a "complete absence of accountability structures." If not attended to, the security vacuum will be filled by nefarious actors who will twist it to their own advantage and eventually overturn initial military successes. The unwillingness to firmly commit in Afghanistan has undermined the potential for stability and made it more difficult for American troops to exit. Not surprisingly then, U.S. military presence is slowly

---

The unwillingness to firmly commit in Afghanistan has undermined the potential for stability and made it more difficult for American troops to exit.

---

spreading to other major cities. But the initial reluctance to use the American military to undertake tasks that smacked of nation-building has cost precious time and will make the job of pacifying and eventually leaving Afghanistan all the more difficult. Afghan warlords have used this time to amass resources and regain some of their former strength.

From Iraq

In Iraq, we are just beginning. The chaos is just emerging. The administration in many ways is better prepared than its predecessors. General Jay Gardner is in the region, ready to go. The military is in place and has known it will have to take on post-conflict tasks. But it is not clear to me that we are any better prepared to under take this than we were when the administration took power. In fact, the reason I wanted UN support going in, or certainly now, is for this aspect, so we can draw on the expertise of others to help with this.

In Iraq we have the advantage that we can use the Iraqi military and police. But they will still have to be retrained and depoliticized.

Let me conclude by returning to the original question. Is nation-building a new American mandate? The answer is yes, and its not new. The mandate has been clear since the early 1990s. In many ways the fact that this administration will be forced to undertake such tasks is actually useful, because it will reduce the constituency of those who believe it's avoidable. But we have to get serious and here is our choice.

1. Get the UN to do it.
2. Do it ourselves. Not just military, but civilians as well.
3. Figure out how to train with the Europeans, who are better organized to take on these tasks.

Those are our choices. Any of them are legitimate, but none of them are easy or cheap. And avoiding the choice is itself a choice, one that we make at our own peril.

New American Strategies for Security and Peace

Hillary Rodham Clinton

U.S. senator (D), New York, 2001– ; born Chicago, IL, October 26, 1947, and raised in Park Ridge, IL, attending public schools there; B.A., Wellesley College, 1969; J.D., Yale Law School, 1973; attorney, Children's Defense Fund, 1973–74; assistant professor of law, University of Arkansas, 1974–77; partner, Rose law firm, 1977–92; lecturer, University of Arkansas Law School, 1979–80; in Senate, member of committees on Budget, Environment and Public Works, Health, Education, Labor, and Pension, and Armed Services; author, It Takes a Village and Other Lessons Children Teach Us *(1996) and* Living History *(2004); Claude Pepper Award of the National Association for Home Care, Martin Luther King Jr. Award of the Progressive National Baptist Convention, and Public Spirit Award of the American Legion Auxiliary.*

Editors' introduction: With the fighting in Iraq continuing, debate in the United States over foreign policy increased significantly throughout 2003. Concerned that the "doctrines and actions by the Bush administration undermine . . . core democratic principles," Senator Clinton maintained that, "if we are to lead this world into a wholly democratic future, we must first be consistent in the principles we champion and the ones we pursue." Senator Clinton addressed New American Strategies for Security and Peace, a conference sponsored by the Center for American Progress, *The American Prospect*, and the Century Foundation. The Center for American Progress is a nonpartisan research and educational institute dedicated to promoting a strong, just, and free America that ensures opportunity for all. *The American Prospect* was founded as an authoritative magazine of liberal ideas, committed to a just society, an enriched democracy, and effective liberal politics. The Century Foundation attempts to educate, provoke, and develop answers to questions raised by public debate.

Hillary Rodham Clinton's speech: Thank you, John, for that introduction. I want to compliment you for all the hard work that you have put into the creation of the Center for American Progress, an institution that I am convinced will be a tremendous force in engaging in the war of ideas so critical to our country's future. And there is no better leader for that effort than John Podesta who has the warrior spirit and strategic mind needed for such an endeavor. I also want to thank Bob Kuttner at *The American Prospect* and Dick Leone at the Century Foundation for their work on this conference.

Delivered on October 29, 2003, at Wardman Park Marriott, Washington, DC.

Today's conference, New American Strategies for Security and Peace, comes at a critical point in our nation's history and I commend the Center for American Progress, *The American Prospect,* and the Century Foundation for putting together from what is, by all accounts, an outstanding program.

Today is a critical moment, not just in our history, but in the history of democracy. As we seek to build democratic institutions in Iraq, and we in this room push for us to reach out to our global partners in this endeavor, this nation must remember the tenets of the democratic process that we advocate.

The issue I'd like to address is whether we apply the fundamental principles of democracy—rule of law, transparency and accountability, informed consent—not only to what we do at home but to what we do in the world. There can be no real question that we must do so because foreign policy involves the most important decisions a democracy can make—going to war, our relations with the world and our use of power in that world.

> *This nation must remember the tenets of the democratic process that we advocate.*

But the fact is that new doctrines and actions by the Bush administration undermine these core democratic principles—both at home and abroad. I believe they do so at a severe cost.

In our efforts abroad, we now go to war as a first resort against perceived threats, not as a necessary final resort. Preemption is an option every president since Washington has had and many have used. But to elevate it to the organizing principle of American strategic policy at the outset of the 21st century is to grant legitimacy to every nation to make war on their enemies before their enemies make war on them. It is a giant step backward.

In our dealings abroad, we claim to champion rule of law, yet we too often have turned our backs on international agreements: The Kyoto treaty, which represents an attempt by the international community to meaningfully address the global problem of climate change and global warming. The biological weapons enforcement protocol. The Comprehensive Test Ban Treaty. This unwillingness to engage the international community on problems that will require international cooperation sends a clear signal to other nations that we believe in the rule of law—if it is our law as we interpret it. That is the antithesis of the rule of law. The administration argues that international agreements, like the Kyoto treaty, are flawed. And the fact is they have some good arguments. When the Clinton administration signed the Kyoto Protocol it said that, working inside the tent, it would try to make further improvements. But rather than try to make further improvements from inside the process, the Bush administration stomped out in an effort to knock over the tent. That is not the prudent exercise of power. It is the petulant exercise of ideology.

In our dealings abroad, we more often than not have promoted, not the principles of international cooperation, but the propensity for an aggressive unilateralism that alienates our allies and undermines our tenets. It deeply saddens me, as I speak with friends and colleagues around the world, that the friends of America from my generation tell me painfully that for the first time in their lives they are on the defensive when it comes to explaining to their own children that America truly is a good and benign nation. Their children, too often, have seen an America that disregards their concerns, insists they embrace our concerns and forces them to be with us or against us. Our Declaration of Independence calls for "a decent respect for the opinions of mankind," yet this administration quite simply doesn't listen to our friends and allies. From our most important alliances in Europe to relations with our neighbors in this hemisphere, this administration has spanned the range of emotions from dismissive to indifferent. Ask President Vincente Fox, who staked his presidency on a political alliance with Mexico's historically controversial ally to the north, only to discover that he got no farther north than Crawford, Texas.

> *This administration quite simply doesn't listen to our friends and allies.*

If we are to lead this world into a wholly democratic future, we must first be consistent in the principles we champion and the ones we pursue.

Nowhere is this more apparent than in the transparency of government decisions. Without such transparency, how can leaders be accountable? How can the people be informed? Without such transparency—openness and information—the pillars of democracy lose their foundation.

Of course in a democracy, there always is tension between the information that the executive branch needs to keep secret and the information that must be provided to the public to have an informed citizenry. There are no easy answers to striking the right balance. But we must always be vigilant against letting our desire to keep information confidential be used as a pretext for classifying information that is more about political embarrassment than national security. Let me be absolutely clear. This is not a propensity that is confined to one party or the other. It is a propensity of power that we must guard against. Because when that happens, we move away from the bedrock principle of informed consent that governs all state actions in a democracy. Getting back, once again, to our founders who I think were not only extraordinary statesmen, but brilliant psychologists—they understood profoundly the dangers and temptations of power. The balance of power that they enshrined in our Constitution and our system of government was a check on all of our human natures and the propensity for anyone, no matter how convinced they are of the righteousness of their cause and view of the world, to be held in a check and a balance by other institutions.

Since 9/11, this question has much more salience since the War on Terror will often be fought in the shadows outside the public limelight. New doctrines of preemption raise profound questions about democratic oversight by making decisions effecting war and peace. They also raise profound questions about the quality of the intelligence information that is not open to public scrutiny. One of the most critical issues that we confront is what is wrong with our intelligence, the gathering and the analysis and the use?

Anybody who follows what is going on Capitol Hill is aware that we are locked in a partisan conflict as to how far to go in analyzing the intelligence with respect to Iraq—with the other side complaining that we can look to the intelligence community, but we cannot look at the decision makers. We can't look at the uses to which the intelligence was put and we can't look at the particular viewpoint that was brought to that analysis. I think that is a profound error and undermining to our democratic institutions.

The American people, and indeed the international community, need to have confidence that when the U.S. government acts, it is acting in good faith—sharing information where appropriate and developing appropriate mechanisms to insure that power is not being abused. A perception that our government is not providing honest assessments of the rationale for war or is unwilling to admit error will diminish the support for U.S. foreign policy of the American people and the international community. The American people will be far more willing to accept the administration's statement's about what is going right in Iraq if they believe that the administration is more forthright about what is going wrong. It is difficult to convince people that everything is fine when we are asking them to essentially shelve their common sense and human experience.

An example that hits close to home for me can be found in the administration's approach to the investigation surrounding 9/11. As Senator of New York, there is no more searing event than what happened to us on September 11th. My constituents have a right to know all the facts of how our government was prepared—or not—for the attacks. Yet, over the weekend, we learned that the 9/11 Commission, charged with the important task of investigating how 9/11 happened, complains that it isn't getting access to all the documents that it needs. This is a hugely important issue and one that must be addressed. The lack of transparency on the part of the Bush administration has forced Governor Kean, the former Republican governor of New Jersey, to threaten subpoenas. This should not be happening.

As bad as it was for Vice President Cheney to keep secret how the administration developed its energy policy, this is far worse. The 9/11 commission is not trying to embarrass the president, any former presidents, or anyone else. It is trying to learn what happened—what went wrong—in hopes that we can become better prepared to protect ourselves from future attacks. In taking this action,

> *We need to level with the American people—the good, the bad and the ugly.*

the administration unnecessarily raises suspicions that it has something to hide—that it might use national security to hide mistakes. That is not necessary or appropriate.

Meanwhile, on Iraq, the Bush administration describes progress on many fronts in direct contravention to what we are hearing every day. There undoubtedly are many instances where U.S. efforts in Iraq are successful. But what is going right should not delude us about what is going wrong. There is too much at stake to treat war as a political spin zone.

We need to level with the American people—the good, the bad and the ugly. For the simple fact is that we cannot fail in Iraq. On that fundamental principle, I am in full and profound agreement with the president. The stakes simply are too high. That means we need to improve our transparency and credibility in Iraq. In the recent $87 billion supplemental appropriations bill passed by the Senate, an amendment that I offered, and which was included in the final bill, would require GAO audits of these opaque supplemental appropriations. Another amendment that I cosponsored with Senator Harkin would require the GAO to examine the level of profits being made by U.S. contractors in Iraq. This is a historic mission that our government has encouraged, going back to George Washington, to make sure that no private company profited off the spoils of war. We need to assure the American people that their money is being spent wisely, assure the Iraqi people that it is being spent in their interest and assure the world that it is not being spent for profiteering by American companies. I understand both of these amendments, my amendment and the one I cosponsored with Senator Harkin, are the subject of some dispute by the administration. And in fact, I understand that the majority party has been advised to ensure the final package doesn't include those amendments. I can only hope that they have a change of mind. They are creating a level of mistrust in our government by our citizens for which we will reap the consequences for years to come.

As we discuss and debate these issues, let us remember the simple fact that we remain at war. That is not a fact lost on the men and women stationed in Iraq. It is not a fact lost on their families who sit at home worrying about their well-being. It should not lead to the administration refusing to release injury figures. We should be willing to admit the price that is being paid by these brave young men and women to pursue this policy. I believe that the executive branch has a strong prerogative on national security issues. As Senator, I have supported that prerogative. But the men and women elected to serve in the Congress also have a great deal of wisdom to bring to bear. And quite honestly, my friends, things have not gone so well in Iraq that we have a single mind to waste.

Recent articles in the *New York Times* and *Newsweek* report that many Republicans share the frustration that comes from lack of genuine consultations—failure to construct a genuine bipartisan consensus for the sacrifices we are asking Americans to make. My Republican colleagues Senator McCain and Senator Hagel, who is speaking at this conference, have cautioned the administration of the dangers of a failure to be open and honest with the American people on the situation in Iraq.

As Senator Hagel and others have suggested, Congress needs be more than just a rubber stamp for the administration's policies. Tell me what war American has won without seeking, achieving, and maintaining a bipartisan consensus.

President Truman worked closely with Senator Vandenberg after World War II to secure U.S. support for the United Nations. President George H. W. Bush consulted closely with Democratic congressional leaders during the first Gulf War. My husband consulted closely with Senator Dole and other Republican leaders during the military action in Bosnia and Kosovo.

In giving Iraqis more of a say and in making transactions and contracting more open, the U.S. simply is practicing the habits of democracy—inclusion, empowerment, and openness. Fundamentally, this is about trust—winning and earning the trust of the Iraqi people and trusting in the Iraqi people who eventually are going to be left to govern themselves and keeping the trust of the American people. I cannot stress strongly enough how significant it is that the American people across the board are beginning to ask such serious questions about our direction in our efforts to pursue a course in Iraq, but also from the Middle East to North Korea as well. An unwillingness of the administration to be more forthright can undermine the greatest capital we have, the capital of human trust between a government and the governed. I think we're on the edge of losing both the confidence of the Iraqi people and of the American people. We can prevent that from happening with a heavy dose of straight talk.

At the same time that we are trying to build a democratic society in Iraq, we must abide by those basic principles that we hold dear and demonstrate that we are willing to be open and have partnerships and build coalitions that are more than just in a name.

I think this moment in American history is wrought with danger and challenge. If you look back at our security and goals in World War II they were clear, the Cold War was clear, the post–Cold War era, prior to 9/11, was a little more muddy because it wasn't as obvious what our strategic objectives were and how we would achieve them.

Now we do have, once again, a very clear adversary. But just proclaiming the evil of our adversary is not a strategy; just assuming that everyone will understand that we are well motivated and people to be trusted is beyond the range of human experiences that I understand. This administration is in danger of squandering not just our surplus, which is already gone in financial terms, but the surplus of good feeling and hopefulness and care and that we had in almost global unanimity after 9/11. We are a resilient, optimistic, and effective people and I'm confident that we can regain our footing, but it needs to be the first order of business, not only for the administration, but also for Congress and the American public. It is my hope this conference will provide more ammunition and more support for those of use who are trying to get back on track and to give America the chance to lead consistent with our values and ideals. Thank you very much.

2004 Annual Kennan Institute Dinner

Colin L. Powell

U.S. secretary of state, 2001– ; born New York City, April 5, 1937, and raised in the South Bronx; graduated Morris High School, New York City, 1954; B.S. in geology, City College of New York, 1958; M.B.A., George Washington University, 1971; U.S. Army, 1958–93, including two tours in Vietnam (1962–63 and 1968–69); assistant to the president for national security affairs, 1987–89; promoted to rank of four-star general, 1989; chair, Joint Chiefs of Staff, 1989–93, overseeing Operation Desert Storm in the 1991 Persian Gulf War; chair, America's Promise—The Alliance for Youth, 1993–2001; author, My American Journey *(1995); two Presidential Medals of Freedom; President's Citizens Medal; Congressional Gold Medal; Secretary of State Distinguished Service Medal; Secretary of Energy Distinguished Service Medal; honorary degrees from several universities and colleges; Purple Heart, Bronze Star, and Legion of Merit Award.*

Editors' introduction: With the fighting in Iraq continuing, and the 9/11 Commission investigation led by Tom Kean and Lee Hamilton ongoing, Secretary of State Powell explained to the National Press Club (NPC) what "three principles" of diplomacy were required for "long-term success in foreign policy." The NPC was founded in 1908 to promote free press and provide benefits to journalists. It has nearly 4,000 members, from bureau chiefs to cub reporters, from journalism professors to first-year students. The Club includes public-relations professionals and others who deal with the media on a regular basis. Members come from 50 states and overseas. Mr. Hamilton introduced Secretary Powell.

Colin L. Powell's speech: Thank you, Lee, for that very warm and kind and short introduction. [Laughter.] We did have some interesting times a couple of days ago before the 9/11 Commission, and you did give me instructions to be here on time tonight, knowing that I had to go to Madrid overnight and come back from Madrid after attending a very moving memorial service.

But in order to follow your instructions, I managed to get myself in trouble. Because when I was in Madrid, after the memorial service, I was planning to see and was invited to see the new Prime Minister of Spain, Mr. Zapatero. And as I was waiting to see him, there were a number of other leaders before me. And for those of you who follow these matters, you will notice in [the] *Financial*

Delivered on March 25, 2004, at around 7:00 P.M., at the National Press Club, Washington, DC.

Times today, there is an article that I was a little bit rude and that I was a little indignant that I was being kept waiting by the president of the French Republic. President Chirac was in with the new Spanish prime minister.

Now, I don't wish to offend my French friends or President Chirac or anyone. But I was anxious, but it had nothing to do with the fact that I was waiting in queue behind President Chirac. It had to do with the very simple fact that my airplane crew was running out of flight time, and if I did not get into this meeting with the new prime minister and out of this meeting with the new prime minister, out to the airport in 15 minutes flat, and back here to the United States, we would have lost 24 hours and I would not be with you this evening. [Laughter.] So with due apologies to [applause] President Chirac, I am here.

Secretary Albright, so many other distinguished guests here, I am quite pleased to be with you all this evening. And Lee, I assume that both you and the dinner chairman, Tom Pickering, had a hand in inviting me here to talk about diplomacy and foreign policy and the Kennan legacy. And it's flattering because I can think of no two other Americans that I admire more with respect to their contributions to diplomacy, to foreign policy, and their dedication to public service. Tom—one of the most able and experienced of all of our Foreign Service Officers, still regarded as something of an icon in Foreign Service [applause] and continuing to do your great work.

And Lee, of course we all know they grow 'em tall and tough, but smart and subtle out in Indiana. And you're a diplomat in so many ways. And you and I have spent some quality time together lately, Lee. And in fact, as I see Madeleine here, and Tom here, and you here, and this nice big table here, we might as well get started again and see what else we can do. [Laughter.]

But I thank you, Lee, for being the vice chairman of the 9/11 Commission. Once again, you're serving your nation. And I know the commission will do its job well and I know the commission will wade through all of the charges and countercharges, comments and commentary that we see going back and forth. The American people want to know exactly what might have been known or not known during this difficult period before 9/11 and over a period of two administrations.

I know that President Bush was committed to doing everything we can do with respect to terrorism and I know President Clinton felt the same way. None of us were unmindful of the threat that this nation was facing overseas and here at home. And I know that as a result of the dedicated work that you and your commission members will put into this and all of the people you have been speaking to, you will come out with the right answer for the American people. The families of the 9/11 victims want that and expect that, and I know you'll provide that to them.

And we also want to know what we can do better in the future. What might we have missed in the past that could have given us more indication of what was about to happen, but just as important, what should we do in the future to prevent a recurrence? And I hope the commission succeeds, and I'm confident that it will under your leadership and with the leadership provided before and by all the members of the commission.

It's a particular honor for me to have been invited to this annual Kennan Institute dinner. Not only does this dinner celebrate the 30th anniversary of the Institute, it also coincides with the Ambassador's 100th birthday.

The Institute is renowned for its sponsorship of scholars examining the former Soviet Union and Russian and Eurasian issues in general. Its work has been of the highest quality, as befits the Wilson Center and the Smithsonian Institution, of which it is a part, and it's still going strong after all these years. Whether it's the Institute's short-term grant program or its research scholarship program, interested top-rate scholars know where to apply. And if it's archives one needs, the NPR / Kennan Institute–founded audio archive is superb.

Now, the Kennan Institute has seen some pretty amazing changes over the 30 years of its life. We have moved from a time when Americans and Russians sat mostly in separate rooms and considered each other as target sets to where we now sit in the same room and target the solution to problems common to us all.

I was in Moscow just a few weeks ago. I can testify to the truth of that statement. Could I have thought 30 years ago or 30-odd years ago, 32 years ago to be precise, when I was a young lieutenant colonel of infantry and I had the chance to visit Russia, the Soviet Union for the first time, could I have imagined back then in the very depths of the Cold War that I'd live to see such a day as this, when an American Secretary, and I'm not just the first, Madeleine has had the same experience, could visit Moscow and be genuinely among friends in high places working on issues of mutual interest, working to strengthen a partnership, disagreeing on some issues but being drawn closer and closer together by those issues in which we have a common interest?

I don't really remember if I could have dreamed of something like that so many years ago. I was too busy at that time defending the Fulda Gap as a young lieutenant. I love to tell the story of being a second lieutenant of infantry and being sent to Germany and being assigned to a rifle platoon that had a section of the Fulda Gap, and having explained to me in the most clear, concrete, crystal terms one can imagine what my job was in the conduct of the strategy of containment. My company commander said to me, "Lieutenant, you see that tree and you see that tree?" "Right, yeah." "Well, you guard between those two trees, and when the Russian army comes, don't let 'em through. You got it?" "Got it." [Laughter.] That's all I needed to know. They shall not pass.

And now these 30-odd years later, just as George Kennan predicted, the Fulda Gap is a tourist attraction. Fulda and Gap—I often joke, maybe Gap means the store, GAP, no longer the Gap that I worried about for all those years. But George Kennan knew there would be such a transformation. He knew it would happen, and he lived to see it. One hundred years old—now that really is something, even in a day of amazing medical breakthroughs.

Most of us, I think, have pondered the secret of what it takes to reach that elusive third digit in our ages. There's certainly lots of lore and humor on the topic to stimulate us, but it's clear to me that one quality that it takes to reach 100 is patience. Living 100 years is something you just can't rush. George Kennan has shown the virtue of patience, but not just by making it to 100 years of age. Ambassador Kennan also demonstrated patience by waiting more than 45 years for his prediction of Soviet collapse to come true. And we could return, as you heard earlier, to a discussion about Russia as our partner.

He suffered though plenty of arguments during those years about the "if"s, "why"s, and "wherefore"s of containment—would it work? Was it more diplomatic or was it more the use of military power and force? But he never changed his mind; he always knew it would happen. He was patient and he was proven right in his own lifetime. And all of us should be so fortunate to get at least one big thing right in our lifetime, and to live to see it come to pass.

All of us might also learn a lesson about diplomacy from Ambassador Kennan's patience. Patience is indispensable to long-term success in foreign policy. And that goes double for a large and wealthy country with a capable military such as the United States. Indeed, patience in a great power goes to the core principle of diplomacy itself, one of three principles that I'd like to talk about this evening.

This first principle concerns the relationship between diplomacy and the power to coerce others, whether military power or economic power. That principle is that power is a necessary condition for foreign policy success, but not always a sufficient one. Power is necessary because using force in statecraft is sometimes unavoidable—as every single American administration and official in any American administration since Pearl Harbor has experienced and knows well. It's just not possible to reason with every adversary that threatens a vital interest.

Fortunately, "jaw-jaw"—as Winston Churchill called diplomacy—is often judged better than war-war. Contests of persuasion form the normal course of events, and that is fortunate. Obviously then, patience is a virtue in diplomacy; but it's not the only virtue. A willingness to use power when necessary is a virtue, also.

But what's the mean, what's the balance, between patience and power? How does a president decide, when everyone knows there are risks and dangers in both directions, risks and dangers of using too much power and of using too little? A president doesn't know. He can't know for sure. No president can. No one can see into the future. A president assembles the best advice he can and then uses his best judgment. Such judgments aren't easy. It's hard to be president. All of our greatest presidents from history have told us so. Every future president will know it, too, or learn it quick enough.

When a president does have to use force, it's a blessing to have the best force around. And the United States military, in the case of military power, is the finest in the world. We're thankful for that and we're proud of it. Our troops and those of our coalition partners performed brilliantly in Afghanistan against the Taliban and Al Qaeda, and in Iraq against the Ba'ath regime—and on that point everyone agrees.

I was in Iraq as well as in Afghanistan last week, and I remember a moment in Baghdad when I was talking to a large group of troops and civilian workers and diplomats in a large hall in the Coalition Provisional Authority room. And after my few remarks, I was taking pictures and shaking hands as all of us like to do, and it's so great to be with those young people. And one young soldier shoved his hand through the crowd and grabbed my hand. And he shook it vigorously and he said, "Not Secretary, but General, stay the course. Stay the course." What he meant by that is he knew why we were there; he knew what we were doing; he knew that the days ahead would be difficult. He knew the dangers, but he also knew that what we were doing was right: the opportunity to bring hope to a people; the opportunity to bring democracy to a people; the opportunity to rebuild a nation that had been devastated by a dictatorial, despotic regime that filled mass graves.

> *When a president does have to use force, it's a blessing to have the best force around.*

I saw that same attitude in Afghanistan when I visited our troops there and saw what they were doing and visited a registration center where women, for the first time, were coming forward, uncovered, in order to sign the necessary forms to get a registration card so they could vote, and vote freely on the basis of the new constitution that had just been passed in Afghanistan by a Loya Jirga.

Stay the course. Even though the days ahead are difficult in Afghanistan and Iraq because the work we do is noble and correct. Stay the course. We stay the course, also, against the threat of terrorism, which all of us are seized with this week. There's no question that the new ideology that threatens us is not called communism or fascism, but it is terrorism. And it affects all of us and no nation can step away from it. No nation can think they're immune from it. No civilized nation dare not be part of this great crusade against the evil of terrorism that afflicts all of us.

We're all in debt to these wonderful young men and women of ours in uniform and also, we're in debt to the thousands of other civilians, diplomats, contractors, who work at their side. That this work goes on illustrates this first principle of democracy. It shows that military victories don't translate automatically into political achievements the day after the war ends.

After the fighting stops, other hard work begins, including political and diplomatic work, rebuilding, transforming a defeated country—something we have experience in from World War II and other events that we have been involved in over the years; so it was after our Civil War, World War II, so it is today. But while the effective use of force doesn't always immediately translate directly into final political success, it does do more than defeat enemies on the battlefield.

Power has a reputation as well that walks before it into the future, affecting what others think about us and what their reactions will be to future events. America never looks for opportunities to exercise power except in defense of our vital interests and the vital interests of our allies. We don't use force just to burnish our reputation or to enhance our credibility. As every president knows, it's better,

---

America never looks for opportunities to exercise power except in defense of our vital interests and the vital interests of our allies.

---

whenever possible, to let the reputation of power achieve policy goals rather than the use of power, especially military power itself. And it's diplomacy that deploys power's reputation to do this in the form of political influence. One of my predecessors and Madeleine's predecessors at the State Department, a great American by the name of Dean Acheson, captured this idea when he wrote that "influence is the shadow of power."

For any administration, any president, real and lasting success in foreign policy frequently comes from deploying the shadow of power as well as, when necessary, from the application of power itself. Moreover, history makes clear that force is only one element of policy success. There are many reasons for this, all embedded firmly in our history books and all very well understood by President Bush.

As he made clear, speaking of Iraq, "all the tools of diplomacy, law enforcement, intelligence, and finance are important. We're working with a broad coalition of nations that understand the threat and our shared responsibility to meet it. The use of force has been, and remains, our last resort." But use it when necessary.

We as a nation are now debating recent history—Afghanistan, Iraq, the campaign against terrorism. We should debate it. It befits a great democracy. We're reviewing judgments that have been made by presidents over the years. That is also appropriate in a great democracy. And there are also broader concerns that we have to look at and which Lee Hamilton and the members of his commission are looking at to make sure that we are structured properly for the times that we live in and the times that we will be living in.

But there is no disagreement in principle about the relationship between power and persuasion in American diplomacy. Everyone who understands that power is necessary, but not always sufficient for foreign policy success knows, too, that force and authority aren't the same. Not all use of force is created equal in diplomatic terms. Others will grant authority to the use of force if it falls within bounds of justice and reason.

Obviously, we still lack universal agreement on what is just and reasonable. There are disagreements, but there is a growing sense of both. Between 1991 and November 2002 the United Nations Security Council passed more than a dozen mostly Chapter 7—use of force—resolutions concerning Iraq; resolutions authorizing the use of force. That matters in a world where principles count. And that's the kind of a world we live in, not least because America, more than most, has tried hard to bring such a world into being.

Diplomacy isn't the opposite of force. Diplomacy without power is just naked pleading.

We're mindful of all this. We've used force when we believed we had to, but not beyond. But it's not just about force. It's about diplomacy. President Bush has stressed that states supporting terrorism are as guilty as terrorists themselves, and he's right—they are. But we were never so unimaginative to think that one approach would work in dealing with all cases. That's why we're determined to make best use of the reputation of American and coalition power to achieve goals without necessarily having to use force.

What do recent decisions of the Libyan government tell us about that effort? What do less dramatic but still noticeable changes in either policy or body language in certain other Middle Eastern countries tell us? I think they tell us that we understand well this first basic principle of diplomacy.

Diplomacy, then, if I may spell it out in a phrase, is the combination of power and persuasion, the orchestration of deeds and words in pursuit of policy objectives. Now, every true diplomat knows this, but not everyone's a diplomat. Some have recently argued that Libya's recent decision to turn away from weapons of mass destruction is an interesting thing, but they see it in terms that remind me of an old beer commercial: "tastes great / less filling, tastes great / less filling." Did they do it because of force? Did they do it because of diplomacy?

And of course, in almost every situation I deal with, it's not either/ or. Diplomacy isn't the opposite of force. Diplomacy without power is just naked pleading. Power without diplomacy is incomplete. Libya's change of heart, in my judgment, wouldn't have happened in the absence of American power as a backdrop. But policy success also required American and British skills at persuasion. In this case, the combination of power and persuasion is what worked. And we all saw on our television sets this afternoon a remarkable scene: Prime Minister Tony Blair sitting in a tent with Muammar Qadhafi. And you also saw this morning, Assistant Secretary of State Bill Burns with Muammar Qadhafi yesterday. Or the day before, I guess it was.

A second basic principle of diplomacy follows from the first: Policy success comes easier when more actors work with you to achieve it than work against you to prevent it.

One of diplomacy's main jobs is to arrange coalitions so that one's power and one's reputation are multiplied. The fact of power alone cannot do this because power repels as well as attracts. A wise diplomacy magnifies power's attractive quality by using power to benefit others as well as oneself. It shows other states that their most important equities will be advanced if they cooperate with you. And the epitome of this principle is a formal alliance.

American diplomacy after World War II exemplified the soundness of this principle. We put our power at the disposal of all who cherished freedom and peace. We did things for others they couldn't do for themselves. We defended others, yes, but we also forgave our former enemies and helped reconcile old adversaries. We advanced common prosperity by building institutions to promote trade and investment.

All this magnified the attractive qualities of American power and legitimized our power in the eyes of others. We were the candyman, the rainmaker, of international politics. And we still are. I know the rap, the charge against this administration's supposed unilateralism. I don't buy it because the facts say otherwise.

Do we not put our power at the disposal of others, including the dozen of allies who stand with us in Afghanistan and Iraq, and the dozens more who work with us in the war against terrorism worldwide? We do not still do for others things they cannot do for themselves, like—do we not still do for others things they cannot do for themselves like organize regional coalitions to bring relief to shattered countries like Liberia and Haiti? We still embrace old enemies with new perspectives, including some in Afghanistan and Iraq, and we still work to reconcile old adversaries, our efforts in the Middle East, in Africa, in South Asia and elsewhere show.

I spent part of last week in India and Pakistan working hard to see these two nations that 18 months, 20 months ago on the verge of war—war that might have been a nuclear war—but the headline this time when I was there was "Pakistan Wins at Cricket," and they're talking to one another. They're exchanging trade ideas and they're exchanging delegations. And they have an agreement underway being executed now to begin conversations that will lead through the thicket of issues that they have to work on, to include Kashmir.

We're no less committed to free trade than we ever were, and we're no less dedicated to our allies either, despite the shifting of the circumstances that gave rise to our oldest and most cherished alliances.

Now, allies aren't always easy to get along with, in war or in peace. But when there's trouble among friends—as we've had over the past year or so—it doesn't follow that the fault always lies on one side. Nor should disagreements among friends surprise or overly excite us.

Nearly every year since 1949, someone has predicted, for example, the end of NATO—over Berlin, over Suez and Hungary, over Vietnam, over the 1973 Middle East war, over the Euromissile ordeal of the 1980s, or something else. But NATO hasn't ended. Quite the contrary, it's enlarging.

I still remember in the early '90s after the Soviet Union ended and I was still chairman of the Joint Chiefs of Staff, and I got to really know some of the Russian generals up close and personal in a way that I couldn't have known them earlier. They would say to me, "Well the Warsaw Pact is gone. You don't need NATO anymore. It only existed for the Warsaw Pact, so why don't you get rid of NATO?"

And I thought about it and gave it some of the most weighty consideration I possibly could, and the simple answer was, it's hard to close down a club when people continue to ask for membership applications. [Laughter.] And this Monday we will add seven more members to this grand alliance. An alliance that is no longer seen as a threat to the Russian Federation, and in fact, the NATO-Russia Council invites Russia to work with NATO. It's a great change in history and it teaches us two things: First, don't fall for the NATO hysteria du jour, that something's about to fall apart; second and more important, it teaches us that alliances based on principles and not just on momentary needs have the ability to adjust when circumstances change. And NATO is such an alliance.

In the late 1940s we worried that Western Europe might be overrun by the Red Army, or subverted by local Soviet-supported communists. We're no longer worried by the dangers that confronted us in the late 1940s, or even the late 1980s. By that measure, if NATO were only a military coalition, serving only Cold War purposes, it would have expired, it should have expired, a long time ago. In the late '40s American statesmen were just as concerned that Europe be rebuilt in such a way that we wouldn't be dragged into a third World War over new European squabbles.

And that's why we were so concerned that postwar Europe be dominated by genuine, stable and prosperous liberal democracies, because liberal democracies don't produce disasters like the First and Second World Wars. So NATO was never just a military alliance. It's been a compact of political principles, too. And that's why NATO can now and has now transformed itself from an alliance devoted mainly to the defense of common territory into an alliance devoted to the defense of common interests and ideals. And that's why it can apply its irreplaceable experience in common defense to dealing with new kinds of threats.

> *Transatlantic ties are as flexible as they are unbreakable.*

That transformation can be tricky. Our common security challenges are no longer as vivid as they were in the days of Soviet military power. Threats are less well defined, more unpredictable. As a consequence we and our allies no longer share common perceptions of threat to the same extent as we did in Cold War times. That's been true even of terrorism, though it's clear now that this threat is global and not simply aimed at America. You can see that in Bali, Madrid, Riyadh, Turkey, so many other places, in Russia itself, in Moscow.

Whatever NATO members today may lack by way of identical definitions of threats, we do more than make up for that through a mature recognition that we share the same vision of a good society and of a better world.

Transatlantic ties are as flexible as they are unbreakable.

So those are the reasons that America's alliance in Europe, in Asia and elsewhere, particularly an alliance that we celebrate this evening a little bit, NATO, become even stronger over the years. We shouldn't let the inevitable stress of dealing with change mislead us or deter us. Our partnerships are growing stronger as they adapt to new realities.

I'll be in Berlin next week for a major conference on Afghanistan. Afghanistan is NATO's first non-European deployment in its history. And Germany is a leader in it. German soldiers head the first provincial reconstruction team in Konduz, under NATO command.

This is the same Germany, with the same German Government that we differed with seriously about Iraq last year. But here we have common cause.

Of course, we don't look forward to disagreements, just so we can feel relieved when we put them behind us—though that is a terrific feeling. I'm feeling it a lot lately. NATO is closing ranks and working well on a whole range of issues, not just Afghanistan, and I hope NATO will find a role to play in Iraq reconstruction as well.

Everyone knows we need each other. We're wrapped up in each other like family, as we have been for so long. We argue with each other in proportion to how much we care about each other. We care a lot—enough to keep our differences in perspective.

Now let me come now to the third principle I wanted to talk about this evening. It's this: Success in diplomacy is often most advantageous when it's incomplete. That may sound strange, but all I mean is that it's possible to overdo things—that there are ways of winning that can turn victory into defeat. Examples of overreach fill history books. Fortunately, there are also examples in those books of getting it right.

Another way to put this principle is that an adversary needs an honorable path of escape if we're to achieve our main policy goals without using force. Some adversaries will never take that avenue of exit, of escape—Saddam Hussein being a perfect example. A cornered adversary may lash out, and our eventual success at arms, if it comes at all, could be a pyrrhic victory. The diplomacy of the Cuban Missile Crisis illustrates this.

By offering to remove U.S. Jupiter missiles in Turkey that we'd scheduled for removal anyway, President Kennedy gave Chairman Khrushchev a way out. He took it. Our success was incomplete. We didn't get the Soviets altogether out of Cuba at that time. We didn't get Fidel Castro out of power, as we know. But our success was the most advantageous one available given the risks and probable costs of seeking more. We did remove a mortal threat to the United States, and we transformed the dynamics of Cold War risk-taking into a positive way.

This third principle of diplomacy remains very much in play. We have a problem in North Korea. Madeleine Albright worked on it. We're working on it. The DPRK North Korean leadership has been trying to generate a crisis atmosphere on the Korean Peninsula. It's part of a pattern of extortion that the DPRK has practiced over many years.

It wouldn't be diplomatic for me to lay out all of our tactics in dealing with North Korea, but it's telling no secrets out of school to say that the president's been very patient. All options remain on the table, but we've focused our efforts on persuasion, so we get back to principle number one.

The president has also gathered allies—principle number two. The main equities of four of our five interlocutors in the six-party talks run parallel to our own. Russia, China, South Korea, Japan—all are committed to the complete, verifiable, and irreversible dismantlement of all North Korean nuclear programs.

By working to bring Japan, Russia, China, and South Korea into our Korean diplomacy, we advance their equities as well as our own. We legitimate our power; we give it greater authority.

We also enhance the prospect that a solution will endure, and we improve our relations with important countries in ways that transcend the stakes in Korea.

To succeed, however, principle number three is key. We're seeking the end of North Korea's nuclear threat. And to achieve that there has to be an exit through which the North Korean leadership can move if it makes the right choices. That exit is called "embark here and now for the 21st century, and to have an honorable place in the world community."

If North Korea's leaders do embark for the 21st century, and if our diplomacy achieves the complete dismantling of North Korea's nuclear programs, we will have gained an important success.

It would still be an incomplete success—knowingly so. As with Cuba, we will achieve the most advantageous success available, given the probable risks and costs of seeking more.

That's the president's policy, and it's the right policy. It doesn't mean we'll ever reward the North Korean regime for oppressing its people and threatening its neighbors, any more than we have rewarded the Cuban regime since 1962.

Those regimes will change, either because the regimes themselves will seek transformation, or because their peoples will change the regime. They are running against the tide of history over a long period of time, just as the Soviet Union did until it realized a better world lay ahead.

Clearly, not every instance of political progress in the world can or should be accomplished by force or arms, certainly not just American force of arms. Of course we stand for universal ideals—we stand for liberty, for freedom, for government of, by, and for the people under the rule of law. But we can't just wave our hands and turn these ideals into reality everywhere at once.

The president knows, we all know, that if we want our power to endure, and the reputation of our power to prevail over the long haul, we must be patient, cooperative, and prudent as well as strong and bold in the face of danger.

As I've tried to describe it this evening, American foreign policy is anchored in a method as well as in its ideals. It's President Bush's method, in which power and persuasion combine in an active diplomacy. It's a method by which we seek partners though whom our power can be both legitimated and used for the greater good.

And perhaps above all, it is a method that recognizes the need to distinguish between what is both desirable and attainable, and what is only one or the other.

I'd like to think George Kennan understands and applauds this description of American diplomacy. After all, to a considerable extent, we all learned much from him, from his example and from his writings.

So let me close, then, by thanking the Wilson Center for the privilege of addressing you this evening, by again congratulating the Kennan Institute on reaching its 30th year—and especially, in the presence of Ambassador Kennan's family, for Ambassador Kennan reaching his 100th year. We are forever in his debt. He remains an inspiration to all of us in the State Department.

Thank you very much. [Applause.]

Security and Strength for a New World

John Kerry

U.S. senator (D), Massachusetts, 1985– , and Democratic presidential nominee, 2004; born Denver, CO, December 11, 1943; B.A., Yale University, 1966; U.S. Naval Reserve, 1966–69, serving in Vietnam and receiving a Silver Star, Bronze Star with Combat V, and three Purple Hearts; national coordinator for Vietnam Veterans Against the War, 1969–71; cofounder and member, Vietnam Veterans of America; M.A. and J.D., Boston College Law School, 1976; assistant district attorney, Middlesex County, Massachusetts, 1976–79; partner, law firm of Kerry and Sragow, 1979–82; lieutenant governor, Massachusetts, 1982–84; U.S. Senate, served on Foreign Relations Committee, chair of Senate Select Committee on POW/MIA Affairs, East Asian and Pacific Affairs Subcommittee; author, The New Soldier *(1971) and* The New War *(1997).*

Editors' introduction: As the fighting in Iraq continued and the 9/11 Commission pursued its investigation into the terrorist attacks of 2001, the campaigns by incumbent George W. Bush and Senator John Kerry for the presidency accelerated. The nation's concern about the war and threats of terrorism at home were echoed in the candidates' speeches. Upon ending two days of campaigning in Seattle, Washington, Senator Kerry told many supporters at McCaw Hall that the Bush administration "looked to force before exhausting diplomacy; they bullied when they should have persuaded." The Kerry campaign advertised this speech as a major policy statement. Gary Hart, former senator from Colorado, introduced the candidate.

John Kerry's speech: Thank you all for being here.

Over the next 10 days, our nation will come together to honor the bravery and sacrifice of past generations of Americans. On Saturday, in our nation's capital, we will dedicate a memorial to the heroes of the Greatest Generation who won World War II. On Memorial Day, we will salute all those who for more than two centuries made the ultimate sacrifice when America's freedom was on the line.

And on June 6th, we will mark the 60th anniversary of D-day by remembering the brave young men who scaled the cliffs on beaches called Omaha and Utah—and brought the light of liberty from the New World to the Old.

Delivered on May 27, 2004, at Seattle, WA.

To me, and to millions of Americans, the days ahead will be filled with the pride of families, the sadness of loss, and a renewed commitment to service. But that is not enough. We must pay tribute.

We must hear and heed the lessons of the Greatest Generation.

Our leaders then understood that America drew its power not only from the might of weapons, but also from the trust and respect of nations around the globe. There was a time, not so long ago, when the might of our alliances was a driving force in the survival and success of freedom—in two World Wars, in the long years of the Cold War—then from the Gulf War to Bosnia and Kosovo. America led instead of going it alone. We extended a hand, not a fist. We respected the world—and the world respected us.

More than a century ago, Teddy Roosevelt defined American leadership in foreign policy. He said America should walk softly and carry a big stick. Time and again, this administration has violated the fundamental tenet of Roosevelt's approach, as he described it: "If a man continually blusters, if he lacks civility, a big stick will not save him from trouble."

> *Today, there is still a powerful yearning around the world for an America that listens and leads again.*

But that is precisely what this administration has done. They looked to force before exhausting diplomacy. They bullied when they should have persuaded.

They have gone it alone when they should have assembled a team. They have hoped for the best when they should have prepared for the worst. In short, they have undermined the legacy of generations of American leadership. And that is what we must restore.

Today, there is still a powerful yearning around the world for an America that listens and leads again. An America that is respected, and not just feared.

I believe that respect is an indispensable mark of our nation's character—and an indispensable source of our nation's strength. It is the indispensable bond of America's mighty alliances.

I'm running for president because, abroad as well as at home, it's time to let America be America again. By doing so, we can restore our place in the world and make America safer.

It's time for a new national security policy guided by four new imperatives: First, we must launch and lead a new era of alliances for the post 9-11 world. Second, we must modernize the world's most powerful military to meet the new threats. Third, in addition to our military might, we must deploy all that is in America's arsenal—our diplomacy, our intelligence system, our economic power, and the appeal of our values and ideas. Fourth and finally, to secure our full independence and freedom, we must free America from its dangerous dependence on Mideast oil.

These four imperatives are a response to an inescapable reality: War has changed; the enemy is different—and we must think and act anew.

Today, we are waging a global war against a terrorist movement committed to our destruction. Terrorists like Al Qaeda and its copycat killers are unlike any adversary our nation has faced. We do not know for certain how they are organized or how many operatives they have. But we know the destruction they can inflict.

We saw it in New York and in Washington; we have seen it in Bali and in Madrid, in Israel and across the Middle East; and we see it day after day in Iraq.

This threat will only be magnified as the technology to build nuclear and biological weapons continues to spread. And we can only imagine what would happen if the deadly forces of terrorism got their hands on the deadliest weapons in history.

Everyone outside the administration seems to understand that we are in deep trouble in Iraq. Failure there would be a terrible setback. It would be a boon to our enemies, and jeopardize the long-term prospects for a peaceful, democratic Middle East—leaving us at war not just with a small, radical minority, but with increasingly large portions of the entire Muslim world.

There is also the continuing instability in Afghanistan, where Al Qaeda still has a base, and Osama bin Laden is still at large, because the Bush administration didn't finish him off at the battle of Tora Bora. And in East Asia, North Korea poses a genuine nuclear threat, while we have begun to strip American troops to relieve the overburdened forces in Iraq.

In the coming week, I will also offer specific plans to build a new military capable of defeating enemies new and old, and to stop the spread of nuclear, biological, and chemical weapons. But first, here today, I want to set out the overall architecture of a new policy to make America stronger and respected in the world.

The first new imperative represents a return to the principle that guided us in peril and victory through the past century—alliances matter, and the United States must lead them.

Never has this been more true than in the war on terrorism.

As president, my number one security goal will be to prevent the terrorists from gaining weapons of mass murder. And our overriding mission will be to disrupt and destroy their terrorist cells.

Because Al Qaeda is a network with many branches, we must take the fight to the enemy on every continent—and enlist other countries in that cause.

America must always be the world's paramount military power. But we can magnify our power through alliances. We simply can't go it alone—or rely on a coalition of the few. The threat of terrorism demands alliances on a global scale—to find the extremist groups, to guard ports and stadiums, to share intelligence, and to get the terrorists before they get us. In short, we need a "coalition of the able"—and in truth, no force on earth is more able than the United States and its allies.

We must build that force—and we can. We can be strong without being stubborn. Indeed, that is ultimately the only way we can succeed.

Building strong alliances is only the first step. We cannot meet the new threats unless our military is adapted for new missions. This is my second new imperative.

As president, on my first day in office, I will send a message to every man and woman in our armed forces: This commander in chief will ensure that you are the best-led, best-equipped, and most respected fighting force in the world. You will be armed with the right weapons, schooled in the right skills, and fully prepared to win on the battlefield. But you will never be sent into harm's way without enough troops for the task, or asked to fight a war without a plan to win the peace.

And you will never be given assignments which have not been clearly defined and for which you are not professionally trained.

This administration has disregarded the advice, wisdom, and experience of our professional military officers. And often ended the careers of those who dared to give their honest assessments. That is not the way to make the most solemn decisions of war and peace. As president, I will listen to and respect the views of our experienced military leaders—and never let ideology trump the truth.

In the past, when our leaders envisioned the use of force, they had in mind the unleashing of massive numbers of American troops, battleships, and aircraft in confrontation with the uniformed military of an enemy nation. Of course, a conventional war to halt conventional aggression still remains a possibility for which we must prepare. But there are other urgent challenges.

I will modernize our military to match its new missions. We must get the most out of new technologies. We must reform training and update the way we structure our armed forces—for example, with special forces designed to strike terrorists in their sanctuaries, and with national guard and reserve units retooled to meet the requirements of homeland defense.

This strategy focuses not only on what we must do, but on what we must prevent. We must ensure that lawless states and terrorists will not be armed with weapons of mass destruction.

This is the single gravest threat to our security. Any potential adversary should know that we will defend ourselves against the possibility of attack by unconventional arms. If such a strike does occur, as commander in chief, I will respond with overwhelming and devastating force. If such an attack appears imminent, as commander in chief, I will do whatever is necessary to stop it. And, as commander in chief, I will never cede our security to anyone. I will always do what is necessary to safeguard our country.

The Justice Department said yesterday that terrorists may be planning to attack the United States again this summer—some believe that Al Qaeda would use an attack to try and influence the outcome of the November election.

I have a message today for Al Qaeda or any terrorist who may be harboring these illusions: We may have an election here in America. But let there be no doubt—this country is united in its determination to destroy you. And let me be absolutely clear: As commander in chief, I will bring the full force of our nation's power to bear on finding and crushing your networks. We will use every available resource to destroy you.

> *We should never wait to act until we have no other choice but war.*

But not all problems should be viewed through a military lens. We should never wait to act until we have no other choice but war. That brings me to my third new imperative.

In this new world, beyond military power, we must deploy all the power in America's arsenal.

We need to employ a layered defense to keep the worst weapons from falling into the worst hands. A strategy that invokes our non-military strength early enough and effectively enough so military force doesn't become our only option.

As president, I will launch a global initiative to fully secure the materials needed for nuclear weapons that already exist and sharply limit and control future production.

This initiative will include changes in international treaties, sharing of intelligence, and setting conditions for economic sanctions and the interdiction of illegal shipments. The key is for America to lead: to build an international consensus for early preventive action, so that states don't even think of taking the nuclear road, and potential traffickers in nuclear and biological technology fear the consequences of getting caught.

We must also have the best possible intelligence capabilities. Nothing is more important than early warning and specific information when dangerous technologies are being developed or sold. Whether it was September 11th or Iraq's supposed weapons of mass destruction, we have endured too many intelligence failures. That is why I will do what this President has failed to do: reform our intelligence system by making the next director of the CIA a true director of national intelligence, with true control over intelligence personnel and budgets all across the government.

All the levers of power will be deployed to overcome the 21st-century dangers we face. I intend to discuss this initiative in detail early next week.

Finally, a new national security policy demands an end to our dependence on Mideast oil. That is my fourth new imperative. For too long, America has lost its voice when talking about the policies and practices of some governments in the Persian Gulf.

We have been constrained by their control over the oil that fuels too large a part of our economy. This is a weakness that this administration has ignored—and one that must be addressed.

I have proposed a plan for energy independence from Mideast oil in the next ten years. It invests in new technologies and alternative fuels. It provides tax credits to help consumers buy and manufacturers build fuel efficiency cars. It will tap America's initiative and ingenuity to strengthen our national security, grow our economy, and protect our environment.

If we are serious about energy independence, then we can finally be serious about confronting the role of Saudi Arabia in financing and providing ideological support of Al Qaeda and other terrorist groups. We cannot continue this administration's kid-glove approach to the supply and laundering of terrorist money. As president, I will impose tough financial sanctions against nations or banks that engage in money laundering or fail to act against it. I will launch a "name and shame" campaign against those that are financing terror. And if they do not respond, they will be shut out of the U.S. financial system.

The same goes for Saudi sponsorship of clerics who promote the ideology of Islamic terror. To put it simply, we will not do business as usual with Saudi Arabia. They must take concrete steps to stop their clerics from fueling the fires of Islamic extremism.

Let me now turn to a subject that I know is on the minds of all Americans—the situation in Iraq.

The stakes in Iraq couldn't be higher. Earlier this week, the president again said he wanted to create stability and establish a representative government in Iraq. He did acknowledge what many have known all along—that we would be far better off if our allies were with us. What's important now is to turn these words into action.

In the coming weeks, President Bush will travel to Europe and meet with the members of the G-8 here in the United States. There will be speeches, handshakes, and ceremonies. But will our allies promise to send more troops to Iraq? Will they dedicate substantially more funding for reconstruction there? Will they pledge a real effort to aid the transformation of the Middle East. That is what we need. But the day is late and the situation in Iraq is grim.

Attracting international support in a situation like Iraq is a clear test of presidential leadership. It is what capable and confident presidents do. I urge President Bush to make a sustained effort. He should start at the Summit in Istanbul by persuading NATO to accept Iraq as an alliance mission, with more troops from NATO and its partners. He should seek help in expanding international support for training Iraq's own security forces, so they can safeguard the rights and well-being of their own people.

And he should propose the creation of an International High Commissioner to work with Iraqis in organizing elections, drafting a constitution, and coordinating reconstruction.

Over the last year, we've heard from the president that our policy should simply be to stay the course. But one thing I learned in the navy is that when the course you're on is headed for the shoals, you have to change course.

If President Bush doesn't secure new support from our allies, we will, once again, feel the consequences of a foreign policy that has divided the world instead of uniting it. Our troops will be in greater peril, the mission in Iraq will be harder to accomplish, and our country will be less secure.

I have spoken today about the architecture of a new national security policy. But at issue here is not just a set of prescriptions; at stake is a vision of an America truly stronger and truly respected in the world. This is not a partisan cause. Patriotism doesn't belong to any one party or president. And if I am president, I will enlist the best among us, regardless of party, to protect the security of this nation.

And I will call on the whole nation to let America be America again.

My father was a pilot during World War II. A year before Pearl Harbor, he was on active duty and he later served in the South Pacific.

And for the rest his life, he served in one capacity or another—whether nationally or locally, by vocation or as a volunteer.

He told me shortly before he died that the "human conscience, when it works, is the most divine thing in our small segment of the universe."

In today's world, conscience marks the difference between tolerance and terror.

In an earlier era, it was the difference between honor and holocaust.

Much has been written about the Greatest Generation.

The question before us now is what will be said about our own.

Because, for better or worse, as Abraham Lincoln once said, we cannot escape the judgment of history.

We do not have to live in fear or stand alone. We don't have to be a lonely "watchman on the walls of freedom." We can, once again, lead a great alliance. That is how we can honor the legacy of the Greatest Generation and restore respect to the greatest country—the United States of America.

Thank you and God bless America.

Progress in the War on Terror

George W. Bush

President of the United States, 2001– ; born New Haven, CT, July 6, 1946, and raised in Midland and Houston, TX; attended Phillips Academy, Andover, MA; B.A., Yale University; M.B.A., Harvard Business School, 1975; F-102 pilot, Texas Air National Guard, 1968–73; oil and gas business, Midland, TX, 1975–86; senior adviser in father's presidential campaign, 1987–88; owner and managing general partner, Texas Rangers baseball team, 1989–94; governor of Texas, 1995–2000.

Editors' introduction: As president and commander in chief of the United States military, George W. Bush chose to proceed with the fighting in Iraq while attempting to justify that policy to citizens and voters at home. Responding to criticism from John Kerry, Democratic presidential nominee, that the administration depended inordinately upon military might in its foreign policy, President Bush defended what he characterized as a "new approach in the world." He told some 200 employees and local officials at the Oak Ridge National Laboratory that "we're determined to challenge new threats, not ignore them, or simply wait for future tragedy."

George W. Bush's speech: Thank you for the warm welcome. I realize the Y-12 National Security Complex doesn't get a lot of visitors—[laughter]—so thanks for the special arrangements. I'm also glad to have the opportunity to thank each one of you for the vital work you do here. And please pass the word to your fellow employees, many of whom were waving, I want you to know, as we drove in, for which I'm thankful. The nation counts on your great expertise and your professionalism in producing, protecting, and maintaining material that is critical to our security. America is safer because of your service at Oak Ridge. You need to know our nation is grateful for that service. [Applause.]

I appreciate our Secretary of Energy Spence Abraham. He traveled with me today. Thank you, Mr. Secretary, for your service. I want to thank Jeffrey Wadsworth, who's the director of Oak Ridge National Laboratory. It's not the first time I've met Jeffrey. I appreciate Jon Kreykes. I want to thank all the people who helped make this visit a successful visit. I want to thank Senator Lamar Alexander, the other members of the United States Congress who are traveling with us today—strong supporters, by the way, of Oak

Delivered on July 12, 2004, at around 11:18 A.M., at Oak Ridge National Laboratory, Oak Ridge, TN.

Ridge. I appreciate the mayor being here, David Bradshaw. Mr. Mayor, I appreciate you taking time to come. I want to thank my fellow citizens for giving me a chance to come and visit.

I've just had a close look at some of the dangerous equipment secured in this place. Eight months ago, the centrifuge parts and processing equipment for uranium were 5,000 miles away in the nation of Libya. They were part of a secret nuclear weapons program. Today, Libya, America, and the world are better off because these components are safely in your care.

These materials are the sobering evidence of a great danger. Certain regimes, often with ties to terrorist groups, seek the ultimate weapons as a shortcut to influence. These materials, voluntarily turned over by the Libyan government, are also encouraging evidence that nations can abandon those ambitions and choose a better way.

Libya is dismantling its weapons of mass destruction and long-range missile programs. This progress came about through quiet diplomacy between America, Britain, and the Libyan government. This progress was set in motion, however, by policies declared in public to all the world. The United States, Great Britain, and many other nations are determined to expose the threats of terrorism and proliferation—and to oppose those threats with all our power. [Applause.] We have sent this message in the strongest diplomatic terms, and we have acted where action was required.

Every potential adversary now knows that terrorism and proliferation carry serious consequences, and that the wise course is to abandon those pursuits. By choosing that course, the Libyan government is serving the interests of its own people and adding to the security of all nations.

America's determination to actively oppose the threats of our time was formed and fixed on September the 11th, 2001. On that day we saw the cruelty of the terrorists, and we glimpsed the future they intend for us. They intend to strike the United States to the limits of their power. They seek weapons of mass destruction to kill Americans on an even greater scale. And this danger is increased when outlaw regimes build or acquire weapons of mass destruction and maintain ties to terrorist groups.

This is our danger, but not our fate. America has the resources and the strength and the resolve to overcome this threat. We are waging a broad and unrelenting war against terror, and an active campaign against proliferation. We refuse to live in fear. We are making steady progress.

To protect our people, we're staying on the offensive against threats within our own country. We are using the Patriot Act to track terrorist activity and to break up terror cells. Intelligence and law enforcement officials are sharing information as never before. We've transformed the mission of the FBI to focus on preventing terrorism. Every element of our homeland security plan is critical, because the terrorists are ruthless and resourceful—and we know they're preparing to attack us again. It's not possible to guarantee perfect security in our vast, free nation. But I can assure our fellow Americans, many fine professionals in intelligence and national security and homeland security and law enforcement are working around the clock doing everything they can to protect the country. And we're grateful to them all. [Applause.]

To overcome the dangers of our time, America is also taking a new approach in the world. We're determined to challenge new threats, not ignore them, or simply wait for future tragedy. We're helping to build a hopeful future in hopeless places, instead of allowing troubled regions to remain in despair and explode in violence. Our goal is a lasting, democratic peace, in which free nations are free from the threat of sudden terror. Our strategy for peace has three commitments: First, we are defending the peace by taking the fight to the enemy. We will confront them overseas so we do not have to confront them here at home. [Applause.] We are destroying the leadership of terrorist networks in sudden raids, disrupting their planning and financing, and keeping them on the run. Month by month, we

---

We're determined to challenge new threats, not ignore them, or simply wait for future tragedy.

---

are shrinking the space in which they can freely operate, by denying them territory and the support of governments.

Second, we're protecting the peace by working with friends and allies and international institutions to isolate and confront terrorists and outlaw regimes. America is leading a broad coalition of nations to disrupt proliferation. We're working with the United Nations, the International Atomic Energy Agency, and other international organizations to take action in our common security. The global threat of terrorism requires a global response. To be effective, that global response requires leadership—and America will lead. [Applause.]

Third, we are extending the peace by supporting the rise of democracy, and the hope and progress that democracy brings, as the alternative to hatred and terror in the broader Middle East. In democratic and successful societies, men and women do not swear allegiance to malcontents and murderers; they turn their hearts and labor to building better lives. And democratic governments do not shelter terrorist camps or attack their neighbors. When justice and democracy advance, so does the hope of lasting peace.

We have followed this strategy—defending the peace, protecting the peace and extending the peace—for nearly three years. We have been focused and patient, firm and consistent. And the results are all now clear to see.

Three years ago, the nation of Afghanistan was the home base of Al Qaeda, a country ruled by the Taliban, one of the most backward and brutal regimes of modern history. Schooling was denied girls. Women were whipped in the streets and executed in a sports stadium. Millions lived in fear. With protection from the Taliban, Al Qaeda and its associates trained, indoctrinated, and sent forth thousands of killers to set up terror cells in dozens of countries, including our own.

Today, Afghanistan is a world away from the nightmare of the Taliban. That country has a good and just president. Boys and girls are being educated. Many refugees have returned home to rebuild their country, and a presidential election is scheduled for this fall. The terror camps are closed and the Afghan government is helping us to hunt the Taliban and terrorists in remote regions. Today, because we acted to liberate Afghanistan, a threat has been removed, and the American people are safer. [Applause.]

Three years ago, Pakistan was one of the few countries in the world that recognized the Taliban regime. Al Qaeda was active and recruiting in Pakistan, and was not seriously opposed. Pakistan served as a transit point for Al Qaeda terrorists leaving Afghanistan on missions of murder. Yet the United States was not on good terms with Pakistan's military and civilian leaders—the very people we would need to help shut down Al Qaeda operations in that part of the world.

Today, the governments of the United States and Pakistan are working closely in the fight against terror. President Musharraf is a friend of our country, who helped us capture Khalid Sheik Mohammed, the operational planner behind the September the 11th attacks. And Pakistani forces are rounding up terrorists along their nation's western border. Today, because we're working with the Pakistani leaders, Pakistan is an ally in the war on terror, and the American people are safer. [Applause.]

Three years ago, terrorists were well-established in Saudi Arabia. Inside that country, fundraisers and other facilitators gave Al Qaeda financial and logistical help, with little scrutiny or opposition. Today, after the attacks in Riyadh and elsewhere, the Saudi government knows that Al Qaeda is its enemy. Saudi Arabia is working hard to shut down the facilitators and financial supporters of terrorism. The government has captured or killed many first-tier leaders of the Al Qaeda organization in Saudi Arabia—including one last week. Today, because Saudi Arabia has seen the danger and has joined the war on terror, the American people are safer. [Applause.]

Three years ago, the ruler of Iraq was a sworn enemy of America, who provided safe haven for terrorists, used weapons of mass destruction, and turned his nation into a prison. Saddam Hussein was not just a dictator; he was a proven mass murderer who refused to account for weapons of mass murder. Every responsible nation recognized this threat, and knew it could not go on forever.

America must remember the lessons of September the 11th. We must confront serious dangers before they fully materialize. And so my administration looked at the intelligence on Iraq, and we saw a threat. Members of the United States Congress from both political parties looked at the same intelligence, and they saw a threat. The United Nations Security Council looked at the intelligence, and it saw a threat. The previous administration and the Congress looked at the intelligence and made regime change in Iraq the policy of our country.

In 2002, the United Nations Security Council yet again demanded a full accounting of Saddam Hussein's weapons programs. As he had for over a decade, Saddam Hussein refused to comply. In fact, according to former weapons inspector David Kay, Iraq's weapons programs were elaborately shielded by security and deception operations that continued even beyond the end of Operation Iraqi Freedom. So I had a choice to make: Either take the word of a madman, or defend America. Given that choice, I will defend America every time. [Applause.]

> *Although we have not found stockpiles of weapons of mass destruction, we were right to go into Iraq.*

Although we have not found stockpiles of weapons of mass destruction, we were right to go into Iraq. We removed a declared enemy of America, who had the capability of producing weapons of mass murder, and could have passed that capability to terrorists bent on acquiring them. In the world after September the 11th, that was a risk we could not afford to take.

Today, the dictator who caused decades of death and turmoil, who twice invaded his neighbors, who harbored terrorist leaders, who used chemical weapons on innocent men, women, and children, is finally before the bar of justice. [Applause.] Iraq, which once had the worst government in the Middle East, is now becoming an example of reform to the region. And Iraqi security forces are fighting beside coalition troops to defeat the terrorists and foreign fighters who threaten their nation and the world. Today, because America and our coalition helped to end the violent regime of Saddam Hussein, and because we're helping to raise a peaceful democracy in its place, the American people are safer. [Applause.]

Three years ago, the nation of Libya, a longtime supporter of terror, was spending millions to acquire chemical and nuclear weapons. Today, thousands of Libya's chemical munitions have been destroyed. And nuclear processing equipment that could ultimately have threatened the lives of hundreds of thousands is stored away right here in Oak Ridge, Tennessee. Today, because the Libyan government saw the seriousness of the civilized world, and correctly judged its own interests, the American people are safer. [Applause.]

Three years ago, a private weapons proliferation network was doing business around the world. This network, operated by the Pakistani nuclear scientist, A. Q. Khan, was selling nuclear plans and equipment to the highest bidder, and found willing buyers in places like Libya, Iran, and North Korea. Today, the A. Q. Khan network is out of business. We have ended one of the most dangerous sources of proliferation in the world, and the American people are safer. [Applause.]

Breaking this proliferation network was possible because of the outstanding work done by the CIA. Dedicated intelligence officers were tireless in obtaining vital information, sometimes at great personal risk. Our intelligence services do an essential job for America. I thank them for their dedication and hard work. [Applause.] The Senate Intelligence Committee has identified some shortcomings in our intelligence capabilities; the Committee's report will help us in the work of reform. Our nation needs more intelligence agents—what is called human intelligence—to cover the globe. We must have the best, cutting-edge technology to listen and look for dangers. We must have better coordination among intelligence services. I need, and the Congress needs, the best possible intelligence in order to protect the American people. We're determined to make sure we get it.

Three years ago, the world was very different. Terrorists planned attacks, with little fear of discovery or reckoning. Outlaw regimes supported terrorists and defied the civilized world, without shame and with few consequences. Weapons proliferators sent their deadly shipments and grew wealthy, encountering few obstacles to their trade.

The world changed on September the 11th, and since that day, we have changed the world. [Applause.] We are leading a steady, confident, systematic campaign against the dangers of our time. There are still terrorists who plot against us, but the ranks of their leaders are thinning, and they know what fate awaits them. There are still regimes actively supporting the terrorists, but fewer than there used to be. There are still outlaw regimes pursuing weapons of mass destruction, but the world no longer looks the other way. Today, because America has acted, and because America has led, the forces of terror and tyranny have suffered defeat after defeat, and America and the world are safer. [Applause.]

All this progress has been achieved with the help of other responsible nations. The case of Libya's nuclear disarmament is a good example. In the fall of 2003, American and British intelligence were tracking a large shipment of nuclear equipment bound for Tripoli aboard a German-registered cargo ship. We alerted German and Italian authorities, who diverted the ship to an Italian port where the cargo was confiscated. We worked together. These events helped encourage Libya to reconsider its nuclear ambitions. That was a dramatic breakthrough, achieved by allies working together. And the cooperation of America's allies in the war on terror is very, very strong.

We're grateful to the more than 60 nations that are supporting the Proliferation Security Initiative to intercept illegal weapons and equipment by sea, land, and air. We're grateful to the more than 30 nations with forces serving in Iraq, and the nearly 40 nations with forces in Afghanistan. In the fight against terror, we've asked our allies to do hard things. They've risen to their responsibilities. We're proud to call them friends. [Applause.]

We have duties and there will be difficulties ahead. We're working with responsible governments and international institutions to convince the leaders of North Korea and Iran that their nuclear-weapons ambitions are deeply contrary to their own interests. We're helping governments fight poverty and disease, so they do not become failed states and future havens for terror. We've launched our Broader Middle East Initiative, to encourage reform and democracy throughout the region, a project that will shape the history of our times for the better. We're working to build a free and democratic Palestinian state, which lives in peace with Israel and adds to the peace of the region. We're keeping our commitments to the people of Afghanistan and Iraq, who are building the world's newest democracies. They're counting on us to help. We will not abandon them. [Applause.] Delivering these nations from tyranny has required sacrifice and loss. We will honor that sacrifice by finishing the great work we have begun. [Applause.]

In this challenging period of our history, Americans fully understand the dangers to our country. We remain a nation at risk, directly threatened by an enemy that plots in secret to cause terrible harm and grief. We remain a nation at war, fighting for our security, our freedom, and our way of life. We also see our advantages clearly. Americans have a history of rising to every test; our generation is no exception. We've not forgotten September the 11th, 2001. We will not allow our enemies to forget it, either. [Applause.]

We have strong allies, including millions of people in the Middle East who want to live in freedom. And the ideals we stand for have a power of their own. The appeal of justice and liberty, in the end, is greater than the appeal of hatred and tyranny in any form. The war on terror will not end in a draw, it will end in a victory, and you and I will see that victory of human freedom. [Applause.]

I want to thank you all for coming. Thank you for your dedication. May God bless you and your families, and may God continue to bless our great country. Thank you very much. [Applause.]

III. The American Veteran

Veterans Day 2003

Harold J. "Bud" Seifert

Assistant principal, 2003– , and English teacher, 1997–2003, Leander High School, Leander, TX; born Rhinelander, WI, July 25, 1948; commissioned a 2nd lieutenant of armor, U.S. Army, upon graduation from the U.S. Military Academy, 1970; master's degrees in management, University of Central Texas, and in English, Syracuse University; postgraduate work in educational administration, Southwest Texas State University; army assignments in South Korea, Germany, and the continental United States, including four postings in Texas; command assignments, armored cavalry troop in Korea, a tank company and later a tank battalion, Ft. Hood, TX, and a readiness group assisting Army National Guard and Reserve units, New York and New Jersey; senior army advisor to the adjutant general of Texas and the Texas Army National Guard, Camp Mabry, Austin; army's Legion of Merit and Meritorious Service Awards, the New York State Award for Conspicuous Service, and the Texas Distinguished Service Award.

Editors' introduction: As a teacher and student advisor, Colonel Seifert sees his role "as that of a mentor, guiding and supporting students who are framing their futures by achieving the best high school education they can, while helping them to develop and maintain high standards of discipline and ethical conduct." Teaching English to Military Academy Cadets at West Point and battalion-level combat operations planning and synchronization to mid-career army officers at the Command and General Staff College fostered Colonel Seifert's interest in public education. In his Veterans Day address to some 500 students, staff, and faculty in the Performing Arts Center at Leander High School, Colonel Seifert reminded that "preservation of peace and security comes only at great cost." He asked audience members to support programs beneficial to veterans, express appreciation to those who served their country, and visit servicemen and women in hospitals.

Harold J. "Bud" Seifert's speech: Good morning. Thank you, Mrs. Serna, for the introduction, all of you for the warm reception, and Ms. Humphreys's third year American sign language students for signing the presentation. I am again honored by your invitation to speak to you today, this day we call Veterans Day.

The word veteran came into our language through French from the Latin word *veteranus*, a complimentary, sometimes even honorific adjective meaning old and of long experience. Used in English since the early 16th century, the title veteran has gener-

Delivered on November 11, 2003, at 10:45 A.M., at Leander, TX. Reprinted with permission of Harold J. "Bud" Seifert.

ally identified soldiers of long service. But in modern, especially American usage the term also applies to most members of our armed services who serve beyond the period of their initial, entry-level training.

An American service member earns the title veteran not by length of service but rather by demonstrated competence and the willingness to abide by our military forces' Code of Conduct in all circumstances. Adopted in 1955 and changed only minimally since, the Code defines our nation's fundamental expectations of its warriors. It states in part:

> I am an American soldier (or sailor, airman, or marine) fighting in the forces which guard my country and our way of life. I am prepared to give my life in their defense.
>
> I will never surrender of my own free will. If in command, I will never surrender the members of my command while they still have the means to resist.
>
> If I am captured, I will continue to resist by all means available. I will make every effort to escape and to aid others to escape. I will accept neither parole nor special favors from the enemy.
>
> I will never forget that I am an American, fighting for freedom, responsible for my actions, and dedicated to the principles which made my country free. I will trust in my God and in the United States of America.

The Code's simplicity of diction and syntax belies the complexity of its ideas and the depth of commitment necessary to carry it out. Yet many have served honorably in response to its declarations. According to the United States Department of Veterans Affairs, more than 50 million men and women have served in our armed forces since our nation's founding 227 years ago. Securing, protecting, and defending the peace and freedom we cherish, they have trained for, supported, and fought our nation's military conflicts from the Revolutionary War through the War on Terrorism.

Our military veterans have also enhanced the security of our country by planning, leading, executing or supporting missions as diverse as peace keeping in the Balkans and the Middle East, building schools, roads, airfields, and hospitals in South America, providing emergency assistance to victims of natural disasters, dredging navigable waterways, building and operating flood control systems, fighting forest fires in the Pacific Northwest, guarding prisoners in Cuba, and securing American embassies around the world.

The efforts and sacrifices of America's veterans have helped to preserve our nation's freedom, peace, and security for over two centuries, but as the terrorist attacks in our own country on September 11, 2001, and almost daily in places such as Iraq, Afghanistan,

Saudi Arabia, or elsewhere in the world horrifically remind us, freedom will never be free, and the preservation of peace and security comes only at great cost.

As we honor our veterans today, we realize that they have always paid a portion of these costs personally and sometimes painfully. Some 25 million military veterans are alive today in our country, and some of these need

> *Most veterans need and ask little or nothing in repayment for their service.*

their country's assistance, as it has gladly accepted theirs. Whether afflicted with the lingering effects of service connected wounds, injuries, and illnesses; or simply struggling to survive the hardships of age and infirmity, these veterans need and deserve our continued and compassionate concern and care.

In addition, nearly one million American veterans have died in combat or combat related events throughout our nation's history. These veterans have paid the highest price, giving what Abraham Lincoln termed "[their] last full measure of devotion" for their country, and our tribute to them must also include compassion for their families.

In his second inaugural address, given in 1865 after the end of America's bloody civil war, President Lincoln emphasized this responsibility, promising that America would "care for him who shall have borne the battle and for his widow and his orphan." Today that promise is the motto of the U.S. Department of Veterans Affairs, the organization charged with the mission of looking after America's veterans and, within the guidelines of applicable law, their families, as well.

But most veterans need and ask little or nothing in repayment for their service. We can honor and pay tribute to them simply by recognizing and remembering on this day their contributions, achievements, sacrifices, and their resolve to keep America strong and free. Recognition begins with an understanding of how our Veterans Day came into being.

In November of 1921, three years after the end of World War I, the remains of an American soldier—his name "known only to God"—were buried on a Virginia hillside overlooking the Potomac River and the city of Washington, DC. The tomb of this Unknown Soldier in the Arlington National Cemetery has since become the most visible symbol of America's honor and respect for its veterans. Similar ceremonial burials occurred in England and in France, where other unknown soldiers' remains were interred in the Westminster Abbey of London and in the Arc de Triomphe in Paris.

These memorial services all took place on November 11, in symbolic remembrance that the signing of the armistice ending hostilities in World War I happened at 11 o'clock A.M., November 11,

1918. In 1926 the United States Congress proclaimed November 11 Armistice Day in America, and 12 years later Congress made the day a national holiday.

Ironically, even as our Congress proclaimed a holiday celebrating the end of a war once hoped to be the "the war to end all wars" the seeds of war were again being sown in Africa, Asia, and Europe. Only three years later World War II would engulf the world. Sixteen and one half million Americans would participate; more than 400,000 would die; nearly 75 percent of those deaths would result directly from combat.

Then in 1954, following World War II and the Korean War, Congress proposed a holiday honoring all of America's veterans, and President Eisenhower signed a proclamation naming November 11 Veterans Day. Since then remains of unknown soldiers killed in more recent wars have been buried alongside their World War I counterpart. The U.S. Army's 3rd Infantry (nicknamed The Old Guard) stands guard at the Tomb of the Unknown Soldier day and night. This morning, just about an hour ago, a memorial service at the Tomb included the salute of a joint color guard representing all of our military services, placement of a presidential wreath in symbolic tribute to America's service members killed in battle, and the playing of "Taps," a musical military salute which Colonel Joseph Magruder will describe for us a few minutes from now.

Our ceremony here is one of many taking place today around the United States and the world in recognition of Veterans Day. If you have a chance later to walk through the atrium, please pause for a moment among the beautiful plants Ms. Tomlinson has graciously let us borrow, and look at the map of France the French club has created in the room's southeastern corner. Placed in the region of Normandy is a small American flag, which marks the location of the Normandy American Cemetery, one of many overseas sites at which ceremonies will occur today in honor of American veterans.

"But what else can I do?" you might ask, "to recognize our veterans?" The answer is not difficult, and you have already done some things of which you should be proud. Although your attendance here this morning was not in most cases fully voluntary, you have voluntarily honored me and the other veterans gathered on this stage by your respectful attention and applause.

Additionally, many of you made stars identifying veterans and displayed them at the main entrance to our school. Some of you or your families contributed items for the displays the Social Studies Department put together in the cabinets near the library. For these things I thank you.

There are other things you can do, as well. First, some of you are old enough to vote, and all of you are old enough to influence someone who votes. Please vote in support of veterans' programs and for candidates who favor such programs.

Second, when you go home tonight, make a call, write a letter, or send an e-mail to a relative or friend serving somewhere in our military services. Say you appreciate what he or she does, and that you care. And don't forget about their families. Call, write, visit. Throughout history it has been an unavoidable, often harsh, and sometimes cruel reality of military life that "they also serve who stay at home and wait."

Third, visit a veterans hospital or medical clinic. There is a VA hospital in Temple, a large medical clinic in south Austin, and a smaller clinic that opened this past year in Cedar Park on Whitestone Boulevard next to the Seton Health Care Center. Simply walk around, smile, say hello to the veterans you see. They will appreciate your attention and kindness more than you know.

For something different, stroll through a national cemetery. There is one at Ft. Sam Houston in San Antonio and one planned for Ft. Hood, near Killeen. Or, alternatively, walk one of the battlefields of the Revolutionary, Civil, Mexican-American, or Indian Wars. Move slowly, silently, meditatively, and listen for an echo of President Lincoln's words at Gettysburg, "The world will little note nor long remember what we say here, but it can never forget what they did here."

Next, when Mr. Washburn asks you tomorrow and in the days that follow to stand for the pledge of allegiance to the flag of the United States of America, do so sincerely and willingly. If you feel so inclined place your hand over your heart, proudly executing the traditional salute of people not in uniform, then join your voice with his and recite the pledge. But even if you choose, as a matter of conscience or otherwise, neither to salute nor to recite the pledge aloud, at least stand quietly and respectfully, mindful of the reality that under our flag nearly one million American veterans have died, 50 times that many have served, and nearly three million are serving today to defend and preserve your right to make that choice.

And finally, as you sit back down tomorrow morning for our minute of silence after the pledges, please think about this. For many Americans the word veteran is little more than a nameless abstraction. For some, veterans are just those old guys who wear funny caps and pieces of old uniforms and walk in 4th of July parades, or who stand out in front of Wal Mart and distribute paper poppies on Memorial Day. And for others, veterans are merely the pictures of young soldiers, sailors, airmen, or marines staring back blankly from the front page of *USA Today*, the *New York Times*, or the *Austin American-Statesman* stacked neatly in the box in front of McDonald's or Starbucks that we glance at briefly as we wait in line for our morning coffee.

But for some Americans the word veteran means much more. You might have seen last Saturday's newspaper article about General Robert M. Shoemaker High School in Killeen. At least 800 of that school's students, nearly 40 percent of its student body, have one or both parents serving in Iraq now or in receipt of orders to go to Iraq just after the first of next year. And nearly one half of Shoemaker's staff and faculty have a spouse, parent, or child similarly deployed or preparing to deploy.

And, yes, even here at Leander High School many of us know more personally the meaning of the word veteran. In a few minutes members of our faculty who are veterans or relatives of veterans will be introduced, but as I complete my presentation, I want us to recognize some of our students who also have a personal understanding of what it means to be a veteran. Students, if you have a family member or a friend in one of our military services who is currently involved in or supporting operations in Iraq, Afghanistan, or one the other trouble spots in the world, please stand and remain standing. [Pause.] If you have a family member or a friend who is currently serving on active military duty, or in the national guard, or in a military reserve organization but is stationed somewhere other than the trouble spots I mentioned, please stand, also. [Pause.] And last, if you have a family member or a friend who served in any branch of our military forces in the past, please stand. Look around you, please, and consider the number of people standing. Thank you. Please be seated.

During our minute of silence tomorrow morning, think about the students and faculty members you will have seen stand in here today. For these people the word veteran can never be abstract. For them it is a prideful but sometimes also frightening and sorrowful complement for other titles it can never replace—grandfather, grandmother, aunt, uncle, nephew, niece, sister, brother, dad, mom, wife, husband, son, daughter, classmate, friend.

Again, you have honored us by your presence here this morning and by your attention; it has indeed been my pleasure to talk with you. May almighty God bless you, our veterans and their families, and all who serve to bring about a just and lasting peace in our world.

Thank you.

Hope and Freedom

Nicole Webb

Sixth-grader, West Ridge Middle School, Austin, TX; born and raised in Austin, TX; attended Barton Creek Elementary School, Austin, TX, for six years.

Editors' introduction: The administration at Barton Creek Elementary School in Austin, Texas, celebrates Veterans Day annually with a special assembly. In 2003 all fifth-grade students were asked to write an essay expressing what they thought about veterans. The essay by Miss Webb, a student in Ms. Doris Hunnicutt's honors language arts course, was judged by the fifth-grade teachers to be best. Veterans Day has always been special for Miss Webb because it is also her birthday. She was asked to read her essay to the school's annual Veterans Day assembly held in the cafetorium and attended by parents, teachers, and students of all grade levels. Other speakers at the assembly were a retired air force chaplain and a national guardsman who had recently returned from Iraq. Reminding those attending the assembly how veterans had given up "life luxuries" for the benefit of others, Miss Webb suggested that it was time now to "say thank you."

Nicole Webb's speech: What is a hero? Is a hero a professional athlete? Is a hero a musician? To me a hero is someone who helps or gives up one of his or her life luxuries for another. The soldiers we have in Iraq probably don't have baths or showers every day or get nice food, but we do. We have so many things that right now our soldiers don't have.

Can you imagine having someone in your family or even you leave to go fight in a war? Our soldiers and especially our veterans are so brave to go out and fight for our country. We wouldn't have the freedom that we have today if it weren't for our veterans.

Have you ever asked a veteran to tell you the story of their life when they were in the war? Sometimes they will tell you a lot of interesting things. You'll be looking at them just waiting to see what is next in the story. But have you ever looked really close at them? You can sometimes see them living their story over again.

Most people that you ask fought in World War II, some Vietnam, some even from the one going on right now in Iraq. It's scary to think how many people have fought to earn and save our freedom. Is there even a number high enough to say how many people have fought even died in the wars that the U.S. has fought in? We have

Delivered on November 11, 2003, at Austin, TX. Reprinted with permission of Ms. Shelly Jones.

had so many people in our country go and give up their lives. Most of them have done it because they would rather die than to see their divine country die. Most of them probably don't care about getting an award or being recognized. They do it because they love their country and want to keep everyone in it safe. Some are there because they feel that it's their duty to fight for their nation.

In our national anthem the "Star Spangled Banner" it says, ". . . the land of the free and the home of the brave." It would not be able to say that if it weren't for our veterans. This song once started as a poem. Someone who had been trying to help a friend captured by the enemy in the War of 1812 wrote this miraculous poem. He could see all of the bombing out of his window. The poem slowly arose. Someone then came along and wrote the tune for it. That's how our national anthem was born.

Our veterans suffered, are suffering, some died, some are dying, and some went through immense pain. But they never gave up and now look where we are. We're in a beautiful country, with great families. We would not be anywhere without our wonderful veterans.

Eddie Rickenbacker, a fighter pilot, once said, "Courage is doing what you're afraid to do. There can be no courage unless you're scared." Mark Twain said another one that I liked a lot. He said, "Courage is resistance to fear, mastery of fear, not absence of fear." What these men are trying to say is that the heroes and heroines who went to go fight in any war are scared but they still want to do it for their country. No matter if they will die or not.

One person can do a lot but two people can do more. Go up to a veteran that is here today and say thank you. They have saved your life.

Veterans Day Speech

Jerry Barnes

Retired middle school art teacher, Lexington Middle School, Lexington, NE, 2004– ; born Richmond, CA, February 23, 1944; B.A. in art, University of Wyoming at Laramie, 1967; commissioned in ROTC as 2nd lieutenant in the army and stationed at Ft. Eustis, VA, 1967, 32nd Transportation Company, Ludwigsburg, Germany, 7th army support command Headquarters, Boebligen, Germany, and Vietnam, 1969–70, in 444 Transportation Company; promoted to captain and reassigned to Qui Nhon headquarters; M.A. and teaching certificate, University of Wyoming, 1972; art teacher, junior high and high school, Lexington, NE, 1973–2004; tank unit, national guard, 1977–97; assists friend with Veteran's History Project, interviewing veterans of World War II and later, with more than 100 statements archived at the Heartland Military Museum, Lexington, WY.

Editors' introduction: Although most Americans today have come to appreciate the sacrifices made by men and women in military uniform, longtime teacher and former army captain Jerry D. Barnes recalled how he and fellow soldiers returning from Vietnam were "harassed and hassled." He explained to some 600 middle school students, invited veterans, faculty, and interested members of the public why he and others home from that conflict "did not talk about it for 30 years." In his speech at a Veterans Day ceremony in the Lexington Middle School auditorium, Mr. Barnes contended that "you have to give back to your country and serve it to feel good about yourself." Mrs. Lisa Fricke of the eighth-grade team organized the event, which included speeches and patriotic songs, followed by a parade through downtown Lexington. Military vehicles furnished by the local Heartland Military Museum were also on display. Barnes says he has received a "great response to the speech, even to this day."

Jerry Barnes's speech: I want to thank Mrs. Fricke for asking me to be the guest speaker today and thank the teams for helping to organize such a great assembly, it has been a long time since we had one.

I wasn't much older than you when I saw President Kennedy on a grainy black and white TV set in the high school auditorium speaking at his inaugural address to the nation. He mentioned "to not ask what your country can do for you but what you can do for your country."

Delivered on November 14, 2003, at 1:30 P.M., Lexington, NE.

That was the guidance that most in my generation followed, joining the armed forces, the Peace Corps, or working for the government.

I went through the ROTC program in college and was commissioned a second lieutenant in the U.S. Army in 1967. I served two years in Germany and a year in Vietnam.

Vietnam was a turning point in our history; it changed our country, some in good ways, some that were not.

Wars have always caused dissension in our country—we have the freedom to protest. There have been protests to all the wars our country has been in—from the Revolutionary War to today's war in Iraq, something that we need to remember today. That is why it is so important for us to know our history so we don't repeat the mistakes of the past.

It is fine to protest a war—that is one of our rights as Americans—but you should not be against the individual soldier.

My wife had returned to college while I was in Vietnam, but due to the campus unrest at the time over the war, did not mention to anyone that she was the wife of a soldier serving in Vietnam. I was not very happy to hear about that.

It is fine to protest a war—that is one of our rights as Americans—but you should not be against the individual soldier; he joined to fight for his country and for freedom, but does not choose the wars or engagements.

Soldiers who came home from Vietnam were harassed and hassled by people who protested the war, thus most, including me, did not talk about it for 30 years.

After Vietnam, patriotism fell out of favor in the United States and it became a country of people who did not believe in serving their country but were only interested in what they could get—a very selfish attitude centered on themselves and our country suffered because of this "me first" attitude. It took September 11 to change that. It is a tragedy that all those people had to die to wake up the citizens of America to what they had and what could be lost.

We enjoy freedom here in the United States and that is why so many people come here, but many that are already here do not appreciate their freedoms and rights that we have. I hope the new immigrants that we have will embrace our country, its traditions, and find it a country to fight for and join the service and become citizens.

As many veterans can tell you, "Freedom is not free." You have to give back to your country and serve it to feel good about yourself. You can't just sit there and take and take and give nothing back. It has been said that "war is hell" and that is certainly true. Soldiers are killed and maimed physically and mentally—sometimes long after. Some Vietnam vets I know are just now being hit by stress syndrome 30 years after the war.

Wars are not started by soldiers—politicians do that—but they need to have the resolve to stick it out through all the controversy that revolves around war and end it with a victory. The soldiers who gave up their lives and bodies for the cause are owed a proper finish to the war or their lives were wasted in vain.

Some people, politicians and newscasters have been comparing the war in Iraq with Vietnam and it is not. In Vietnam you had two large countries, China and Russia, supplying the North Vietnamese with supplies—you do not have that in Iraq. The Vietnamese were fighting a civil war over a political system and to reunite the country. In Iraq you have thugs fighting to get back in power so they can continue terrorizing the citizens who are now happy to be free.

I am proud of my service in the army; I followed my grandfather and father who also served in the military and proud that my sons chose to follow me in that family tradition of serving their country also.

Because I had been in Vietnam my wife was not very happy about John, our oldest son, going into the national guard, but once she saw how much being in the service developed his character through the experience she was all for Eric, our youngest son, joining up also. The old recruiting slogan the army used to have, "To be all you can be," is certainly true.

I never felt more alive than when I was in Vietnam doing the best job I could.

I never felt more alive than when I was in Vietnam doing the best job I could to make sure my convoys delivered their supplies to the troops. Being on the side of the road in "Ambush Alley," all alone in the silence, trying to get a broken down truck moving again was quite an experience. As was being awoken in the night to a mortar and rocket attack.

If you do not serve your country you will not be aware of what your capabilities are, thus you never will be the person you could have been. So when you see a soldier, you know that they are doing more than they ever thought possible and you should at least respect that.

A funny thing has developed lately; people who were never in Vietnam are now claiming that they were there, even though they did not serve and indeed tried their best to avoid serving. We call them "wanna be"s, so don't be one of them. Follow your fellow patriotic Americans and serve your country as so many have before you.

One of the more moving experiences in my life was visiting the World War II cemeteries in Europe—those rows and rows of thousands of crosses extending as far as the eye can see really brings home to you how many have given their lives for our freedom. If you have seen the movie *Saving Private Ryan* you have experienced some of this; you can see an actual military cemetery at Ft. McPherson right here in Nebraska.

When they came back from war veterans seldom mentioned their experiences and I was one of them. We had fought for a life of freedom and then put war behind us to get on with living. The soldier's families never knew what they did in the war and that was a shame. That is why Mr. Sankey's interviews that he and his classes are doing are so important to the veteran, his family, and our nation. You can see those at the Heartland Military Museum.

I have gotten involved with Vietnam veteran groups and individuals since the Internet got going. I had not thought of Vietnam or talked to anyone about it for 30 years; now I have been meeting fellow veterans on the Internet and this summer went to a reunion of Vietnam Gun Truckers at Ft. Eustis, Virginia. It was a celebration of our survival and a new book a friend of mine had written about the gun trucks that protected our convoys.

Meeting all the guys was great and sharing our experiences and stories was very good for all involved; many had not talked about it at all and it was a good release.

I now do art work from the photos I took in Vietnam and just recently donated most of it to the Transportation Museum at Ft. Eustis, Virginia—the home of the Transportation Corps. You can see it on display there.

Locally, we have a group of veterans, who through their interest in restoring military vehicles have built that into the great museum that we have out on the interstate, the Heartland Military Museum. They have some of their vehicles here today for you to look at after school and will be in the parade today; I urge you to look at them and take your family out to the parade and the museum.

America has been lucky to not have a war on its soil since the Civil War, but since 9/11 that has all changed and the war on terrorism began. That is making veterans of us all.

Women During the War

Gale Norton

Secretary, U.S. Department of the Interior (the first woman to head that department), 2001– ; born Wichita, KS, March 11, 1954; B.A., magna cum laude, 1975, and J.D., with honors, 1978, University of Denver; assistant to the deputy secretary of agriculture, 1979–80; senior attorney, Mountain States Legal Foundation, 1979–83; associate solicitor of the U.S. Department of the Interior, overseeing endangered species and public-lands legal issues for the National Park Service and the Fish and Wildlife Service, 1985–87; as attorney general of Colorado, 1991–99, negotiated $206-billion national tobacco settlement for Colorado and 45 other states as part of the largest lawsuit settlement in history; senior counsel, Brownstein, Hyatt and Farber, 1999–2001; national fellow, Hoover Institution, 1983–84; environment committee chair, Republican National Lawyers Association; general counsel, Colorado Civil Justice League.

Editors' introduction: The National Women's History Museum's (NWHM) exhibition *Partners in Winning the War, Women in World War II* opened at the Women's Memorial at Arlington National Cemetery on May 30, 2004, with Gale A. Norton delivering the keynote address. The day before, the National World War II Memorial to which Secretary Norton refers was dedicated. Through posters, pictures, video clips, and quoted statements, *Partners in Winning the War* honors women who served America during World War II at home and at the front. In her speech, Secretary Norton stated, "The women of the World War II generation . . . open[ed] the doors through which my generation walked. By helping the war effort, they advanced the role of women in ways that have finally become clear."

Gale Norton's speech: This has been a wonderful weekend of honoring the World War II generation. Yesterday's ceremony was moving—not just for the events on-stage, but for the people in the audience.

The new World War II Memorial will become a unit of the National Park Service. Because my department now becomes the custodian, I was privileged to sit on-stage. There were tens of thousands in the audience. They included veterans who had donned their old uniforms or their VFW or American Legion hats, and traveled thousands of miles to join in the ceremony. In wheelchairs, or with walkers, they showed the same determination they did 60 years ago.

Delivered on May 30, 2004, at Arlington National Cemetery, across the Potomac from Washington, DC.

There were spouses sharing the experience of celebration just as they had shared the times of fear and anxiety.

Sons and daughters came along and joined the celebration to honor their parents. There were youngsters here who we hope will remember it 60 years from now.

> *I am inspired by the women of the World War II generation.*

The phenomenon that was World II was not just the military efforts. What sets it apart from our other modern experiences of war was the way everyone pulled together.

It is ironic that long before live satellite coverage of battles gave us minute-by-minute ringside seats in our living rooms, World War II involved everyone in the war effort.

The war effort on the home front has been too often forgotten. I am inspired by the women of the World War II generation, and I want to be sure their stories are preserved and told.

The generation of women who accomplished so much—in the military, as nurses, as workers on the home front—did not toot their own horns and did not demand attention. They modestly viewed themselves as doing their small part while men served on the front lines.

Some events seem huge at the time they occur, but quickly fade into obscurity in the context of history. Winning the World Series or an Academy Award is certainly notable, but someone else will do the same thing next year.

But other occurrences are not fully appreciated or understood at the time they happen. In retrospect, their impacts truly changed the world. The World War II–era home front created exactly this type of situation.

How many generations experience truly revolutionary change? We are fortunate to live in one of those times. The roles of women have changed dramatically over the past six decades.

The suffragettes successfully campaigned for the right to vote—and got it in 1920. Their role has been well-recognized in women's history. Yet the major changes in the daily lives of women received their most significant push during World War II.

The women of the World War II generation deserve recognition for opening the doors through which my generation walked. By helping the war effort, they advanced the role of women in ways that have finally become clear. It is time we tell the enduring story of the women of World War II.

During the war years of 1941 to 1945, one often heard the Andrews Sisters on the radio singing, "Don't Sit Under the Apple Tree with Anyone Else but Me."

The message was, of course, to stay true to your loved one. But there was an underlying message to a nation of women left behind—that while their husbands, fathers, and sweethearts were at war, they were to keep the home fires burning.

The women of the Greatest Generation did exactly that. From chopping wood to changing the oil in their cars, they assumed new and different tasks and responsibilities, while they kept their traditional roles and held families together by "accentuating the positive."

It was a time in our history when the mission was clear, the patriotism was palpable, and the enemy was not in dispute.

Nearly one in five families had a loved one in the military. Sixteen million Americans served and people pulled together in ways that today's generation probably cannot comprehend.

Americans created victory gardens and recycled materials like aluminum foil and scrap metal—before they knew the term "environmentalist." They went without things like gasoline, coffee, sugar, beef, oils, and some canned foods. They created meatless Tuesdays and came up with recipes that made use of things they had in abundance—like carrots from those victory gardens.

A person in uniform standing in line for tickets at a movie theater would find that the person ahead of them had already paid for their ticket. Many servicemen and women reported not having to pay for meals at restaurants. The generosity was a way of saying "thank you," but it was also a hope that wherever their loved one or friend might be, he or she might receive similar care.

Perhaps the closest this generation has come to experiencing this extraordinary singleness of purpose and feeling, is the outpouring of generosity and caring that flowed from the American people after 9/11.

That day we must have felt for a moment the same anger, resolve, and commitment that Americans felt after Pearl Harbor. The difference was that the casualties from 9/11 were finite. For the World War II generation, casualties were a daily list. Friends and relatives clung together as a blue star in the window was exchanged for a gold star that signified a death.

With our young men fighting and dying in the trenches, it soon became apparent that mobilization of the entire population in support of the war was a necessity. Women began going into the workplace in unprecedented numbers.

Women helped keep the trains going, became taxi drivers and streetcar conductors. Poet Maya Angelou became the first black streetcar conductor in San Francisco.

Women were business managers, journalists, photographers, and more. They even played professional baseball—remember the movie *A League of Their Own*?

These were women who wore curls and waves and bright red lipstick. They wore hats and gloves and black velvet collars; and they learned to draw a very fine line on the back of their legs with an eyebrow pencil to simulate the seams in nylon stockings they couldn't have.

But they stuffed those curls under a bandana, dressed in slacks, rolled up their sleeves, packed a lunch pail, and began to answer to a time clock—all for the war effort.

As this change was afoot, American art legend Norman Rockwell created a character known as "Rosie the Riveter." With her sleeves rolled up and her show of muscle, Rosie became a symbol of the government's campaign to encourage women to join the war effort. Almost 3 million women answered the nation's call to serve in defense plants.

Women like Lois Turner who worked as a mechanic at Bell Aircraft in Niagara Falls, New York, from 1943 to 1945. Lois's small hands enabled her to do the safety wiring in areas of planes that others couldn't reach. She often was held upside down for 15 minutes at a time to get to especially tight spots. You could say Lois stood on her head for her country!

I met Lois this month at a Capitol Hill reception in honor of the Rosie the Riveter World War II Home Front National Historical Park located in Richmond, California.

Rosie's influence goes beyond the war. A later poster of Rosie in a bandana, designed by J. Howard Miller, contained the slogan, "We Can Do It!" That spirit is etched into the nation's consciousness as a symbol of the increased independence of American women. The Rosies not only changed the history of our nation, but they changed its culture.

In fact, by 1945 the number of female workers rose by 50 percent from 12 million to 18 million. The total women in the national work force increased from 8 percent in 1940 to 25 percent in 1945.

Most well known of the war employees were probably those who went to work in the factories making ships, planes, tanks, and ammunitions.

For example, Caryl McIntire of Laurel, Maryland, answered an ad for shipyard welders at the Boston Navy Yard at Charlestown, Massachusetts. She worked the nightshift welding the huge steel bulkheads for ships. Some nights in winter 20 below zero. One day an overhead crane malfunctioned while moving one of the bulkheads, resulting in the death of a woman welder.

Women also stepped into government jobs that had been reserved for men. By 1944 women accounted for more than a third of the available civil service jobs. The so-called "government girls" understood that they could hold their jobs until the national emergency was over, when the men who were drafted would be able to reclaim those positions.

Washington was inundated by young, single women from all over the country answering the call of the posters they saw: "V for Victory," "Uncle Sam Needs You," "Do Your Part."

Many held clerical positions and moved mountains of paper during the course of the war.

These multifaceted women of the war years maintained that strained balance among their femininity, their intellect, and their traditional values, and they opened a new path for their daughters to follow.

A perfect example was Hazel Bishop. She was an organic chemist at Standard Oil who as a part of her contribution to the war effort discovered the causes of deposits affecting aircraft engine superchargers. To solve the problem, she helped develop a new kind of gasoline for airplanes.

After the war she founded a cosmetic company and came up with a very different use for petroleum products: the "kissable lipstick."

Before the war, women found it almost impossible to find a job in scientific research or engineering. It was considered man's work.

Women who did not have paying jobs helped win the war with their hours of volunteerism.

But the war turned "man's work" into "woman's work," in many ways.

In coastal communities women joined civil defense organizations, serving as air raid wardens and joining the Civil Air Patrol both as pilots and technical support staff.

A letter went out to other female pilots in 1941 that they were needed to ferry trainers and light aircraft from the factories to the airfields. Nancy Harkness Love trained and commanded these pilots in the Women's Auxiliary Ferrying Squadron, or WAFS.

With all the stories of Rosies and pilots and even scientists, we need to remember that only one in six women was employed outside the home during the conflict.

But women who did not have paying jobs helped win the war with their hours of volunteerism. It was a time when we took care of each other and didn't expect government to provide all of our needs.

Women's organizations provided a nationwide network that mobilized millions of women to do myriad tasks. Members of American Women's Voluntary Services were trained to drive ambulances, fight fires, and provide emergency medical aid.

At-home moms volunteered to make and repair clothing, knit socks and other items, and assemble packages of food and personal hygiene items to be sent to troops overseas.

More than 200,000 women participated in the Red Cross Volunteer Nurse's Aide Corps, pledging a minimum of 150 hours annually to perform non-technical nursing services. The Gray Lady Corps helped with recreational services at military and veterans hospitals—many a GI remembers a smile and a new novel to read.

Six private organizations formed the United Service Organizations, or USO, to provide recreation for military personnel while on leave. The USO camp shows are probably the most enduring image, but single women spent a great deal of time with GIs over doughnuts and coffee, or dancing to Glenn Miller or Artie Shaw.

In fact, my mom and dad met at a USO in South Texas. He was an aircraft mechanic in the Army Air Corps, and she was a native Texas girl.

Finally there were the women who actually signed up for the military and served in the Women's Army Auxiliary Corps, the Women's Naval Reserve, Marine Corps Women's Reserve, the Women's Air Force Service Pilots, or WASPs, and the Coast Guard's SPARS—a name that was developed from the Coast Guard motto, Semper Paratus, or "always ready."

There was a huge recruitment campaign that encouraged women to join and to "free a man to fight."

More than 400 military women lost their lives during the war. Army and navy nurses were captured and kept in prisoner of war camps in the Philippines. Nurses received more than 1,600 medals, citations, and commendations during the war.

All of these women—military and civilian, paid and volunteer—played a pivotal role in defending and supporting the nation.

As I relate these stories of the women of the era, I owe a debt of thanks to Susan Jollie and her staff at the National Women's History Museum. They conceived of and created the exhibit that is displayed here at the Women in Military Service for America Memorial. It is aptly entitled *Partners in Winning the War: American Women in World War II*.

Their exhibit begins with the statement that "Women Are America's Secret Weapon."

It concludes with a strange testament to that fact.

After the war ended, Albert Speer, head of Nazi war production, observed, "How wise you were to bring your women into your military and into your labor force. Had we done that initially, as you did, it would have affected the whole course of the war. We would have found out as you did, that women are equally effective, and for some skills, superior to males."

The Rosies, the volunteers, the victory gardeners, the government girls, and the women in the military all have forged a path for their daughters and granddaughters.

Today, young women recognize that a woman can be an air force brigadier general like Wilma Vaught [Editor's note: Vaught took part in the event] or the president's national security advisor like Condoleeza Rice.

Women will continue to make history and contribute to the nation and the world, because Rosie taught us: "We Can Do It."

We are grateful to them all.

Tuskegee Airmen Dinner

John D. Hopper Jr.

U.S. Air Force's senior ranking African American officer, and vice commander of Air Education and Training Command, 2000– ; born Clarksville, TN, November 16, 1946; U.S. Air Force Academy, 1969; M.S. in logistics management and distinguished graduate, Air Force Institute of Technology, 1977; Air Command and Staff College distinguished graduate, 1982; Industrial College of the Armed Forces, 1988; Syracuse University Maxwell School of Citizenship and Public Affairs, and Johns Hopkins University Nitze School of Advanced International Studies, 1997; command pilot with more than 3,900 flight hours in 12 different aircraft; combat tours as a C-130 pilot in Vietnam and wing commander in the Persian Gulf War; commanded at the squadron, group, wing, and numbered air force levels; U.S. Air Force Academy commandant of cadets; joint staff at the Pentagon; Defense Distinguished Service Medal, Distinguished Service Medal, Defense Superior Service Medal, Legion of Merit with two oak leaf clusters, Distinguished Flying Cross, Meritorious Service Medal with three oak leaf clusters, Air Medal with two oak leaf clusters, and the Air Force Commendation Medal with oak leaf cluster.

Editors' introduction: Lt. General John D. Hopper Jr. addressed an estimated 1,000 people at Rosenblatt Stadium at the City of Omaha Military Appreciation Ceremony and Tuskegee Airmen Incorporated National Convention held in Omaha, Nebraska. General Hopper discussed the implications of the Tuskegee Experiment for the integration of the armed forces, for *Brown v. Board of Education*, for the Civil Rights Act of 1964, and for today's air force culture. He concluded that "you can rest assured the Tuskegee legacy lives on in the air force core values of integrity, service, and excellence." After the speech, Mayor Fahey presented General Hopper with the key to the city of Omaha.

John D. Hopper's speech: Thank you for that kind introduction. I'm humbled to be here tonight to talk about our African American heritage and the legendary Tuskegee airmen.

When Mayor Fahey asked me to speak at this ceremony, I had a couple of thoughts. First was what a wonderful thing for the great city of Omaha to do. This truly is the heartland and no one does a better job of supporting our men and women in uniform—past and present. Second, and this is a little more selfish, is the great honor I feel that you would ask me to share this time with you. My third thought was the eternal prayer of every speaker. It is short and

---

Delivered on August 6, 2004, at 7:00 P.M., at Rosenblatt Stadium, Omaha, NE. Reprinted with permission of John D. Hopper Jr.

simple and is one of several variations that goes something like "Wow, I can't believe they asked me." Followed quickly by "Oh Lord, don't let me screw this up!"

Although I'm excited to be a part of these activities, I promise not to let my remarks resemble a Texas longhorn. You know, a point over here . . . a point over there . . . and a lot of bull in between.

I promise to do my best to avoid a lot of extra bull . . . but since the theme tonight is "heroes all . . . share the legacy," I thought I would talk briefly about the Tuskegee legacy as I see it, and focus on three of these early heroes.

In April 1941, First Lady Eleanor Roosevelt visited Alabama's Tuskegee Institute. There, she met a black, self-taught flight instructor named Charles "Chief" Anderson—at that time, he was the only licensed African American pilot in our country.

It's true that Jacques Bullard, an African American, had flown in the Lafayette escadrille during World War I; and in 1921, Bessie Coleman had become our first female black pilot; however, "Chief" Anderson was the first to earn our nation's prestigious commercial air transport certificate.

You see, before World War II, most of the public thought African Americans lacked the discipline and aptitude to fly—but not "Chief" Anderson; and, certainly not the First Lady, who astonished the secret service when she asked Chief for a ride.

The story goes that Mrs. Roosevelt's' secret service agents were so taken back by her request, they raced for the phone to ask the president what they should do. The president, like any smart husband, replied, "There's nothing you can do but tell her to buckle in and have a good flight!"

It proved to be not just a good flight, but an historic one; one that became the catalyst for change. On the heels of the First Lady's celebrated sortie, the war department agreed to train African Americans to fly. Thus began what was called the Tuskegee "experiment." The real story is it was much more than that.

Students in the audience know that experiments are normally performed without bias, where all outcomes are possible; but this was not the case with this experiment. The Tuskegee experiment was done under pressure, and the only expected outcome was failure. Fortunately for our nation, those expecting failure were disappointed.

Even with the cards stacked against them, 966 black pilots, bombardiers, and navigators successfully completed army air corps training.

By October of 1942, just 18 months after Pearl Harbor, the all-black 99th Pursuit Squadron was trained and ready for combat. Once deployed to Europe, the 99th was joined by three other units to form the renowned 332nd fighter group—the "Red-Tailed Angels."

Together these black airmen earned a wartime record of almost mythical proportions: they destroyed over 250 enemy aircraft, sunk a nazi destroyer with just their machine guns, and never lost a single allied bomber to enemy fighters.

I just gave a talk to the Fort Worth, Texas, chapter of the Air Force Association, during which they honored the veterans of World War II. After it was over, one of the World War II veterans asked if I knew Colonel Charles McGee. I said, "Yes, of course; Tuskegee airman; air force pilot in three wars—World War II, Korea, and Vietnam—and past president of TAI." Well, he was excited because he had been a pilot in one of those bomb squadrons escorted by the Red-Tailed Angels, and they had just confirmed that Colonel McGee would be the speaker at their bomber reunion!

I'm positive that if we asked the Tuskegee airmen with us today, they could tell thousands of stories about courage and character—both their own stories and the stories of their fallen comrades . . . and, I encourage you to do that before you leave tonight . . . but, let me talk briefly about three legendary Tuskegee airmen, beginning with general Benjamin O. Davis Jr.

Ben Davis Jr. was the son of a career soldier. His father was one of only two black combat officers in the U.S. Army. Davis Sr. fought some pretty tough odds to become the army's first African American general.

> *Together these black airmen earned a wartime record of almost mythical proportions.*

As a patriot, General Davis Sr. passed on two very important traits to his son: love of country and hatred of discrimination. From his dad, Davis understood that segregation was not only harmful to black soldiers, but to the nation as a whole. When young Davis accepted his 1932 appointment to the U.S. military academy at West Point, he hoped—perhaps naively—that his classmates would accept him based on his abilities and his character. Sadly, he was wrong.

Throughout his four years at West Point, Cadet Davis was silenced—meaning no one, from his fellow cadets to his superior officers, spoke to him unless acting in an official capacity. He roomed alone; he ate alone. He traveled separately and sat by himself at army football games. This cruel treatment was designed to break him. But, according to Davis, "What they didn't realize was that I was stubborn enough to put up with their treatment to reach the goal I had come to attain."

He was determined to succeed; and in 1936, he graduated number 35 in a class of 276! He went on to earn his wings at the Tuskegee army airfield and then to command the 99th pursuit squadron during World War II.

Davis's path would parallel his father's footsteps as he became our air force's first African American general—nearly 50 years ago.

General Davis's legacy is one of perseverance and integrity. Unfair and seemingly overwhelming obstacles may come in our way, but with persistence and determination, we can overcome these barriers and reach our goals.

Certainly, General Davis's story may be well known to some of you. But there is another individual equally as inspiring, but perhaps less known. I've mentioned him before—Charles "Chief" Anderson.

Earlier I mentioned Chief Anderson's flight with the first lady. But his lasting contribution was bigger than just one successful sortie.

Like General Davis, Chief fought to overcome obstacles, but he also believed in teaching others.

Because African Americans were prohibited from military flight training, Chief decided to teach himself. Of course to learn to fly you need access to an airplane, so you can see Chief's problem. He started by borrowing $2,500 from his relatives and friends in order to buy a monoplane—that's quite a sum considering the average monthly wage was around $50.

Although he faced opposition and criticism, he fulfilled a dream and became the first black commercial pilot. Yet, that wasn't where his dream ended—no, Chief wanted to teach other African Americans to fly as well. In 1940, he set up a flight school at the Tuskegee Institute and began instructing and serving others.

With his love of aviation, and devotion to his students, he was able to teach hundreds of Tuskegee airmen to fly. Without a doubt, hundreds of black aviators owed their aviation skills to Chief Anderson.

Chief's life demonstrated the importance of teaching and training—his legacy was one of serving others. He understood there were issues more important than himself. Today, we call this "service before self." Not too long ago, I had the pleasure to fly with his son, Chief Master Sergeant Jim Anderson, a C-141 flight engineer. I can attest that Chief passed on his love of aviation and service. His legacy continues today.

Now, the final Tuskegee airman I want to discuss was completely different from the previous two, but only on the outside. Inside, he possessed the same strong character and determination that drove the others. Colonel Noel F. Parrish stood out, not only by the color of his skin, but also by his dedication to fairness in the pursuit of excellence.

Colonel Parrish was the Southern-born and educated white officer chosen to lead the Tuskegee experiment. As the white commander at Tuskegee, he faced a moral test. Colonel Parrish could likely have freely hindered the development of these black aviators. I imagine the pressure to do so must have been high.

Instead, however, he created an atmosphere where black cadets developed into professional officers—an atmosphere of aviation excellence.

By all accounts, Colonel Parrish was tough but fair. He believed that everyone, regardless of race, deserved an equal opportunity. He insisted on high standards and strict discipline—the same foundation that sustained the Red-Tails in combat.

Regarding the integration of the armed forces, Colonel Parrish once wrote, "The more rapidly officers in the air corps learn to accept these practical matters [meaning integration] . . . the

> *The Tuskegee legacy shows us that sometimes the so-called norms of society can be wrong.*

better the position of everyone concerned. The answer is wider distribution."

He saw diversity as a "practical matter" with the solution being increased diversity. Surely, he must have risked ostracism at least, if not his career, because of his views. Military law review would later describe Noel Parrish as "courageous and farsighted" and I agree. His legacy is one of leadership and strength of character.

So, what lessons can we take from the Tuskegee experiment, these three legendary airmen, and the heroes seated among us tonight?

The Tuskegee legacy shows us that sometimes the so-called norms of society can be wrong. But even more importantly, that sometimes people, collectively and individually, can, and must, change society's views. Perhaps not all at once, but over time individuals can create cracks that eventually bring down unfair barriers; just as a house built on a flawed foundation will eventually come crashing down.

In 1941, Chief Anderson and Eleanor Roosevelt convinced the army to try an "experiment"—the first crack. Then the Tuskegee airmen widened that crack with their heroic performance in combat.

In over 15,000 combat missions, they destroyed or damaged 409 enemy aircraft. They were awarded over 744 air medals, 150 distinguished flying crosses, 14 bronze stars, and 3 distinguished unit citations. The bomber crews began to call them "guardian angels" because they knew they were safe whenever those Red-Tails appeared as their escorts.

Their success was a testament to their training, skill, and courage. But it also came at a high price: sadly, 66 Tuskegee airmen were killed in action and 32 were captured as prisoners of war.

By World War II's end, the impressive combat record of the Tuskegee Airmen could not be denied—the small cracks had begun to spread. Soon that flawed foundation would be so weak it would no longer sustain the barriers of segregation.

In 1948, President Truman completely integrated the military. Six years later, the Supreme Court integrated public schools in *Brown v. Board of Education.* Finally, the Congress and President

Johnson codified racial integration in the Civil Rights Act of 1964—all because of the cumulative impact of individuals such as the Tuskegee airmen.

This nation, and the world, are far better thanks to their legacy.

That legacy is a military that integrated a decade before the majority of society. A military that values diversity for the strength it brings.

Today, over 15 percent of our air force is made up of African Americans, over 6 percent is Hispanic, and almost 20 percent women. But, we still have work to do—of the more than 12,000 pilots in the air force, roughly only 2 percent are African American, and unfortunately that number has been static for nearly a decade.

When you remember that Tuskegee produced 966 African American aviators in only four years, as well as nearly 10,000 of the world's best support officers and NCOs, it's clear we need to do more.

And, we are doing more: We're aggressively recruiting across all minority groups. We've boosted some of our minority aviation programs at HBCUs by nearly 300 percent, and just last month I met with HBCU presidents to solicit their help in encouraging minorities into operational fields. This past March, the secretary of the air force and chief of staff signed a joint letter to all commanders emphasizing the importance of diversity.

Do we still have some challenges in this area? Sure we do. But the Tuskegee airmen left us a strong legacy that we have built upon and will continue to push forward.

And let me tell you, the Tuskegee legacy is alive and well. Today the 332nd air expeditionary wing—descended from the 332nd fighter group Red-Tails—proudly fly their flag over Balad Air Base, Iraq. As I speak, today's Tuskegee airmen are operating inside hostile territory supplying humanitarian aid and stability to the liberated people of Iraq.

Ladies and gentlemen, you can rest assured that the Tuskegee legacy lives on in your air force's core values of integrity, service, and excellence; and as the strong champion of democracy overseas.

Thank you for the honor of speaking with you this evening. May God bless you, and may God continue to bless the United States of America.

IV. Intellectual Property

The Moral Imperative

Jack Valenti

Recently retired as chair and chief executive officer, Motion Picture Association of America, 1966–2004; born Houston, TX, September 5, 1921; B.A., University of Houston; M.B.A., Harvard University; lieutenant in the army air corps in World War II, flying 51 combat missions as the pilot-commander of a B-25 attack bomber with the 12th air force in Italy; awarded Distinguished Flying Cross, the Air Medal with four clusters, the Distinguished Unit Citation with one cluster, and the European Theater Ribbon with four battle stars; cofounder, advertising/political consulting agency of Weekley and Valenti, 1952; special assistant to President Lyndon B. Johnson, 1963–66; author, Bitter Taste of Glory *(1971),* A Very Human President *(1976),* Speak Up With Confidence: How to Prepare, Learn and Deliver an Effective Speech *(1982), and the political novel* Protect and Defend *(1982); has written extensively for prominent newspapers and magazines; Legion d'Honneur (France); a star on Hollywood's Walk of Fame; Life Member of Directors Guild of America; honorary doctorate, University of Oklahoma.*

Editors' introduction: Founded in 1922, the Motion Picture Association of America (MPAA) is the voice of the American motion picture, home video, and television industries, and for 38 years Chairman Jack Valenti was its advocate. A few weeks before testifying on the gravity of the digital piracy situation before the U.S. House of Representatives Subcommittee on Courts, the Internet, and Intellectual Property, Mr. Valenti spoke to a Duke University audience. Envisioning the "collision of values" experienced by many using the Internet, Mr. Valenti advised, "If choices chosen by young people early in their learning environment are infected with a moral decay, how then can they ever develop the judgment to take the right fork in the road?"

Jack Valenti's speech: No free, democratic nation can lay claim to greatness unless it has constructed a platform from which springs a moral compact that guides the daily conduct of the society and inspires the society to believe in civic trust. That "moral imperative" connects to every family, to every business, every university, every profession, and to government as well. It is defined by what William Faulkner called "the old verities," the words that define what this free and loving land is all about. Words like *duty, service, honor, integrity, pity, pride, compassion, sacrifice.*

Delivered on February 24, 2003, at Durham, NC. Reprinted with permission of Jack Valenti.

If you treat these words casually, if you find them un-cool, if you regard them as mere playthings which only the rabble and the rubes, the unlearned and the unsophisticated, observe and honor, then we will all bear witness to the slow undoing of the great secret of America.

> *The digital world is not necessarily a better world, but it is surely a different one.*

Newspapers have been full of sordid stories of unbounded avarice by some corporate executives, whose acts soiled the moral compact. But their dishonesty did not indict the free market system. The system works. What was so contemptibly wrong was the breakage of civic trust by some within the system who knew they were cheating and stealing from employees and stockholders, but because it was easy to do, because they had the power to do it, they did it.

It was a cynical, coarse defiance of the moral imperative. But the exposure of this fiscal perfidy made most of us think hard and long about the lack of any moral reference within those corporate malefactors.

Most Americans with very little don't resent those who have a lot more. Most Americans believe if they work hard, educate themselves, and play by the rules, they will by their own effort rise to higher places and have more tomorrow than they have today. That is the sanity and the beauty of the American dream.

But the belief by the average citizen in the American moral compact is demolished by the brute reality that some who have more got theirs through treachery and trickery, which so cruelly mocked all those "fools" who trusted them.

There is no larger objective in this country than the reassembling of civic trust, the reaffirmation of honorable conduct by the most powerful among us; in short, holding fast to the sustenance of civic trust. How then does the university insert within the young "the old verities" so that students not only understand and believe in the compact but also live it in their daily moral grind? That's the grand question as we enter the new digital world. It's a question that every guardian of the university's purpose must answer.

Someone once said that all movement is not necessarily forward nor is all change necessarily progress. So it is that the digital world is not necessarily a better world, but it is surely a different one. The divide between the digital world and the analog world is a vast chasm. To put it another way, in Mark Twain's words, the difference between digital and analog is the difference "between lightning and the lightning bug." The digital Internet has the potential to become the greatest communications delivery system ever known on this planet. It has the promise of allowing people to find new ways to do new things, and do them with dazzling speed.

The nation's universities, including Duke, are equipped with large pipe, high velocity broadband state-of-the-art computer networks. None better, none faster. They produce vast benefits to the university, allowing instant delivery of information and knowledge for professors and research experts within the academy. They are also accessible to students who are privy to not only this avalanche of data—but also to

> *Sad to report, a large chunk of . . . Internet abuse occurs on college campuses by students.*

movies. This is an Open Sesame opportunity for some students to take creative property that does not belong to them with effortless ease and speed. And because they have the power to do it, many, but not all of them, do it.

That is why today I choose to chat with you about the interlacing of the moral compact, digital technology—and American movies—and to introduce you to a view of the collision of values brought on by the migratory magic of digital ones and zeros.

One value says, "Digital technology gives me power to roam the Internet; therefore whatever is available, I can take, no matter who owns it." The other value says, "The fact that digital technology gives me power to use, doesn't make it right for me to use it wrongly." That is where the collision of values takes place.

So it is we confront a contradiction that puts to hazard the moral compact that guides the nation. How does the society deal with it? Importantly, how does the university react to this challenge to civic trust flung down by the best and the brightest?

Viant, a Boston-based research firm, estimates that between 400,000 to 600,000 movies are being illegally downloaded every day! Sad to report, a large chunk of that Internet abuse occurs on college campuses by students who are hourly visitors to the digital realms of KaaZa, Morpheus, Grockster, Gnutella, etc.—so-called "fileswapping" sites—and fill their hard drives with new movies, free of charge.

But there is a larger, darker issue here. Students would never enter a Blockbuster store and with furtive glance stuff a DVD inside their jacket and walk out without paying. They know that's shoplifting, they know that's stealing. They know they can find themselves in big-ass trouble if they're caught. That's why they don't do it. Then why would those same young leaders-to-be walk off the Internet with a movie inside their digital jacket? Why? Is it because digital shoplifting is at this moment a "no risk" activity? If that is so, why is it so? Is it because Ambrose Bierce's definition of conscience as "something you refer to when you are about to get caught" is an unwanted truth? Are the words *ethics—morality—principle*—alien words, exiled from the student lexicon? It's a sizeable question.

There are some critics who say, "Come on, movie industry, get with it. Stop your whining and get a new business model."

Fine, except no business model ever struck off by the hand and brain of man can compete with "free." And if critics don't understand that, it's because they just love the status quo. When a new multimillion dollar film, just released, is suddenly on the Net being abducted by millions of visitors to file-swapping sites, then that, dear friend, is "the status quo." Not a congenial status. Not a pleasant quo.

About two years ago, when Napster was in full blossom, I spoke to some 200 students, the finest of the breed, at one of the most prestigious universities in the land. My subject was "The Changing American Presidency." In my opening remarks, I said, "Before we talk about the White House, I have a question. Music is not my turf. Movies are. But I wonder how many of you have bought a CD in the last several months?" Some three or four hands were upraised. "All right, how many of you have been on Napster the last several months?" Every hand shot up.

I fixed my gaze on a young man who I was told was going to graduate near the top of his class. "You are," I said, "about to graduate from one of the best schools in the world. You are now an educated, civilized human being, those best fitted to meet life's changes and challenges with versatility and grace. Now tell me, how do you square that with the fact that you're stealing?"

He was crestfallen at first. Then his face brightened and he said, "Well, maybe it is a kind of stealing, but everyone else is doing it and besides music costs too much." I smiled as I thought to myself, "For this version of a moral value, parents are paying a small fortune in tuition."

Making choices is a daily experience for Americans. Making the right choice emerges from a process that is rooted in instinct and intuition which leap from unshakable values. When you come to a fork in the road, which way do you go? If choices chosen by young people early in their learning environment are infected with a moral decay, how then can they ever develop the judgment to take the right fork in the road? How will you, when many of you are in leadership roles in the future, deal with younger employees who have learned as students that if you have the power to take what doesn't belong to them, you do it? As the leader of the enterprise, how will you come to grips with that? You'll be face-to-face with the breakage of the moral compact and, guess what, it's on your dime.

That's why the university cannot stand aloof from this progression since administrators and professors set the final design before its graduates—in the words of that old cliché—go on to "face life."

I am pleased to report the movie industry is now meeting with a committee representing the nation's colleges and universities. The objective of these meetings is to urge the construction of a Code of Conduct for students when they use the university broadband system, a Code of Conduct solely within the confines and the authority of the university. Those discussions are going well. The university representatives have a clear vision of this issue. Many of them have developed or are in the process of creating a Code of Conduct.

While digital technology is a hyper-modern phenomenon, its molecular connection to the moral rostrum has an ancient ancestry. Many years ago, the British philosopher William Hazlitt wrote: "Man is the only animal who both laughs and weeps for he is the only animal who understands the difference between the way things are and the way they ought to be."

The digital world has the capacity to unlock knowledge hidden behind doors previously only partially open, and mostly closed to all but a few. What is yet to be put in place is a clear understanding of how to conduct yourself when you have digital power available to you that you will not use because it causes injury to others. William Hazlitt summed up that choice for us better than anyone else.

Privacy and Piracy

James V. DeLong

Senior fellow and director, Center for the Study of Digital Property, Progress and Freedom Foundation, 2002– ; born Evanston, IL, September 7, 1938; B.A. cum laude in American history, Harvard College, 1960; J.D. magna cum laude, Harvard Law School, 1963; book review editor, Harvard Law Review; *attorney, O'Melveny and Myers, Los Angeles, CA, 1963–66; special assistant, U.S. Dept of Housing and Urban Development, 1966; analyst, Program Evaluation Office of the U.S. Bureau of the Budget, 1966–70; deputy director, Drug Abuse Council (private foundation), 1970–74; assistant director for special projects, Bureau of Consumer Protection, U.S. Federal Trade Commission, 1974–78; research director, Administrative Conference of the United States, 1978–81; independent consultant and author, 1981–99; vice president and general counsel, National Legal Center for the Public Interest, 1999–2000; senior fellow, Competitive Enterprise Institute, 2000–2002; author,* Property Matters: How Property Rights Are Under Assault—And Why You Should Care *(1997), and numerous articles and monographs; Web site* http://www.ipcentral.info/print/index.html.

Editors' introduction: The ease with which movies and music are downloaded for personal use and sharing with others has produced enormous conflict between producers and consumers. Mr. DeLong addressed these issues before the Permanent Subcommittee on Investigations, a Senate Committee on Governmental Affairs, at a hearing entitled "Privacy and Piracy: The Paradox of Illegal File Sharing on Peer-to-Peer Networks and the Impact of Technology on the Entertainment Industry." Others testifying included Jack Valenti, then president of the Motion Picture Association; Jonathan Moreno, director of the Center for Biomedical Ethics, University of Virginia; and recording artist LL Cool J. Mr. DeLong told about 200 senators, Congressional staff, and Washington representatives, "The true interest of consumers is in having a strong system of intellectual property rights and well-functioning markets that makes available a wide variety of products and that enables consumers to vote with their payments to influence what is produced."

James V. DeLong's speech: My name is James V. DeLong. I am senior fellow and director of the Center for the Study of Digital Property at the Progress and Freedom Foundation in Washington, DC.

Delivered on September 30, 2003, in the morning, Dirksen Senate Office Building, Washington, DC. Reprinted by permission of James V. DeLong.

PFF is a market-oriented think tank that analyzes the digital revolution and its implications for public policy. For more information about us, a copy of our mission statement is attached to the end of this statement.

It is a pleasure to be here today to talk about intellectual property, peer-to-peer (P2P) file sharing, and private and public responses. The Digital Age has the potential to foster the creation of an immense quantity and variety of intellectual riches of all kinds—music, books, journals, software, movies, video. Whether this potential is fulfilled depends largely on whether appropriate property rights and markets are developed and enforced, so this issue meshes neatly with the issues of regulatory policy and the protection of markets that PFF has addressed during its decade of existence.

I will focus first on a question that receives too little attention, in my view. It is: What is the true interest of consumers in this controversy?

Much of what I read on the issue of intellectual property generally, including much that is written by "consumer representatives," treats the issue as a zero sum conflict between creators of intellectual property on the one hand and consumers on the other. Such work often talks about the need to "balance" the interests of the two groups. The underlying assumption seems to be that the consumer interest lies in getting creative work for free—indeed, it is often portrayed as virtually a right to get things for free—and that society grudgingly chips away at this consumer interest so as to give producers some incentive to produce.

This view of the world is erroneous—as a matter of economics, morality, and law.

> *The true interest of consumers is in having a strong system of intellectual property rights and well-functioning markets.*

The true interest of consumers is in having a strong system of intellectual property rights and well-functioning markets that makes available a wide variety of products and that enables consumers to vote with their payments to influence what is produced. The only question worthy of consideration by Congress is what it can do to help us ensure that such a market system exists.

Let me use three thought experiments designed to illustrate the absurdity of the "information ought to be free" line of argument, and the reasons why it seems obvious that the true interest of consumers is in property rights and markets.

First, consider an information service here in Washington called *TechDaily*. I am sure most people at this hearing are familiar with it. It is an e-newsletter issued twice a day that covers developments in the tech world. It is comprehensive, well-written, thoughtful. It is accessed by password and it's not cheap, in absolute terms, but my organization's site license is spread over several of us so my access to it costs a couple of bucks a day, which is a true bargain.

Now, suppose a "consumer representative" decides, after "balancing the consumers' interest" against that of the producer, that *Tech-Daily* charges too much. After all, the marginal cost of adding me, or any other individual, to the distribution list is zero. So every day this "consumer representative" cuts-and-pastes the newsletter and blasts it out to the world at large. Of course, *TechDaily* soon goes out of business. Or it is forced to revert to the pre-Internet mode of operation, in which it is printed up, each night on flimsy pastel paper (to discourage photocopying) and hand-delivered in the wee hours of the morning, thus becoming both less timely and more expensive.

I am the consumer here. On what possible theory can the "consumer representative" who caused this carnage call himself my friend?

To extend this thought experiment further, suppose *TechDaily* wants to stop this practice. Should the "consumer representative" be able to claim that to allow the company to ascertain his identity is a violation of his right to privacy on the Internet? Suppose that such a privacy claim were upheld; the losers would include not just *Tech-Daily*, its investors, and employees, but me—the consumer—and all my fellow consumers, who have been deprived of a valuable service for which we were paying a quite reasonable price.

To extend the analysis another step, consider the effect of this chain of events on the structure of this city. My organization is a small one. It, like other small organizations and individuals, cannot afford the legion of reporters needed to produce a work like *Tech-Daily*. Nor can it afford the price of a newsletter produced according to the old-fashioned print-and-hand-distribute methods. So one effect of eliminating e-distribution as an option would be to ensure that only large organizations, those which can spread overhead across a wide base, could survive. The creative impetus that can be provided by individuals and small businesses would be lost.

This example may seem extreme, because almost no one would admit openly to wanting to destroy the intellectual property rights that make *TechDaily* possible. But if you dissect the rhetoric of many of the consumer groups you will find that their proposals would have precisely this impact. For example, they would say that *TechDaily* should not be allowed to encrypt its product in a way that inhibits someone from making a backup copy, or from shifting the use in space or time, because these constitute "fair use." In effect, of course, destroying the ability to encrypt or to control access would have the effect of destroying the property right entirely, and the advocates of such positions are fully aware of this. Much advocacy of "fair use" is in fact a torpedo attack on the very concept of intellectual property rights.

Thought experiment number two concerns the common grocery store. Would anyone ever claim that consumers should get groceries for free, and that we must "balance the interests" of consumers against the interests of food producers and grudgingly allow producers to charge something (but not too much)?

We would regard such a statement as absurd on its face. The interest of consumers lies in being able to pay for things, so that producers are induced by their own interests to produce food. Then these producers become consumers of other goods and pay other producers who then become consumers, and so on in that great chain we call the free market.

The same logic applies to intellectual creations. The argument that these are somehow different and thus should be subject to different rules rests upon misinterpretations of economic principles concerning marginal cost pricing and upon such economic concepts as "non-rivalry" and "exhaustion."[1] These concepts are indeed important, but they do not undercut the elementary truth that products of the intellect, like physical goods, are best produced by market incentives, and that propositions that are absurd on their face when applied to groceries do not become sensible when applied to the world of creativity.

Thought experiment number three is based on my personal experience walking through book stores. I see many a work that I might like to read, or perhaps read part of to see if I want to read it all, that I pass by because I will not lay out the $25 to $40 price. Suppose a system existed whereby I could tailor my investment. For a dollar, I could access it for a day to decide if I am seriously interested. For $4 or $5, I could read it once. For $30, I could add it to my permanent library. Clearly, I as a consumer would be better off to have all of these options available.

Yet, again, self-styled "consumer representatives" want to deny me this choice. They raise the horrible possibility that the book industry might impose "pay per use," whereby the level of payment would be tied to the intensity of the use made of the work. Why, where would this end? Next thing you know, people will be renting videos rather than being forced to buy them; perhaps grocery stores would even start charging more for a gallon of ice cream than for a quart!

As in the case of *TechDaily*, or the grocery store, how can people call themselves my friends when they want to deny me options that, in my judgment, make me better off?

The logic of these three thought experiments applies to the music business, the entertainment business, or any other product. Obviously, any individual consumer would be best off if everyone else paid for things while he or she got things for free. Equally obviously, the economy and the social system do not work this way, and only very small children and psychopaths think it should. The rest of us know that societies and economies are built on reciprocity.

You produce something, I produce something, and we trade. Or, in anything beyond a barter economy, we both trade with a number of third parties using money and the market as the intermediary mechanism for achieving this state of reciprocity.

The Internet is a wonderful invention for the distribution of intellectual creations because it vastly reduces the transaction costs, thus allowing these reciprocal arrangements to take place with minimum friction. One sends bits over fiberoptic cable instead of putting them on pieces of plastic and shipping them by truck.

The Internet also expands the potential dimensions of markets to include the whole world, which will greatly increase the variety of creations available. Those who say that music can be free while bands make money from concerts miss a crucial point. If a band can sell its music over the Internet, all it needs to support itself is enough paying fans scattered all over the world. If it can exist only through concert sales, then it must have a critical mass in every city. So only the most popular acts would be able to exist at all, and the people in small areas lacking a critical mass would get no music.

> *Those who say that music can be free while bands make money from concerts miss a crucial point.*

Unfortunately, getting to this happy state of Internet markets is not easy. The outlines of what is needed are clear, though, even if the exact path is not, and a workable long-term system for music will include:

Legitimate Downloading Services

Clearly, music and other intellectual products must be available on a paying basis through legitimate channels. The music industry knows this as well as anyone, and is working to make it happen. But this is not easy. Music copyrights are a tangled mess, and it is very difficult to negotiate out all the interests involved. In addition, the existence of the unauthorized downloading services substantially discourages investment in legitimate channels.

As a matter of ethics, an individual consumer could take the view that it is up to the industry to figure out how to make music available online and that the consumer will be happy to pay when this is achieved, but that he is not willing to pay to put bits on plastic and move them around the country by truck when this has ceased to be necessary. But as the online services are indeed coming into existence, this rationale is losing force.

Digital Rights Management

Legitimate channels must have a way of collecting money, which means that the product must be controlled by some method of electronic locks and keys. Furthermore, consumers will be better off if they are presented with options containing different packages of rights offered at different prices. Such packages require DRM. It is very important that DRM not be undermined by abstractions about "fair use." If DRM allows producers of IP to tailor their offerings to the desires of consumers, we will all be better off. Let a hundred business models bloom.

Education

The affected industries are sponsoring education programs on why unauthorized downloading is wrong. Education should go further: it should also emphasize fundamental explanations why property rights and markets are important, and why we are all better off if they are enforced and observed. In the end, as noted above, each individual would be better off if he got to cheat while others played by the rules, but this is not the way societies work. The downloading issue presents a Prisoner's Dilemma problem, and as author William Poundstone noted, "Study of the prisoner's dilemma has great power for explaining why animal and human societies are organized as they are. It is one of the great ideas of the twentieth century, simple enough for anyone to grasp and of fundamental importance."[2] The consumer who downloads music through unauthorized channels is cheating his or her fellow consumers because the practice involves free riding on their payments. Of course, if everyone tries to free ride on everyone, the system does not work at all.

The consumer who downloads music through unauthorized channels is cheating his or her fellow consumers.

Enforcement

It is not possible to do without enforcement efforts. No matter how well-protected by DRM, intellectual products such as music must be channeled through an output device, and they can be captured, redigitized, and sent out over the Internet. The problem can never be eliminated, but, hopefully, as legitimate services become plentiful, enforcement can be relegated to the minor role in the system that it plays in other areas, such as the protections against shoplifting in the retail system.

No one likes the current enforcement offensive, least of all, I suspect, the RIAA, but there is a serious chicken and egg problem. Why should anyone invest in legitimate services if they will be forced to compete with free, which is the road to bankruptcy? On the other hand, unless legitimate services exist, consumers will feel justified in using the unauthorized ones. In my view, one strong reason for the RIAA to launch its current enforcement effort was to signal potential investors that the industry is serious about supporting efforts to create legitimate channels. This will help us get through the awkward chicken-and-egg problem as quickly as possible.

Benign Neglect by Congress

This body is under continuing pressure to enact temporary fixes in response to the perceived crises of the day. It should resist. Most of the proposals are bad ideas that will inhibit the creativity of the market system and damage everyone. They are backed by slogans rather than analysis. Such proposals also compound the aura of uncertainty that surrounds the area, and thus inhibit the investment and effort needed to establish legitimate channels and get the whole problem behind us.

I am an optimist. The problems can be solved, and we can indeed reach the promised land of a vibrant system of intellectual creativity sparked by property rights and the market. But it will take steadiness on the part of the Congress, and a willingness to support the fundamental values involved.[3]

Finally, while most of this statement has concerned the interests of consumers, some very fundamental rights of creators are at stake as well. In 1972, the Supreme Court was confronted with an argument that "mere" property rights should be treated as unworthy of constitutional protection. It responded:

> [T]he dichotomy between personal liberties and property rights is a false one. Property does not have rights. People have rights. The right to enjoy property without unlawful deprivation, no less than the right to speak or the right to travel, is in truth a "personal" right, whether the "property" in question be a welfare check, a home, or a savings account. In fact, a fundamental interdependence exists between the personal right to liberty and the personal right in property. Neither could have meaning without the other.[4]

Intellectual property is encompassed by the constitutional protections of property, and by these principles.[5] And as a higher proportion of society's collective effort is devoted to the production of information goods rather than physical goods, the need to defend the rights of creators, and their support network of employers and financiers, grows apace.

In closing, it is worth emphasizing that there is no conflict between the rights and interests of producers of intellectual property and the interest of consumers. As Justice Ginsburg said in her majority opinion in the recent Supreme Court decision *Eldred v. Ashcroft*:[6]

> As we have explained, "the economic philosophy behind the [Copyright] Clause . . . is the conviction that encouragement of individual effort by personal gain is the best way to advance public welfare through the talents of authors and inventors." *Mazer v. Stein*, 347 U.S. 201, 219, 98 L. Ed. 630, 74 S. Ct. 460, 1954 Dec. Comm'r Pat. 308 (1954). Accordingly, "copyright law celebrates the profit motive, recognizing that the incentive to profit from the exploitation of copyrights will redound to the

public benefit by resulting in the proliferation of knowledge. . . . The profit motive is the engine that ensures the progress of science." *American Geophysical Union v. Texaco Inc.*, 802 F. Supp. 1, 27 (SDNY 1992). aff'd, 60 F.3d 913 (CA2 1994). Rewarding authors for their creative labor and "promoting . . . Progress" are thus complementary; as James Madison observed, in copyright "the public good fully coincides . . . with the claims of individuals." The Federalist No. 43, p. 272 (C. Rossiter ed. 1961). Justice Breyer's assertion that "copyright statutes must serve public, not private, ends" *post*, at 6, similarly misses the mark. The two ends are not mutually exclusive; copyright law serves public ends by providing individuals with an incentive to pursue private ones.

Notes:

1. James V. DeLong, "Marginalized," *TechCentralStation*, 29 July 2003 *<http://www.techcentralstation.com/072903D.html>.*

2. William Poundstone, *Prisoner's Dilemma*, (New York: Doubleday Anchor, 1992), 9.

3. For further discussion of many of these issues, see James V. DeLong, *Intellectual Property in the Internet Age: The Meaning of Eldred*, Progress and Freedom Foundation Progress on Point No. 10.5, February 2003 *<http://www.pff.org/publications/POPIO.5.pdf>.*

4. *Lynch v. Household Finance Corp.*, 405 U. S. 538, 552 (1972).

5. *E.g., Ruckelshaus v. Monsanto Co.*, 467 U.S. 986 (1984).

6. *Eldred v. Ashcroft*, 537 U.S. 186 (2003).

Mitigating the Impact of Intellectual Property Theft and Counterfeiting

James B. Comey Jr.

Deputy attorney general, U.S. Department of Justice, 2003– ; born Yonkers, NY, December 14, 1960; B.S. with honors in chemistry and religion, College of William and Mary, 1982; J.D., University of Chicago Law School, 1985; law clerk for then–U.S. District Judge John M. Walker Jr. in Manhattan; with Gibson, Dunn and Crutcher, New York City; partner, McGuire Woods, LLP, Richmond, VA, 1993–96; managing assistant U.S. attorney in charge of the Richmond Division of the U.S. Attorney's Office for the Eastern District of Virginia, 1996–2001; adjunct professor of law, University of Richmond; U.S. attorney, Southern District of New York, 2002–2003, eventually serving as deputy chief of the Criminal Division.

Editors' introduction: On February 5–6, 2004, the U.S. Chamber of Commerce sponsored a Strategic Leadership Forum on Mitigating the Impact of Intellectual Property Theft and Counterfeiting. This forum assembled key executives from the most influential companies and senior government officials to develop a shared vision toward combating intellectual property theft and counterfeiting. Deputy Attorney General Comey addressed this forum. While "pirates and counterfeiters . . . have found new and more sophisticated ways to hide their illegal activity," Mr. Comey assured, "we have worked, and will continue to work closely with American rights holders to ensure that we continue to respond to this threat."

James B. Comey's speech: It is a pleasure to be here today to discuss the growing problem of intellectual property theft and counterfeiting and the role law enforcement can play in protecting intellectual property rights.

First, let me emphasize that protecting intellectual property rights is an important part of the Department of Justice's mission. IP industries represent the fastest growing sector of the American economic engine. IP industries contribute approximately 5 percent to our Gross Domestic Product, having more than doubled in size in the last 25 years. These companies employ millions of people in high-paying jobs. The Business Software Alliance estimates that the United States software industry supplies 70 percent of the world's demand for legitimate software products. The American movie industry has a positive trade balance with every other nation around the world. American music and games continue to be as pop-

---

Delivered on February 5, 2004, at Washington, DC.

ular abroad as they are at home. Indeed, it would be difficult to overstate the importance of intellectual property rights to the continued economic well-being of the United States.

The digital era, in which we all live, provides intellectual property rights holders with unprecedented opportunities to distribute their works to a worldwide audience. Unfortunately, these same technologies that provide the

We believe that criminal enforcement to protect intellectual property rights is appropriate.

benefits of increased public exposure and access to protected works also have a down side. They have greatly expanded the opportunity to commit piracy and widespread copyright infringement and trademark counterfeiting. Millions of copyrighted songs and hundreds of thousands of copyrighted movies are illegally copied every day. Those who create software and games suffer significant losses from illegal copying. Technology is also being misused by trademark counterfeiters who create near perfect or perfect replicas of well known trademarks and append them to shabby knock-offs. In many instances, resourceful criminals use technology to violate both trademark and copyright, creating and selling products, such as software, which to the average consumer appear legitimate when in fact they are not.

For almost 100 years, the United States has recognized a limited, though important, role for the criminal law enforcement with regard to intellectual property rights. The vast majority of intellectual property rights enforcement in the United States has always been, and should remain, civil in nature. For the most part, property rights holders are capable of enforcing their intellectual property rights through civil law suits, and law enforcement authorities must be careful about how they utilize scarce resources in the post–September 11th era. However, where the level of piracy is particularly egregious, where public health and safety are put at risk, or where civil remedies fail to adequately deter illegal conduct, we believe that criminal enforcement to protect intellectual property rights is appropriate.

For example, a few years ago we successfully prosecuted a criminal for selling counterfeit luxury items, including fake Rolex watches and designer handbags. What is significant about this case is that before the United States prosecuted him, he had almost 16 million dollars in civil judgments against him. Because the criminal ignored the civil judgments and continued his illegal activity, this case was a clear choice for criminal prosecution.

We are at a pivotal time in the history of intellectual property rights enforcement. A number of factors have come together to create unprecedented challenges to intellectual property rights holders and to law enforcement:

- The increasing value of intellectual property
- The massive worldwide digital reproduction and distribution of copyrighted products is cheap and easy
- Millions of copies can be disseminated around the world with the simple click of a button
- The ability of pirates to create unlimited generations of perfect copies
- The ease with which criminals avoid detection by victim companies or law enforcement
- The sporadic or inconsistent enforcement throughout the world
- Criminals are no longer motivated solely by profit
- The emergence of organized crime syndicates in international piracy and counterfeiting

During the past two years, the Department of Justice has waged the most aggressive campaign against counterfeiting and piracy in its history. Since the beginning of his tenure, Attorney General Ashcroft has worked diligently to ensure that the prosecutorial resources needed to address intellectual property crime are in place. Shortly after becoming the Attorney General, he expanded Computer Hacking and Intellectual Property (or CHIP) Units in major U.S. Attorney's Offices across the nation. These specialized units consist of dedicated federal prosecutors whose primary focus is prosecuting high-tech crimes, including IP crimes.

The CHIP Units complement the existing network of Computer and Telecommunications Coordinators (CTCs) that serve in every United States Attorney's Office. The CTCs regularly receive specialized training in the investigation and prosecution of high-tech crimes, including intellectual property crimes. Many of the 94 U.S. Attorneys Offices have two or more CTCs to help meet the growing demand for trained high-tech prosecutors.

Attorney General Ashcroft has also significantly expanded the Criminal Division's Computer Crime and Intellectual Property Section, also known as CCIPS. CCIPS is a highly specialized team of over 35 lawyers who focus exclusively on computer and intellectual property crime. CCIPS attorneys are involved in all facets of criminal intellectual property rights enforcement. The expansion of CCIPS has allowed us to devote additional resources to address piracy both here and abroad. For the first time, CCIPS has a Deputy Chief whose sole responsibility is to oversee and manage the attorneys in the section dedicated to IP enforcement. At present, there are 12 CCIPS attorneys working exclusively on the IP program. Working in concert, CCIPS, the CTC Network, and the CHIP Units create a formidable, multi-pronged approach to prosecuting intellectual property crimes. We are already beginning to see the positive results of their efforts.

We are making substantial impact on piracy and counterfeiting—both in regard to online and traditional hard goods activities. We have made significant inroads into online piracy, which has grown precipitously in lockstep with the phenomenal growth of the Internet, file compression technology, and broadband Web access. We have successfully targeted some of the most egregious online offenders, including the international organizations that have placed the latest, hardest to obtain, and highest quality pirated products on the Internet. Working in cooperation with law enforcement counterparts overseas, our collective efforts, which are ongoing, have dismantled many of the most prominent online piracy groups and resulted in the substantial prison sentences ranging, for first offenses, from 33 to 47 months for the core conspirators.

We have also successfully prosecuted trademark violations. Just last month, an Alabama man pled guilty to 28 counts of counterfeiting and pesticide misbranding charges pending against him. The defendant sold mislabeled and adulterated pesticides used to control mosquitos and West Nile Virus to various municipalities.

The potential consequences of intellectual property offenses . . . cut right at the heart of public health and safety.

As this case illustrates, the potential consequences of intellectual property offenses go beyond lost sales, but cut right at the heart of public health and safety.

Another emerging area of intellectual property rights enforcement that may be of interest to you are recent successful prosecutions for the theft of trade secrets under the Economic Espionage Act. Recent prosecutions have involved the theft of such trade secrets as satellite encryption technology, confidential pricing information used as part of the government contracting process, proprietary customer databases, and various mechanical processes used by American manufacturers to produce goods and services. Many of these trade secrets are critical to the economic viability of the victim companies. Since its inception in 1996, this statute has risen to prominence on the intellectual property landscape as stolen trade secrets have become an increasingly attractive commodity on the black market. As this threat increases, American industry has taken steps to protect its trade secrets from theft. Criminal enforcement of trade secret law has become an important aspect of protecting these vital intellectual property rights.

Although we have had great success in each of these important areas, piracy is a continually evolving crime. We know there is much work to be done. I would like to touch on just a few of the more prominent issues that loom on the horizon.

Organized crime syndicates have begun to use piracy and counterfeiting as a means to fund their illicit activity. Traditionally, piracy operations were small, often run by individuals or a loose collection of people trying to make a quick buck in what has been perceived to be a fairly risk-free criminal enterprise. This has all changed. Piracy has become big business: it is a worldwide, multibillion-dollar illicit economy which robs legitimate industries and creators of income, while driving up costs for consumers. It is against this backdrop that criminal organizations are playing a more prominent—and dangerous—role in piracy around the globe.

Highly organized criminal syndicates have significant resources to devote to their illegal operations, thus increasing the scope and sophistication of their criminal activity. Further, by nature, these syndicates control international distribution channels which allow them to move massive quantities of pirated goods, as well as other illicit goods, throughout the world. As one might expect, these groups do not hesitate to threaten or injure those who attempt to interfere with their illegal operations. Industry representatives in Asia report that they have been threatened and their property has been vandalized by members of these syndicates when their antipiracy efforts strike too near the illegal operation. Government officials have also been threatened. These criminal syndicates, which are not limited to Asia, are formidable foes, but must be dealt with to truly attack the problem of intellectual property theft.

As the emergence of organized crime illustrates, IP crime has reached global proportions. The Internet has created a borderless community for online pirates. Online cases almost inevitably involve co-conspirators located outside of the United States. We must increasingly rely on foreign governments for much of the enforcement effort in this area. To this end, we have successfully engaged a number of foreign countries to assist in prosecuting criminals both here and abroad. We have taken the unprecedented step of seeking extradition of one such criminal for his leadership role in an international piracy ring.

Finally, although we are making inroads in this battle, pirates and counterfeiters are also refining their own illicit techniques. In response to our aggressive enforcement activities, organizations and individuals have found new and more sophisticated ways to hide their illegal activity. The quality of counterfeit and pirated goods is near perfect. In some instances, even representatives of victim companies have difficulty distinguishing counterfeit goods from legitimate ones. That is how sophisticated this illicit industry has become. We have worked and will continue to work closely with American rights holders to ensure that we continue to respond to this threat.

While there are many challenges ahead, we look forward to meeting them head on. The harm caused by piracy is real. It robs our economy of vital resources and ignores the fundamental notion that innovation should be rewarded. The American intellectual property rights community is second to none. American products are sought the world over. The Justice Department is committed to working with all of you to ensure that the intellectual capital of this nation receives the protection it deserves. Thank you for allowing me to speak with you this morning on this important topic.

The Digital Piracy Dilemma

Graham B. Spanier

President, Pennsylvania State University, 1995– ; born Capetown, South Africa, July 18, 1948; B.S., 1969, and M.S., 1971, Iowa State University; Ph.D. in sociology, Northwestern University, 1973; associate dean and professor, Pennsylvania State University, University Park, 1973–82; vice provost for undergraduate studies, State University of New York at Stony Brook, 1982–86; provost and vice president for academic affairs, Oregon State University, 1986–91; chancellor, University of Nebraska–Lincoln, 1991–95; family sociologist, demographer, and marriage and family therapist; host, To the Best of My Knowledge, *on public television and radio; authored more than 100 scholarly publications, including 10 books; founding editor,* Journal of Family Issues; *former chair, board of directors, the National Association of State Universities and Land-Grant Colleges; chair, Big Ten Conference Council of Presidents/Chancellors; vice chair, Worldwide Universities Network.*

Editors' introduction: In March 2004 an Intellectual Property Task Force, commissioned by Attorney General John Ashcroft, began to examine how the Department of Justice handled intellectual property issues in order to develop recommendations for the future. Leaders in government, industry, and education also sought legal and economic practices that would help alleviate the problem of piracy, which had caused a 31 percent decrease in music sales between 1999 and 2002. In addressing the *Financial Times* New Media and Broadcasting Conference, President Spanier stated, "As a place where knowledge is created, shared, and cherished, a university must be the champion and protector of intellectual property rights in order to carry out our mission of educating students and to stimulate more creativity."

Graham B. Spanier's speech: It's a pleasure to be here to discuss higher education and its role in the entertainment industry, particularly with regard to the piracy of music and movies.

The entertainment industry is now facing a serious challenge—particularly from our youth, who have grown up believing that everything—especially music and movies—is free on the Internet.

As one high school student recently said, "Who wouldn't want to do this? It's totally free and it's easy."

Technology has made copying music and other protected works far easier than ever before and it is this ease of replication that has made digital piracy a mainstream activity practiced by millions of people on any given day. About 60 percent of these "file sharers"

Delivered on March 3, 2004, at London, England. Reprinted with permission of Graham B. Spanier.

are in the United States alone. A recent report from the BBC indicated that Hong Kong is the world leader in the number of songs illegally downloaded—130 million over the last two and a half years.

Across the globe, more than 2 billion files are illegally downloaded every month, and those of you in this room know what that has done to the music industry and now threatens to do to the movie industry as well.

In fact, in the less than 15 minutes I will spend talking today, about $672,000 dollars worth of songs will be downloaded in the United States alone.

As president of the Pennsylvania State University, one of the world's largest universities, with an enrollment of more than 83,000 students and 36,000 employees, why should I care about digital piracy? It's not just that I'm still waiting for my big break in show business.

Universities are one of the primary producers of intellectual prop-

---

Universities are one of the primary producers of intellectual property and so have a vested interest in nurturing and protecting creative works.

---

erty and so have a vested interest in nurturing and protecting creative works—not only those that have come from our own institutions, but also innovations that are being discovered by those outside our gates.

As a place where knowledge is created, shared, and cherished, a university must be the champion and protector of intellectual property rights in order to carry out our mission of educating students and to stimulate more creativity.

As many of you know, copyright law started right here in England with "The Statute of Anne," a law passed by the British Parliament in 1710. Like today, that statute was prompted in part by a technological advancement—the printing press—laying the groundwork for intellectual property policies that still hold today.

Without copyright protection, the works of J. K. Rowling, John Meaney, Robert Bolt, the Beatles, the Darkness, and even Benny Hill, would be up for grabs.

In the U.S., online intellectual property is governed by a number of laws, most notably the Digital Millennium Copyright Act, enacted in 1998. Violators can face civil and criminal penalties, including up to five years in prison and fines of up to 250,000 U.S. dollars—equivalent to about 134,000 pounds, or over 199,000 euros.

The law covers a number of areas from fair use to the liability of online service providers, and even bans the dissemination of technology whose main purpose is to get around copyright protections. While the Recording Industry Association of America has filed lawsuits under a basic copyright law passed in 1976, the Digital Millennium Copyright Act has helped expedite the process for gathering the names of those stealing music. Such lawsuits have become an important aspect of our nation's deterrence efforts.

So as the Web has enabled intellectual property to flow more freely than ever before, universities—which are the defacto Internet service providers for millions of people—have found themselves in somewhat of a dilemma. In essence, we're providing the networks that allow pirated information to be shared. Most universities have been reluctant to admit that they were part of the problem. But I believe that we surely must be part of the solution.

Piracy is particularly prevalent at universities because the institutions are among the most wired in the world. Most students and employees have unrestricted Internet access at the broadest bandwidths, and there is a widespread lack of knowledge about copyright laws, making online theft an effortless and accepted activity.

> *One of the most compelling reasons that universities should help find a solution to digital piracy is because it's just plain wrong.*

Clearly, this is not what university administrators had in mind when they provided high-speed Internet access as part of the educational package.

But one of the most compelling reasons that universities should help find a solution to digital piracy is because it's just plain wrong. As recording artist Elvis Costello recently said, "If you make something and someone steals it, that's theft. That's all you need to say about file sharing. Where's the ambiguity?"

The technology of peer-to-peer file sharing has greatly facilitated such piracy, both conceptually and legally. There are, of course, quite innovative, academically sound, and legally appropriate uses for P2P technologies.

Unfortunately, using peer-to-peer file sharing for piracy has given infringers linguistic cover. "Sharing" is something we teach our kids to do but sharing stolen goods is another matter. What we communicate to the next generation will largely determine if we will live in a just society. Honesty, integrity, respect for individual achievement, and working for the common good are all values that students should have when they leave college. It's our obligation to educate students about ethical behavior.

While testifying before the United States Congress on the issue of digital piracy, I was told, as the leader of higher education's efforts in this arena, to fix this problem, or Congress would fix it for us with laws we wouldn't like.

So—what are we doing about digital piracy?

First and foremost, we are educating our students, faculty, and staff about copyright issues, and we have seen a huge sea change over the last year in awareness levels. Before receiving an Internet access account, everyone within our university, for example, must read and sign a statement saying they will abide by our policies and the laws related to copyright infringement. They also receive a document discussing the issue of digital piracy. They are advised of bandwidth limitations, a restriction that was instituted to ensure that users doing legitimate work would not be hindered. At the same time, these restrictions limit the bandwidth availability needed for egregious levels of downloading.

In addition, over the last year or so, we have sent several e-mails to every member of the university community, again discussing copyright law, music piracy, the responsibilities of the computer user, and repercussions for illegally downloading and distributing copyrighted material. We let our students know in no uncertain terms that Penn State follows the Digital Millennium Copyright Act and that they may also be subject to university-imposed sanctions—including expulsion.

As part of our enforcement efforts, we have assigned a designated agent to respond to reports alleging copyright infringement on our servers and we respond expeditiously to remove access to the stolen material.

Currently, we are deploying firewalls on all residence hall network systems. The firewalls will prevent access to pirated peer-to-peer traffic, while at the same time providing greater protection against viruses, worms, Trojan horses, and the like. We continue our bandwidth shaping practices and our assessment of evolving technologies.

In addition to education, enforcement, and network management procedures, Penn State also has undertaken something that no other university has. We launched a program to make online music legally available to our students.

After reviewing proposals from several music subscription services, we selected Napster, which has a music library of more than 500,000 tracks.

This legitimate alternative to music piracy was rolled out several weeks ago for about 17,000 students in our residence halls on several of our campuses. By fall 2004, about 75,000 students at more than 20 of our Penn State campuses will have access to this music service. Faculty and staff also will be able to pay for the service at a discounted rate, and we are working on a concept to serve our alumni as well.

As the first U.S. university to provide a sponsored legal alternative to illegal downloading, Penn State faced considerable skepticism from many corners, but we had done our homework by talking to groups of students who made it clear they wanted instant access to hundreds of thousands of music files. Student input was core to the development of this program and we even hired a 22-year-old on to the staff to advise us. I personally spoke to scores of students.

Working in partnership with Cary Sherman, president of the RIAA, we pushed the industry—from the songwriters to the copyright holders to the recording companies—to cooperate with this effort.

To date, evidence suggests that access to Napster's legal download site at Penn State has substantially diminished the use of services such as KaZaa and Grokster.

Our students are streaming or downloading to their computers more than 100,000 songs per day. This is free to them, since Penn State pays for the subscription. Students pay 99 cents per track if they wish to burn the track onto a CD and own it.

The notion that universities should take stronger action to stop digital piracy on their networks is catching on. Last month the University of Rochester in New York also signed on to offer access for its students. Several dozen other schools have begun such discussions.

The work on this issue at Penn State emanates from the work of the Committee on Higher Education and the Entertainment Industry, a national group that Cary Sherman and I cochair. The committee's efforts over the past year have focused on legal, technical, educational, and legislative issues.

I am proud of the work we have accomplished through this unprecedented relationship among higher education leaders and music and motion picture executives.

The free-range design of the Internet combined with the victimless feel of downloading has meant the re-education of a generation, as well as a change in attitude for all computer users.

Solving the digital piracy dilemma will take creativity and patience. Universities must be part of the solution.

Through continuing educational efforts, increased enforcement, technological advances, and legal alternatives, perhaps we can stem the underground swapping of movie and music files and, in the process, restore ethical behavior to our youth and put our energies toward the legitimate uses of technology for teaching and learning.

Coalition of Entertainment Retail Trade Associations (CERTA) Congressional Fly-In Media Briefing

Jim Donio

Acting president, National Association of Recording Merchandisers (NARM), 2003– ; B.S. in journalism, Temple University; at NARM: director of creative services, 1988; communications director, 1991; vice president of communications and events with oversight for conventions and conferences, 1995; prior to joining NARM, held a variety of editorial, public relations, and event-related positions for the Association of Information Systems Professionals (AISP); active in Philadelphia-area TV and cultural events, winning a local Emmy Award in 1986 for Outstanding Cultural Programming.

Editors' introduction: Illegal downloading of movies, music, and other properties had become so prevalent that Senator Patrick Leahy (D-Vt.) sponsored the Pirate Act, which passed the Senate in June 2004. This legislation would authorize the U.S. attorney general's office to file civil suits and collect damages "against any person who engages in conduct constituting copyright infringement." A few weeks earlier, Mr. Donio, acting president of the National Association of Recording Merchandisers (NARM), told the Coalition of Entertainment Retail Trade Associations (CERTA) that "education about copyright infringement is paramount—for consumers, for businesses, for law enforcement professionals, and for legislators as well. . . . Simply put, our businesses are being damaged and this cannot continue unabated." CERTA is comprised of four national trade organizations who share common interests, such as combating entertainment product piracy and increasing consumer awareness of entertainment product ratings and labeling.

Jim Donio's speech: The music retailing community has long supported efforts to protect intellectual property and to thwart the piracy that hurts our industry.

NARM has worked very closely and collaboratively with the Recording Industry Association of America (RIAA) for many, many years to identify and shut down operations manufacturing pirated music product. We have also partnered with RIAA and the Motion Picture Association of America to strengthen state true name and address statutes to help prevent piracy.

Delivered on April 20, 2004, in a briefing room at the U.S. Capitol Building, Washington, DC.
Reprinted with permission of Jim Donio.

NARM's hundreds of retail, wholesale, distributor, and supplier member companies and individual industry professionals are fully apprised of the latest initiatives to combat this threat to their future. We have shared information via our committees and councils, at events and most recently through Web site postings and links.

Music retailers and wholesalers know only too well about grappling with the challenges of dealing with product stolen not just by consumers, but by unscrupulous business owners and presumptuous entrepreneurs.

We have applauded and strongly endorsed RIAA's blitz targeting retail outlets that don't play by the rules because retailers who willfully engage in commercial pirating of music should be held accountable for their actions. Legitimate, law-abiding businesses are the ones that must thrive and grow. NARM's Bylaws are crystal clear and unequivocal—anyone convicted of piracy forfeits their right to be a member of the Association.

> *Education about copyright infringement is paramount—for consumers, for businesses, for law enforcement professionals, and for legislators as well.*

And now piracy is so much easier to accomplish. With the advent of rampant digital piracy, NARM became a member of the MUSIC Coalition spearheaded by RIAA. NARM's members believe RIAA has the right to act on behalf of copyright holders and recording artists to protect their rights, their interests, and their creative works as the law provides.

Today, I am very proud to be standing shoulder to shoulder with my fellow entertainment retail trade associations to deliver a very important message. It's not enough for us to simply continue to "echo" the sentiments and support the efforts of our sister organizations in the supplier community in this piracy battle. It is essential—and we believe that even more can be accomplished—if we add our own unique voices to the dialogue.

Education about copyright infringement is paramount—for consumers, for businesses, for law enforcement professionals, and for legislators as well. The MUSIC Coalition and "What's the Download" industry Web sites provide helpful information. Laws must clearly be enforced. Simply put, our businesses are being damaged and this cannot continue unabated.

But I must also stress that lawful uses of sampling, sharing, or copying copyrighted material—as well as the consumer's right to privacy—must be preserved as well. We must strike a balance.

The retailing community must be an equal partner in providing legal alternatives for consumers. But to legally give consumers what they want, both physical stores and online ventures need the content to do so.

We don't wish to inhibit technological advances. On the contrary, we look to embrace them and use them to encourage a more vibrant and competitive retail landscape. With this in mind, NARM has recently created an In-store CD-burning Task Force to explore with our supplier partners new legal opportunities for music retailing.

We're committed to do what it takes to fight the good fight against entertainment piracy. We need your help to serve the consumers who can make the difference in the long-term health of our members' businesses.

Thank you.

V. Challenges to the Environment

National Press Club Luncheon

Gaylord Nelson

Counselor, the Wilderness Society, 1981– ; born Clear Lake, WI, June 4, 1916; B.A., San Jose State College, 1939; LLB, University of Wisconsin Law School, 1942; lieutenant, U.S. Army, serving four years in the Okinawa campaign; attorney, Madison, WI, 1946–58; Wisconsin Senate, 1948–58; governor of Wisconsin, 1959–62; U.S. senator (D), Wisconsin, 1963–81, serving as chair, Select Committee on Small Business, and member, Special Committee on Official Conduct, and Interior and Insular Affairs Committee; founder of Earth Day, 1970; author, America's Last Chance *(1970),* What Are Me and You Gonna Do?: Children's Letters to Senator Gaylord Nelson About the Environment *(1971), and* Beyond Earth Day: Fulfilling the Promise, *with Susan Campbell and Paul Wozniak (2002); Presidential Medal of Freedom, 1995; UN's Environmental Leadership Award, 1982 and 1992; Gaylord Nelson State Park established in Madison, WI.*

Editors' introduction: In 1970 Senator Gaylord Nelson founded Earth Day, a commitment to learn about ecology and to protect the environment. In 1993 *American Heritage Magazine* called Earth Day "one of the most remarkable happenings in the history of democracy." On the first Earth Day, April 22, 1970, some 20 million Americans participated in one form or another, and by 2000 some 500 million people from 167 countries were swept up in the event. In the speech below, Mr. Nelson stated, "The public is prepared and, in the end, will support those measures necessary to forge a sustainable society if the president and Congress have the vision to lead us to that goal."

Gaylord Nelson's speech: Forging and maintaining a sustainable society is the overarching challenge for this century and beyond. At this point, no nation has managed to evolve into a sustainable society. We are all pursuing a self-destructive course of fueling our economies by drawing down our natural capital—that is to say, by degrading and eroding our resource base and counting it on the income side of the ledger. This, obviously, is not a sustainable situation over the long term.

Since the first Earth Day, we have tried a lot of things. We have learned a lot, and we have achieved a lot but we still have a long way to go.

After 33 years of discussion, debate, legislation, and education since the first Earth Day, there has evolved a new level of concern over what is happening around us. The public is prepared and, in

Delivered on April 22, 2003, at Washington, DC. Reprinted with permission of Gaylord Nelson.

the end, will support those measures necessary to forge a sustainable society if the president and Congress have the vision to lead us to that goal.

The necessary "vision" is not currently present in either the Congress or the executive branch. The fact is, the political system will not effectively move to address the challenge of sustainability until the president and the Congress articulate the necessity of moving in that direction. They, after all, are the elected representatives of the political system. If they don't lead, who will?

The ultimate key to sustainability is population. A sustainable society may be described as one whose activities do not exceed the carrying capacity of its resource base; or one that manages its environmental and resource systems so that their ability to support future generations is not diminished.

In the past 10 years there have been three United Nations Conferences that revolved around the issues of population and sustainability—Rio in 1992, Cairo in 1996, and Johannesburg in 2002.

The fact is, the political system will not effectively move to address the challenge of sustainability until the president and the Congress articulate the necessity of moving in that direction.

At the Cairo Conference some 170 nations, including the U.S., endorsed the concept that it is the responsibility of each nation to stabilize its own population. While the U.S. is the fastest growing country among the industrial nations it has done nothing to stabilize its own population.

Thirty years ago, in 1972, the president's commission on population growth and the American Future published its five-volume report called the Rockefeller Report. The bottom line conclusion of the report was that the commission could not identify a single value in American life that would be enhanced by any further population growth. The commission recommended that the U.S. move vigorously to stabilize our population of‘ 200 million as rapidly as possible.

Since the Rockefeller Report, the U.S. population has ballooned from 200 million to 282 million and still growing. At the current growth rate, U.S. population will reach 500 million about 2060 or '70. In the second half of the next century, or sooner, we will join China and India as the third member of the one billion population club.

What does it all mean? It means that when we double our population in a few decades we will of necessity double our total infrastructure—twice as many houses, schools, colleges, hospitals, prisons, airports, traffic jams, freeways; twice as much crowding and half as much open spaces. When we again double our population in the next century that will require that we multiply by a factor of four the current infrastructure—four times everything.

Of course not everything would increase by the same factor as population—when the population doubles some things may increase by a factor of three or four and some by a factor of one half, more or less.

For example, there are now about 215 million cars and light trucks on our highways and the U.S. Department of Energy projects that 317 million passenger vehicles will be on the road by about 2050–60. That will put an additional 100 million cars on our highways within the next 50–60 years or so. Where will we put them? How many more parking lots and miles of roads and city streets will that require? How much will it cost? How will we manage it all? Can we do it and maintain that quality of life we cherish? Open spaces, scenic beauty, adequate habitat for song birds and people?

Indeed, when we double the population in the next few decades and double again during the second half of the next century the result will be nothing less than a revolutionary transformation of how we and future generations will live and at what quality of life. In short, we are headed into this century with no discussion, understanding, or plans for a future that will double and quadruple our population in a very short time frame.

In 1992 the United States National Academy of Sciences and the Royal Society of London, two of the world's leading scientific bodies, addressed the state of the planet in the following words:

> If current predictions of population growth prove accurate and patterns of human activity on the planet remain unchanged, science and technology may not be able to prevent either the irreversible degradation of the environment or continued poverty for much of the world.

On January 10, 1990, Pope John Paul II delivered a message on Peace and the Environment. A few words describe his concern about what is happening to the natural world around us. The message said in part:

> Faced with the widespread destruction of the environment, people everywhere are coming to understand that we cannot continue to use the goods of the earth as we have in the past. . . . The ecological crisis has assumed such proportions as to be the responsibility of everyone. . . . The ecological crisis is a moral issue.

The road to sustainability will be long and sometimes rocky. Neither political party is prepared to tackle the challenge directly. It involves too many controversial issues and too few political rewards. It is much easier to postpone any action to some infinite future date—and that is just what the political system has done for the past several years and will continue to do until it is too late to avoid irreparable environmental damage.

> *A national dialogue over sustainability will clarify the major issues that we must address.*

There is, however, a politically sound practical way to address the issue of forging a sustainable society that will get us where we need to go. It simply involves the president and the Congress initiating a national dialogue on sustainability—what is it? Why is it important? How do we achieve it?

The president should set the standard and the precedent by delivering an annual message to Congress on the "state of the environment" including a list of recommended priorities we need to address. This message should follow the traditional State of the Union message. To crank up the political machinery for a move down the path to sustainability, someone has to spark the engine. The president is in the best position to do that. He owns the bully pulpit; he is the chief educator of the nation, the superstar, the only one who can command top billing in the papers and on television and radio, whenever he wishes. An annual State of the Environment address to the Congress and hearings on sustainability would inspire the kind of public dialogue that must precede major decisions on controversial matters.

In about the same time frame Congress should begin a series of educational hearings—I would suggest one hearing a month, on each of the multiple issues involved in forging a sustainable society. The annual presidential message and the Congressional hearings would finally let the public know that the political leadership ranks sustainability high on its list of priorities. As of this date, the president and the Congress have been silent on the issue of sustainability. How would the public know that the issue was important?

Of necessity, sustainability hearings must range over all significant issues on the environmental spectrum. That will include exploring: how we make a transition from our overwhelming reliance on fossil fuels to a significant reliance on solar energy; how we move to restore ocean fisheries; how we reduce air and water pollution to a level manageable by nature; how we preserve our magnificent heritage of public lands; how we shrink our excessive reliance on herbicides and pesticides; how we stop over-drafting ground water, reduce soil erosion; how we preserve wetlands, forests, national parks, and biodiversity; and how we stabilize the population within our boundaries as agreed at the Cairo Conference.

A national dialogue over sustainability will clarify the major issues that we must address and provide a political roadmap to the goal of sustainability. Without presidential leadership and extended Congressional hearings we will remain at a political stalemate on The Challenge of our time.

Congressional hearings on sustainability could begin with a focus on any one of at least a dozen issues. One good place to start is on public lands. The U.S. has preserved and protected the largest, most varied collection of natural lands ever assembled by any country. It is an estate of about 620 million acres, almost one million square miles—a vast mosaic of mountains, valleys, seashores, grasslands, deserts, rivers, lakes, and forests.

Tragically, this rare heritage of natural areas is being degraded and despoiled very rapidly by off-road vehicles—snowmobiles, jet skis, ATV's, and other ORV's. In another 25–30 years most of our natural parks, forests, and other public lands will be little more than crowded, noisy, polluted theme parks—the original purpose will have been destroyed. The first celebrated icon to go will be Yellowstone National Park.

The Clinton administration proposed a rule that would eliminate snowmobiles from Yellowstone. The Bush administration reversed that proposal and snowmobiles will not be phased out of Yellowstone. Mike Finley, former superintendent of Yellowstone had this to say about the settlement between the Bush administration and the snowmobile industry: "This is the first time that the opinion of the park was not sought, or solicited, or considered by an administration. This was a top-down decision to settle this lawsuit. . . . What this settlement represents is a repudiation of the American people and a sell-out by the administration." If the Congress and the president want to save this remarkable heritage of public lands there is still a window of opportunity—but it is closing fast.

Tackling Climate Change:
Five Keys to Success

Eileen Claussen

President, Pew Center on Global Climate Change, 1998– , and president and chair, Board of Strategies for the Global Environment; born New York City, June 9, 1945; B.A., George Washington University, 1966; M.A., University of Virginia, 1967; systems analyst, U.S. Navy, Washington, DC, 1967–68; consultant, Booz, Allen and Hamilton, Inc., 1968–69; assistant director, center for commercial development Boise Cascade Corp., 1969–72; director of various programs, Office of Solid Waste at the U.S. Environmental Protection Agency (EPA), 1972–87; director, atmospheric and indoor air programs at the EPA, 1987–93; acting deputy assistant administrator for the Office of Air and Radiation, 1988–89; special assistant to the president and senior director for global environmental affairs at the National Security Council, 1993–96; former assistant secretary of state for Oceans, International Environmental and Scientific Affairs; Timothy Atkeson Scholar in Residence, Yale University; member, board of directors—Environmental Law Institute, Council on Foreign Relations, China Council for International Cooperation on Environment and Development; executive editor, Climate Change: Science, Strategies and Solutions, *and author of numerous publications on environment and development; recipient, Department of State's Career Achievement Award, the Meritorious Executive Award for Sustained Superior Accomplishment, the Distinguished Executive Award for Outstanding Contributions to International Environmental Protection.*

Editors' introduction: In 2003 authorities representing various scientific and sociological disciplines addressed the Fourth Annual Dartmouth Student Science Congress, which was free and open to the general public. Student Science Congresses at Dartmouth College introduce participants to timely, complex, and often controversial topics centered on human biology, where they are encouraged to explore issues from a variety of perspectives, taking an interdisciplinary approach. At the conclusion of the discussions, students vote on a series of questions as a way to gauge their opinions and provoke further discussion. Contending that "global warming is shaping up as one of the most important challenges of the 21st century," President Claussen attempted to provide those attending the Congress with "a clear idea of where we stand today in the effort against global climate change."

Eileen Claussen's speech: Thank you very much. It is a pleasure to be here at Dartmouth for the Fourth Annual Student Science Congress. I understand that as part of these proceedings, students

Delivered on May 2, 2003, at 7:30 P.M., in the Rockefeller Center, Hanover, NH. Reprinted with permission of Eileen Claussen.

will be voting on a series of ballot questions. I have not yet seen these questions, but tonight I am nevertheless going to try to influence your answers.

For example, if one of the questions is "How serious a problem is global warming?" I encourage you to answer that it is a very serious problem indeed. And, if one of the questions is "Who was your favorite speaker during the Congress?" . . . well, just keep in mind that Claussen sort of rhymes with awesome.

Seriously, I appreciate this opportunity to address your Student Science Congress, and I applaud the organizers of this event for taking on a topic of such pressing importance. Whether we like it or not, global warming is shaping up as one of the most important challenges of the 21st century. It is going to drive far-reaching changes in how we live and work, how we power our homes, schools, factories, and office buildings, how we get from one place to another, how we manufacture and transport goods, and even how we farm and manage forests. It touches every aspect of our economy and our lives, and to ignore it is to live in a fantasy land

---

> *Whether we like it or not, global warming*
> *is shaping up as one of the most important*
> *challenges of the 21st century.*

---

where nothing ever has to change—and where we never have to accept what the science tells us about what is happening to our world.

My goal tonight is to give you a clear idea of where we stand today in the effort against global climate change. To do that, I'd first like to offer you an insider's look at how the world and the United States have responded to this challenge over the last decade.

Then, after the history lesson—and don't worry, there will not be a test—I want to look forward. And I'd like to suggest to you five keys to success—five things we need to do if were are to successfully meet the challenge of climate change.

So, to begin with, let's travel back in time to 1992, when another George Bush was our president, and when the nations of the world gathered in sunny Rio de Janeiro for the United Nations Conference on Environment and Development, affectionately known as the Earth Summit. This was the event, you may recall, where more than 150 countries signed an agreement called the United Nations Framework Convention on Climate Change.

The UNFCCC, as it is known, set an ambitious long-term objective: to stabilize greenhouse gas concentrations in the atmosphere at a level that would—and I quote—"prevent dangerous anthropogenic (or human-caused) interference with the climate system." This is a goal that the United States, and virtually every other nation, has embraced.

As a first step, industrialized countries agreed to a voluntary emissions target: they aimed to reduce their greenhouse gas emissions to 1990 levels by the year 2000. Before long, however, it became clear that the targets would not be met and that voluntary commitments could not deliver genuine action. So the United States and others countries began to negotiate a new agreement, one with binding targets, and they agreed at the outset that these new commitments would extend only to the industrialized countries, which so far have contributed the most to the problem.

The result, negotiated five years after the Rio summit in Kyoto, Japan, is the Kyoto Protocol. The Protocol requires countries to reduce or limit their emissions of greenhouse gases in relation to 1990 levels, with different countries agreeing to different targets. The agreement also includes a number of features advocated by the United States to ensure countries a high degree of flexibility as they work to achieve their targets. They can make actual emission reductions at home, trade emission credits with others who have made reductions, and use "sinks" such as farms and forests to remove carbon from the atmosphere.

During the negotiations in Kyoto, Vice President Al Gore flew to the ancient Japanese capital to help hammer out the deal. And what the U.S. negotiators ultimately agreed to was a binding 7 percent reduction in emissions below 1990 levels by 2012.

The problem was that it was already 1997, and U.S. emissions had already risen over 1990 levels by more than 8 percent. In other words, we had pledged to reduce our emissions by nearly 14 percent and we didn't have any kind of program in place to do this, nor any will to put such a program into place.

Another problem was that the United States Senate, under the Byrd-Hagel resolution, had recently voted unanimously that the United States should not sign any climate treaty that—quote—"would result in serious harm to the economy of the United States" or that did not impose some type of commitment on developing countries as well.

Of course Kyoto did not include commitments for developing countries, because the parties, including the United States, agreed at the outset that it would not. And the target agreed to by the United States was portrayed by those who wished to kill the treaty as clearly harmful to our economy, a charge that was not effectively countered by the administration. So the fact of the matter is that the Kyoto Protocol negotiated by the Clinton administration was about as welcome in the Senate as the proverbial skunk at a lawn party—and senators had no intention of holding their noses so they could tolerate this thing. They just plain didn't want it anywhere near them.

The Clinton administration, for its part, did nothing to try to bring about the ratification of this treaty that its people had made such a big deal of signing. Granted, the president at the time was caught up in a scandal, and Vice President Gore was gearing up for a presidential run of his own and surely wanted to avoid being publicly associated with anything that could be said to pose a threat to the economy. But still, the whole episode of U.S. participation in Kyoto—and, before that, the UNFCCC—was enough to recall the line from Shakespeare: "full of sound and fury, signifying nothing." The bottom line: We clearly were not prepared to deliver at home what we were promising abroad.

But the story does not end there. To fast-forward to 2000, American voters elected another president—another Bush—and within months of entering office his administration made a unilateral decision to reject the Kyoto Protocol out of hand, instead of working to change it and make it better. Needless to say, this decision was not received warmly by other nations that had persevered through years of difficult negotiations and that had acceded to U.S. demands early on that the treaty include trading and other business-friendly mechanisms.

As an aside, I think it is interesting to note that in the recent run-up to the war in Iraq, it was hard to find an article about other countries' perceptions of the United States that did not mention the impolitic way in which this administration rejected Kyoto. It was perceived as a real slap in the face—a confirmation of global fears that the United States, which is responsible for almost one-fourth of global greenhouse has emissions, had no intention of acting seriously on this issue.

As if to confirm these fears, the Bush administration last year announced a climate strategy that was big on rhetoric but not-so-big on results. Here is what this strategy does: It sets a voluntary "greenhouse gas intensity" target for the nation. The idea is to reduce the ratio of greenhouse gas emissions to U.S. economic output, or GDP. But the funny thing about the White House target—an 18 percent reduction in greenhouse gas intensity by 2012—is that it would allow actual emissions to grow by 12 percent over the same period.

What's more, the administration's strategy relies entirely on voluntary measures. This despite the fact that U.S. climate policy has consisted primarily of voluntary measures for more than a decade. And what have these voluntary measures achieved? As of 2001, U.S. greenhouse gas emissions were up 11.9 percent over their 1991 levels. And so now we are more than 10 years removed from the Earth Summit, and we still—still—have no real plan in place to reduce the U.S. contribution to the problem that we and other countries identified back then as—quote—"a common concern of humankind."

The reason I have presented this history lesson is to show that, as the world has set out in the last decade to respond to the problem of climate change, the United States has been both a driver and a drag on the process, a driver in terms of development of a framework for action, a drag because we have made no serious attempt to implement that framework. We are like the boyfriend or girlfriend who says sweet things all the time but will never truly commit. And lately we aren't even saying sweet things any more.

> *We must forge a global response to the problem of climate change.*

The reality is that it is long past the time for playing these sorts of games. We should have committed long ago to serious action on this issue and, having failed, it is all the more urgent that we get serious now. What does that mean? What principles should guide these efforts? I'd like to offer five—five keys to success in meeting the challenge of climate change.

Key number one: We must forge a global response to the problem of climate change. As I already said, the United States is responsible for one-fourth of global greenhouse gas emissions. The 15 countries of the European Union are responsible for another one-fourth. The remainder is divided among other developed nations and rapidly developing countries such as China and India. And, while developed countries clearly are responsible for a majority of these emissions, that will not be the case in the future as emissions continue to grow more rapidly in developing countries than anywhere else.

It is one of the most contentious issues in the debate over global climate change—that is, the perceived divide between the interests and obligations of developed and developing countries. Equity demands that the industrialized world—the source of most past and current emissions of greenhouse gases—act first to reduce emissions. This principle is embedded in both the UNFCCC and the Kyoto Protocol, which sets binding emission targets for developed countries only. However, with the Protocol expected to enter into force sometime this year or next, it is now time to turn our attention to what happens next. And as we do this, we need to think broadly of a framework that will include not only the countries that will be implementing the Kyoto protocol, but also the United States, Australia, and the major emitting countries in the developing world.

I do not claim to know what form this framework should take. But here's what I do know: It must be effective; over the coming decades, it must significantly reduce global emissions of greenhouse gases. It also must be fair. We must recognize who bears responsibility for climate change, and who will bear the brunt of its impacts; and we must arrive at an equitable sharing of responsibility for addressing it. That probably means different kinds of measures for different countries at different times, but all the major emitting countries must do their part. Finally, this new framework must marry our environmental goals with our economic and development objectives. In the developing world in particular, commitments that are not consistent and compatible with raising standards of living and promoting sustainable economic growth have little chance of success. And even in the developed world, all countries will have to be convinced that the environmental goals they agree to, the carbon limits they accept, will not impede their efforts to sustain economic growth. This will mean not only ensuring that countries are given flexibility in how they meet their goals, but also that they can turn over the existing capital stock and acquire more climate-friendly technology at prices that they can afford.

This brings us to the second Key to Success in our efforts to address the climate issue: We need to think in terms of both short-term and long-term actions. There is a great deal we can do now to reduce our emissions. At the same time, we need to be looking ahead to longer-term, and potentially more far-reaching, reductions in the years and decades to come.

At the Pew Center, we are developing a plan we call the 10/50 Solution. The idea is to think ahead to where we need to be 50 years from now if we are going to meet the challenge of climate change, and then to figure out decade by decade how to do it.

Why look 50 years out? Because achieving the necessary reductions in our greenhouse gas emissions will ultimately require innovation on a level never before seen. It will require a massive shift away from fossil fuels to climate-friendly sources of energy. And, as I said at the start of my remarks, it will require fundamental changes in how we live and work and grow our economies.

The 10/50 approach doesn't just look long-term, though. It recognizes that in order to realize that 50-year vision, we have to start right now. We can start with the low-hanging fruit—the countless ways we can reduce greenhouse emissions at little or no cost by simply being more efficient: everything from more fuel-efficient cars and trucks, including hybrids, to energy-efficient appliances and computers, efficiency improvements in industry, and even better management of animal wastes.

In the medium to long term, the challenge is to begin what we have called a second industrial revolution. The Pew Center is just now completing a scenario analysis that identifies several technologies as essential to our ability to create a climate-friendly energy future for the United States. Among them:

- Number one: natural gas. Substituting natural gas for coal results in approximately half the carbon emissions per unit of energy supplied, but we need policies to encourage the expansion of natural gas supply and infrastructure.

- Number two: energy efficiency. We have the ability to dramatically improve the fuel economy of cars and light trucks right now and in the very near future through a combination of advances in the internal combustion engine or through hybrid electric vehicles.

- Number three: renewable energy and distributed generation. The potential here is enormous, but policy support will be essential in promoting investment and breaking barriers to market entry for these technologies.

- Number four: nuclear power. Despite its problems, the fact remains that our carbon emissions would be much higher without nuclear power.

- Number five: geological sequestration. Sequestration holds the potential of allowing for the continued production of energy from fossil fuels, including coal, even in the event of mandatory limits on carbon emissions.

- And number six: hydrogen and fuel cells. The President's recent announcement of a new federal commitment to fuel cell research was a welcome one, but we must have policies that will help pull these vehicles into the market.

The second industrial revolution is not just about responding to the challenge of climate change; it's about creating a common-sense energy future.

Looking down this list, it is hard not to see that most, if not all, of these technologies would be important even in a world where we did not have this pressing obligation to reduce the amount of greenhouse gases in the atmosphere. For energy security and economic growth reasons, and a wide range of environmental reasons as well, these are simply smart things to do. The second industrial revolution is not just about responding to the challenge of climate change; it's about creating a common-sense energy future.

And, in order to create that energy future, we are going to have to keep in mind Key to Success number three: Industry must be a partner in shaping and implementing climate solutions. The Pew Center serves as a convenor of leading businesses that are taking practical steps to reduce their contribution to the climate problem. The 38 members of our Business Environmental Leadership Council represent nearly 2.5 million employees and have combined revenues of $855 billion. They include mostly Fortune 500 firms, and they are deeply committed to climate solutions:

- There is DuPont, for example, which made a voluntary pledge to reduce its global emissions of greenhouse gases by 65 percent by the year 2010. And guess what? Late last year, they announced they had achieved this target eight years ahead of schedule.

- Also ahead of schedule in meeting its target is BP, which in 2002 announced it had reduced global greenhouse emissions by 9 million metric tons in just four years. This marked a 10-percent reduction in the company's emissions—and, like DuPont, BP had originally intended to achieve this goal in 2010.

Over the past several years, it has become clear that there are three types of companies when it comes to the issue of climate change: those that do not accept the science; those that accept the science and are working internally to reduce their contribution to the problem; and those that accept the science, are working internally and are advocating for strong government action to address this issue.

BP, DuPont, and the other companies we are working with at the Pew Center clearly fall into this latter group. And I hope that our government—as well as other governments throughout the world—will take full advantage of their expertise and commitment.

The benefits of active involvement by industry in environmental policy-making first became clear to me during negotiations on the Montreal Protocol—the agreement that set out to address the man-made threat to the Earth's protective ozone layer. An important reason for the success of that agreement, I believe, is that the companies that produced and used ozone-depleting chemicals—and that were developing substitutes for them—were very much engaged in the process. As a result, there was a factual basis and an honesty about what we could achieve, how we could achieve it, and when. And there was an acceptance on the part of industry, particularly U.S. companies, that the depletion of the ozone layer was an important problem and that multilateral action was needed.

I am happy to report that we are seeing the same kind of acceptance and determination to act on the climate issue among the companies we work with at the Pew Center. Their involvement should serve as a reminder that it is industry that will develop the technologies and the strategies that will reduce global emissions of greenhouse gases. It is industry that will have to deliver on government requirements and goals. To ignore this as we try to structure a global response to this enormous challenge is to fail.

Speaking of government, let me introduce a fourth Key to Success in responding to climate change: We have to adopt real, mandatory goals. Voluntary approaches, as I have said, simply have not worked to address this problem. In order to engage the full spectrum of industry and society, we need to set clear, mandatory goals for emission cuts, and at the same time provide sensible, business-friendly rules that give companies the flexibility they need to help meet those goals as cost-effectively as possible.

This is the approach embodied in recent legislation introduced by the bipartisan duo of Senators John McCain and Joe Lieberman. This landmark measure for the first time brings together several features that would be critical to the success of a national climate change strategy. The bill would establish ambitious and binding targets for reducing U.S. greenhouse gas emissions. Equally important, it would provide companies with the flexibility to reduce emissions as cost-effectively as possible—thanks to the creation of a rigorous nationwide system allowing emissions trading and providing some credit for carbon storage. Last but not least, the bill would recognize those reductions that are being made now by the companies that are taking the lead on this issue and provide additional flexibility for these early actors.

Of course, the McCain-Lieberman measure has little chance of becoming law any time soon, but it is an encouraging development nonetheless to see our policymakers in Washington finally coming to grips with exactly what it is going to take to yield real progress toward a climate-friendly future. And what it is going to take is a set of real, enforceable commitments.

This leads us finally, and forgive me if this seems redundant, to Key to Success number five: The United States must be an integral part of the climate solution. Despite having 4 percent of the world's population, we have contributed nearly a third of worldwide emissions of greenhouse gases in the last century, and we continue to be the largest source of these emissions worldwide. And still, we have decided to sit on the sidelines while the world moves forward with a plan to begin addressing this challenge. Even worse, we have yet to develop anything resembling a domestic program to reduce our own emissions and protect the climate.

This problem, quite simply, will not be solved without us. We owe it to ourselves, we owe it to other nations, and we owe it to future generations, to commit American ingenuity and American leadership to meeting this challenge. I think the job begins at home: We must achieve a national consensus on how best to reduce our greenhouse gas emissions. And from there, we must engage constructively with other nations in the searching for a lasting global solution.

So there you have it. Five keys to success: We need to address this issue globally. We need to think and act both short-term and long-term. We need to involve industry. We need mandatory goals. And we need the United States to do its part both at home and abroad.

Yet another key to success, as I have learned over the years, is to keep your remarks to a reasonable length. So I will stop there, and I welcome your questions.

Thank you very much.

Delivering Natural Resource Values: Four Threats to Our Mission

Dale Bosworth

Chief, United States Department of Agriculture Forest Service, 2001– ; born Altadena, CA, 1945; B.S. in forestry, University of Idaho, 1966; forester, Northern Region on the St. Joe National Forest (now part of the Idaho Panhandle National Forest) in Idaho, 1966– ; forester, Kanisksu, Colville, and Lolo National Forests; district ranger, Clearwater National Forest, ID; planning staff officer and deputy forest supervisor, Flathead National Forest, MT; assistant director for land management planning, Northern Region, Missoula, MT; forest supervisor, Wasatch-Cache National Forest, UT, in the Intermountain Region, 1986–90; deputy director, forest management, Forest Service national headquarters, Washington, DC, 1990–92; deputy regional forester, Pacific Southwest Region, headquartered San Francisco, CA, 1992–94; regional forester, Intermountain Region, Ogden, UT, 1994–97; regional forester, Northern Region of the Forest Service, Missoula, MT, 1997–2001; member, Society of American Foresters and the Society for Range Management.

Editors' introduction: Chief Bosworth spoke to the Agricultural Research Organization (ARO) at the Volcani Center campus near Tel-Aviv, Israel. The ARO, the research arm of the Israel Ministry of Agriculture, plans, organizes, and implements the greater part of Israel's agricultural research effort and has helped Israel to achieve among the highest yields in the world. In his address, Chief Bosworth explained how, with Earth Day in 1970, "came a new approach to national forest management. . . . A new set of values also emerged. Today, people in the United States value the outdoors for a higher quality of life. People value places with clean water, scenery, wildlife, and opportunities for outdoor recreation."

Dale Bosworth's speech: It's a pleasure to be here in Israel. I don't often get out of the United States, and I'm finding that opportunities like this are great learning experiences. I believe we can mutually benefit from sharing our experiences and comparing notes.

I've been the main beneficiary so far, because you've been showing me around. But now I guess it's my turn to share some experiences with you. So I'd like to tell you about some of the challenges we face as land managers in the United States.

Delivered on February 10, 2004, in Beit Dagan, Israel.

There are different perspectives on those challenges, depending on whom you ask. If you ask an environmentalist, you'll get a different perspective than if you ask a logger. Even our federal land managers have different perspectives because our missions are so different.

My perspective is from my 38 years of experience in the Forest Service. I'd like to start by telling you a little about our agency's history and purpose. Then I'll go into the main challenges we face today. We call them the four threats: fire and fuels, invasive species, loss of open space, and unmanaged outdoor recreation. Finally, I'll say a little about what we're doing to address each threat.

History and Purpose

Next year, the Forest Service will be a hundred years old. A hundred years ago, most people thought that our nation's forest resources would last forever, no matter how much we cut them and burned them. It took vision to foresee a time of timber shortages and degraded watersheds.

Fortunately, we had visionary leaders at the time, and we weren't the only ones with vision. Awhile back, I participated in a celebration at the Israeli Embassy in Washington. It was the 100th anniversary of the Jewish National Fund, which also had the foresight to restore and manage forests and rangelands in Israel. Our organizations have common roots.

About a hundred years ago, our leaders set aside a system of forest reserves to protect watersheds and timber resources for future generations. Today, the Forest Service manages about 77 million hectares of national forest land, or about 8 to 9 percent of our nation's land base. We also administer state and private forestry programs nationwide, and we have the world's largest research organization for natural resource management.

Our mission is to protect the nation's forests and grasslands for multiple uses—such as water, wildlife, and recreation—and for sustained yields of timber, forage, and other products. Although our mission has stayed the same, our management has changed enormously in the last 30 or 40 years. I'll talk about some of those changes before discussing the four main threats we face today.

One thing that's changed is what Americans want and expect from their national forests and grasslands. Fifty years ago, we thought we faced a timber famine. State and private timber stocks were exhausted following World War II, and there was a huge postwar demand for lumber to help fulfill the American dream of owning a single-family home. For decades, every U.S. administration placed high demands on the Forest Service for national forest timber.

That began to change with the first Earth Day in 1970. We got some new environmental laws, and I think that did us a lot of good as a nation. It gave us some national sideboards and a shared sense of purpose.

Out of that purpose came a new approach to national forest management. It's sometimes called ecosystem management. It has a number of basic features: watershed analysis, landscape-scale planning, collaboration across different ownership boundaries, and adaptive management. It capitalizes on new information technology. It emphasizes working closely with communities— making public involvement

> *Today, people in the United States value the outdoors for a higher quality of life.*

as meaningful as possible through collaborative decisionmaking.

A new set of values also emerged. Today, people in the United States value the outdoors for a higher quality of life. People value places with clean water, scenery, wildlife, and opportunities for outdoor recreation. So our primary job at the Forest Service is to protect the water, the scenic beauty, the wildlife habitat, and everything else that people value for a high quality of life.

Four Threats

That brings me to the four threats. In the past, people focused on timber harvest and roadbuilding as the biggest problems on national forest land. In my view, those just aren't the biggest threats we face. The biggest threats today are fire and fuels, invasive species, loss of open space, and unmanaged outdoor recreation. I'll say a little about each, beginning with fire and fuels.

Since 2000, America has had some of our worst fire seasons in 50 years. Two years ago, we had record fires in four states, and a fifth came close. Last fall, we had a record fire season in southern California. Twenty-four people lost their lives and more than 3,700 homes were destroyed. More people died and more homes were lost in the debris flows that followed when rains fell on slopes where the fires last fall had burned away the vegetation.

Later this week, I will be part of a preliminary discussion at American Independence Park, where we are planning a lasting memorial to interagency wildland firefighters in the United States and Israel who have lost their lives in the line of duty. In the last 10 years alone, we have lost about 180 wildland firefighters in the United States. The relationship between the Forest Service and JNF began about 15 years ago, and it initially revolved around fire management and suppression.

The underlying issue is that so many of our fire-dependent ecosystems have become overgrown and unhealthy. In my view, the answer is to restore ecosystems *before* the big fires break out. Where fire-dependent forests are overgrown, we've got to do some thinning, then get fire back into the ecosystem when it's safe. And in shrubby systems such as chaparral in southern California, we've got to use more prescribed fire to take some of the heat out of those systems.

A second major threat comes from nonnative invasive species, including invasive insects, diseases, plants, and birds. With the globalization of trade in commercial products such as wood and livestock, the United States has gotten a growing number of invasive species. For example, in five western states the number of new weeds generally fell by decade from the 1880s to the 1960s, but it has been rising ever since. Invasive plants now cover about 53 million hectares in the United States. That's an area about a third larger than all of California, and it is expanding at a rate of about 700,000 hectares per year. At that rate, all of Israel would be swallowed up in about three years.

The costs are enormous. By one estimate, all invasives combined cost Americans about $138 billion per year in total economic damages and associated control costs. But the ecological costs are even worse. One study found that invasives have contributed to the decline of almost half of all imperiled species in the United States.

The problems are all across the board. One study of fish species across North America found that two out of three extinctions were at least partially caused by introduced species. Introduced diseases have also affected major forest trees such as western white pine, American elm, and American chestnut. We are losing our national heritage.

A third threat is loss of open space. Every day, the United States loses about 1,600 hectares of open space to development. That's more than 1 hectare per minute, and the rate of conversion is getting faster all the time. In some places, we're losing large, relatively undisturbed forests that endangered mammals like grizzly bear need to survive. In other places, we're losing rangeland that many native plants and animals need to survive, including elk. And where private open space is lost, recreational pressures on public lands tend to grow.

That brings me to the fourth threat—unmanaged outdoor recreation. A good example is off-road vehicles, such as all-terrain vehicles. In the United States, the number of off-road vehicle users has just exploded. It grew from about 5 million in 1972 to almost 36 million in 2000.

Ninety-nine percent of the users are responsible. But with all those millions of users, even the one percent who are the problem can have enormous impacts. Each year, the national forests get hundreds of miles of unauthorized roads and trails created by repeated cross-country use. We're seeing more erosion, water degradation, and habitat destruction. We're seeing more conflicts between users. We have got to improve our management so we get responsible recreational use based on sound outdoor ethics.

Finding Solutions

These are the four main threats we face today—fire and fuels, invasive species, loss of open space, and unmanaged outdoor recreation. These are the main things that keep us from delivering the values that Americans want—clean water, wildlife habitat, and so forth.

We're doing something about them. With respect to fire and fuels, the long-term solution is to restore healthy ecosystems, and we've made a start through a federal program called the National Fire Plan. The area we treat with thinning and prescribed burning together with other federal agencies has gone way up in recent years. In fiscal 2002, it was about 900,000 hectares—twice as much as 5 or 10 years ago.

But we need to do more. A big hindrance has been all the process we need to go through. It's caused huge delays and eaten up our resources. Our forest supervisors often tell me that they spend 60 to 70 percent of their direct resources on planning and assessment, including a lot of needless paperwork.

We're fixing that. Through the Healthy Forests Initiative and a new piece of legislation called the Healthy Forests Restoration Act, we've gotten some new legal and administrative tools for streamlining some of our processes. For example, where we need to move quickly against a threat from fire or insects, we've reduced the need for exhaustive environmental studies. That should also let us redirect some of our resources to the ground, where it counts.

With respect to invasive species, we find that prevention and control can work pretty well if they're done across ownerships on a landscape scale. The Forest Service has some good partnership programs with the states, such as Slow-the-Spread for gypsy moth and weed-free hay certification for animals used to pack in recreationists and other people. We had good success working with the city of Chicago to stop the Asian longhorned beetle. We're now preparing a national strategy for dealing with invasive species. It will probably focus on a few of the worst problems.

With respect to loss of open space, one solution is to keep ranches and working forests in operation. The Forest Service sponsors conservation easements through the states so that willing landowners can keep their lands forested, and we've just had a big increase in funding for that program. For example, we just signed an agreement to protect 132,000 hectares of working forest in Maine through a conservation easement. We also have forage reserves that ranchers can use to give their grazing allotments a rest, and we've gotten new funding for conservation easements on grasslands. Through programs like these, we can work together across the landscape to keep the land whole.

Finally, we're making a big effort to improve our management of outdoor recreation. Over the next several years, all national forests will assess inventories of roads, trails, and areas used by ORVs.

From those inventories, they will designate a system of routes offering the best opportunities for ORV use while still meeting our responsibility to protect the environment. The focus will be on improving our travel management. We also want to engage user groups and get more volunteers involved. We want ORV users to take responsibility for their national forests, to tread lightly on the land, and to pass on a "tread-lightly" ethic to others.

Partners and Friends

These are some of the problems we face and some of the approaches we're taking for more sustainable natural environments in the United States. Before closing, I'd like to say a few words about our relationship with the Jewish National Fund.

The Forest Service and JNF have developed a collaborative relationship around our common responsibility to manage arid and semi-arid wildlands. I mentioned our common roots. Both of our organizations are celebrating a hundred years as responsible stewards of the land.

Both of our organizations are focused on providing a sustainable future for our wildlands in the face of great pressure from this or that special interest.

A hundred years ago, our conservation mandate was this: to provide the greatest good for the greatest number for the longest time. We now talk about the same thing in terms of sustainability. Both of our organizations are focused on providing a sustainable future for our wildlands in the face of great pressure from this or that special interest.

That's why it makes sense for us to work together. Our collaborative work with JNF over the last 15 years has led to progress in both of our countries toward sustainable forests and rangelands. Based on that success, we've decided to expand on our more traditional collaborative projects in wildland management. We are entering a new phase of collaboration. Specifically, we are working closely with the JNF leadership to explore ways of better understanding and adapting to changing public attitudes.

In the past, we tended to see sustainability primarily in terms of the quantitative measures of economic and ecological productivity. Today, we also see sustainability in terms of the value that society places on the lands we manage. The quantitative measures are still important, but both of our organizations are trying to do a better job of understanding how the public values its natural resources and evaluates the job we're doing of sustainably managing those resources. As part of that here in Israel, the Forest Service has agreed to join an International Evaluation Committee that JNF is chartering to look at the professional management of Israel's wild-lands. I am sure we will learn from this experience.

Time for Change

In closing, I'll sum up. In my 38 years at the Forest Service, I've seen some enormous changes. Our forests have changed, society's needs and expectations have changed, and the tools at our disposal have changed.

The way we manage the land has also changed. We've learned that what we leave on the land is more important than what we take away. Today, we focus on delivering the full range of the values that Americans want for quality of life: clean air and water, habitat for wildlife, and all the rest.

What hasn't changed enough is the debate. Too often, we're still debating issues from 20 or 30 years ago—issues like timber harvesting and roads. But we've started to change the debate. I think we're getting more people focused on the real threats we face today—fire and fuels, invasive species, loss of open space, and unmanaged outdoor recreation.

We've made a start in addressing the four threats. The challenge will be to continue the momentum. For the Forest Service, that means implementing the new legal and administrative tools we've gotten in the right way. If we do, I think we'll see steady progress on the ground, at least for fire and fuels. But I think we can also make headway against the other threats.

Maybe we can make some headway together. I am interested in learning more about how our collaboration with the Jewish National Fund is solving these types of problems. I'd be interested in hearing more from you about these problems here in Israel. If we can learn something from you about how to tackle these problems, then maybe we can move forward more quickly in the United States.

I appreciate the opportunity to spend this time with you and would be happy to answer any questions you might have about our situation in the United States.

National Association of Manufacturers

Pete V. Domenici

U.S. senator (R), New Mexico, 1972– ; born Albuquerque, NM, May 7, 1932; worked in father's wholesale grocery business; B.S. in education, University of New Mexico, 1954; pitcher, Albuquerque Dukes, Brooklyn Dodgers farm club, 1954; math teacher, Garfield Junior High, Albuquerque, 1954–55; law degree, University of Denver, 1958; partner, Domenici and Bonham, 1958– 72; elected to Albuquerque City Commission, 1966–68; Commission chair (mayor), 1967; member—Senate Appropriations Committee, Energy and Natural Resources Committee, Committee on Environmental and Public Works, Governmental Affairs Committee, Presidential Avisory Committee on Federalism, and Republican Policy Committee; chair—Senate Subcommittee on Energy Research and Development, Budget Committee, Committee on Indian affairs, and Committee on Energy and Natural Resources; recipient—National League of Cities award for Outstanding Performance in Congress; Distinguished Service award, Tax Foundation, 1986; Legislator of the Year award, National Mental Health Association, 1987; Public Sector Leadership Award, 1996.

Editors' introduction: Senator Domenici spoke to the National Association of Manufacturers (NAM) about rising oil, gasoline, and natural gas prices and the feasibility of mining coal. He predicted that these "very problems" would "create a perfect storm for the passage of an energy bill." The mission of NAM, established in 1895 and now the nation's largest industrial trade association, is to enhance the competitiveness of manufacturers and to improve American living standards by advocating legislation and regulations that would foster economic growth. The group also seeks to increase understanding among policymakers, the media, and the public about the importance of manufacturing to America's economic strength.

Pete V. Domenici's speech: Last week, T. Boone Pickens publicly predicted that we will see oil go up to $50 per barrel before we will see it go below $30 per barrel.

I am not a market forecaster. I don't know if Boone is right or not. It is possible that the recent price hikes are the result of market psychology instead of the relationship between supply and demand or the threat of terrorism to international wells and shipping ports.

If it's market psychology, prices should fall after the summer driving season.

Delivered on May 18, 2004, at Washington, DC.

On the other hand, Boone may be right. We may have moved into an era of extraordinarily high oil prices.

First, several international supply issues could keep prices high: 1. Venezuelan production is down; 2. Nigerian reserves estimates have been lowered; 3. Iraqi production is still low and jeapordized by military and political instability, and; 4. OPEC seems comfortable maintaining production quotas at current levels.

> *I think OPEC sees us for what we are. We are hooked on imported oil.*

I have some additional concerns that will affect oil prices in the near future.

1. Oil is still priced in dollars. That means oil has been insulated from the recent decline in the value of the dollar versus the euro. I worry that OPEC nations might begin trading oil in euros or some other non-dollar denomination. If that were the case today, oil prices would have increased 30 percent in the last year, just based just on the decline in the dollar.

2. I am also very concerned about increase in global demand. China has surpassed Japan to become the second largest importer of oil behind the United States. Chinese crude oil imports rose by a staggering 31 percent last year, at an increased cost of 55 percent.

3. I think we have underestimated the compounding effect of increasing world populations and simultaneously increasing standards of living. These factors increase the global demand for energy at an extraordinary rate. That will have a dramatic and lasting impact on the price we pay for foreign oil.

4. Finally, I am concerned that relations between the United States and Saudi Arabia are not what they were 25 years ago. I think our "friends" in the Middle East take a much more pragmatic, business approach to dealing with us. I also worry that our relative influence in the region is declining. Some have suggested that we "jaw-bone" the Saudis and the rest of OPEC into increasing production. I don't want to discount that idea, but I have to wonder why OPEC would respond to our pleas. There is no consensus in Congress to either decrease our demand by sharply increasing CAFÉ standards or increase our supply by opening ANWR or producing more from the Outer Continental Shelf.

I think OPEC sees us for what we are. We are hooked on imported oil. We now import nearly 60 percent of our oil and expect to import 70 percent by 2025. Gasoline costs more than $2 per gallon in most of the country and the price will likely go up through the summer. These facts don't seem to shock people. There is no public outcry. We seem to have broken through any psychological barrier we may have had to these startling facts and have accepted them as our destiny.

Let me speak to a recent proposal that the president open up the Strategic Petroleum Reserve and start releasing that oil supply into the market. Frankly, I think that's the worst idea I've heard all year. Why would we risk a valuable national security asset for a penny's saving on the price of gasoline? When President Clinton opened SPR to ease gasoline prices, we saw the price of a barrel of oil drop by a few dollars for a few days. But for the next several weeks, gasoline prices dropped by only one penny per gallon.

We are a nation at war. We live in a world dominated, more than ever before, by violence and the fear of terrorism. We face the real possibility of having our oil supplies disrupted if key pipelines, refineries, or tankers are attacked by terrorists.

If we tap SPR now, because gas prices are high, we leave ourselves with no margin for error. If our oil supply is cut, we are powerless to protect our own ongoing commerce.

I believe we must vigilantly protect SPR as a vital national security asset.

Of course, oil prices aren't our only energy challenge.

For the last 20 years, natural gas was the energy of choice for new power plants. It was clean. It was affordable. And was in abundant supply. Now, supplies are tight and prices have been climbing steadily since June 2000. Today, natural gas is almost prohibitively expensive.

In its 2004 forecast, the Energy Information administration predicted that, by 2025, the U.S. would import 30 percent of its natural gas as liquefied natural gas [LNG]. Right now, it looks like local opposition on both coasts may keep us from building LNG import facilities.

Gulf states like Louisiana, Texas, and Mississippi may welcome LNG facilities. They already have a huge natural gas infrastructure from production in the Gulf. But then we have to ship it to the states that use the most natural gas: the same East and West coasts that refuse to import it. The high cost of transporting LNG across country doesn't do much to relieve natural gas prices.

Not surprisingly, utilities are switching from natural gas to coal. That's driving up the price of coal. Wholesale coal prices rose more than 30 percent over the last year.

Over the next 20 years, our demand for coal is expected to exceed our demand for natural gas. The demand will make coal mining more efficient and I think the price of coal will come down over time. But I keep waiting for the other shoe to drop. If we implement proposals to regulate CO_2 or tighten the Clean Air Act, the cost of burning coal could climb sharply.

None of these problems are new. Congress and the administration are keenly aware of them. Three years ago yesterday, the president issued his National Energy Policy Plan. He outlined the challenges ahead, proposed solutions, and called on Congress to pass a comprehensive energy bill that would put his proposals to work.

He called for the development of hydrogen cars and more wind, solar, and geothermal energy. He called for more nuclear energy, increased domestic production of oil, and more clean coal. He outlined a plan that ensured us a supply of clean, abundant, and affordable energy for decades to come.

The House has passed an energy bill three times. It's still struggling in the Senate—mostly because the Senate is very closely divided and Democrats do not want to give the president a victory on this issue.

But I am optimistic that we will get an energy bill this year. The very problems I have identified are combining to create a perfect storm for the passage of an energy bill.

We will do more to produce our own oil in the Gulf of Mexico and from inland wells— helping to stabilize oil prices.

Natural gas prices are so high they are driving tens of thousands of manufacturing jobs overseas. Rising gasoline prices have peeled $31 billion from our economy this past year. Meanwhile, rising crude oil prices caused the stock market to fall this week.

Last summer, we were hit by the worst power outage this country has ever known. Consumers understand electricity better than they did before and they are demanding reliable power. They expect Congress to mandate that reliability.

Energy prices are hitting consumers hard. They are driving up the price of everything, from the silicon chips in your computer—which is made from petroleum—to the price of groceries. These aren't happy events. But I believe they are events that might force Congress to act.

I have an energy bill that will invest nearly $2 billion dollars into the development of hydrogen cars. It will increase by tenfold the production of wind energy. We will see a rise in the production of solar and geothermal energy.

With my bill, we will conserve more energy. The bill offers tax credits for buying energy efficient cars, building energy efficient homes, and manufacturing energy-efficient appliances.

We will build a pipeline that brings the largest, untapped supply of natural gas in this country down from Alaska to stabilize natural gas prices. We will do more to produce our own oil in the Gulf of Mexico and from inland wells—helping to stabilize oil prices.

We will burn coal more cleanly that we imagined was possible 10 years ago. We will mandate electricity reliability and expand and modernize our national grid.

We will produce more, conserve more, and diversify our national energy supply.

Historically, this has been a country that found victory in its darkest hours. We have done so in war. We expect to do so again in this new war against terror. Likewise, our presidents and our Congresses rise to meet our domestic challenges. Despite politics and elections, we have always found a way to solve our biggest problems. I believe that the bigger our energy challenges become, the more likely this Congress will come together to find solutions.

The energy bill isn't perfect. But it's the first big step in solving our energy problems. Delivering this energy bill to the president's desk addresses the immediate crises and sows the seeds for the next generation of energy solutions.

Cumulative Speaker Index: 2000–2004

A cumulative speaker index to the volumes of *Representative American Speeches* for the years 1937–1938 through 1959–1960 appears in the 1959–1960 volume; for the years 1960–1961 through 1969–1970, see the 1969–1970 volume; for the years 1970–1971 through 1979–1980, see the 1979–1980 volume; for the years 1980–1981 through 1989–1990, see the 1989–1990 volume; and for the years 1990–1991 through 1999–2000, see the 1999–2000 volume.

Abrams, Janet, and Laurie Girand, 2001–2002, pp135–138, S.T.O.P.'s Position on FDA's Efforts Toward BSE to Date

Ashcroft, John, 2001–2002, pp99–102, Remarks on the National Security Entry-Exit Registration System

Bailey, Antoinette M., 2000–2001, pp113–138, Thoughts on Building a House for Diversity

Barnes, Jerry, 2003–2004, pp117–120, Veterans Day Speech

Bilchik, Shay, 2002–2003, pp149–154, Opening Remarks to National Conference "Children 2003, Imagine an America"

Blakey, Marion C., 2002–2003, pp171–175, Centennial of Flight Kick-Off Event

Bordogna, Joseph, 2002–2003, pp167–170, Creating a Better Future

Bosworth, Dale, 2003–2004, pp177–183, Delivering Natural Resource Values: Four Threats To Our Mission

Bronson, Rachel, 2003–2004, pp68–73, New Directions in U.S. Foreign Policy?: From Regime Change to Nation-Building

Buchanan, Patrick J., 2000–2001, pp139–145, To Reunite a Nation

Bush, George W., 2001–2002, pp11–18, Address to a Joint Session of Congress and the American People; 2002–2003, pp24–31, Remarks on Iraq; 2003–2004, pp100–106, Progress in the War on Terror

Bush, Laura Welch, 2001–2002, pp26–27, Taliban Oppression of Women and Children

Byrd, Robert C., 2002–2003, pp38–43, The Road to Cover-up Is the Road to Ruin

Cameron, Nigel M. de S., 2001–2002, pp178–188, Biotechnology and the Struggle for Human Dignity: Whatever Happened to the Human Race?

Chao, Elaine L., 2001–2002, pp105–109, State of the Workforce

Chavez-Thompson, Linda, 2001–2002, pp86–89, Immigration Reform

Cheney, Richard (Dick), 2000–2001, pp176–181, Remarks at the Annual Meeting of the Associated Press

Claussen, Eileen, 2003–2004, pp168–176, Tackling Climate Change: Five Keys to Success

Clinton, Hillary Rodham, 2002–2003, pp63–70, "To Provide for the Common Defense"; 2003–2004, pp74–80, New American Strategies for Security and Peace

Comey, James B., Jr., 2003–2004, pp148–152, Mitigating the Impact of Intellectual Property Theft and Counterfeiting

Conko, Gregory, 2001–2002, pp139–148, Behind the Headlines: What Laymen Should Know About Everyday Issues in Science and Health

Daschle, Thomas, 2001–2002, pp110–122, America's Economy: Rising to Our New Challenges

DeGioia, John J., 2002–2003, pp104–108, Principles of Speech and Expression

DeLong, James V., 2003–2004, pp140–147, Privacy and Piracy

Dill, Karen E., 2002–2003, pp155–158, Real Life Unplugged

Dingell, John D., 2001–2002, pp149–154, Food Safety and Bioterrorism Legislation

Dodd, Chris, 2002–2003, pp176–179, Tribute to the Astronauts of the Space Shuttle *Columbia*

Domenici, Pete V., 2003–2004, pp184–188, National Association of Manufacturers

Donio, Jim, 2003–2004, pp158–160, Coalition of Entertainment Retail Trade Associations (CERTA) Congressional Fly-In Media Briefing

Donohue, Mary O., 2001–2002, pp50–56, Maria College Commencement

Donovan, John B., 2000–2001, pp105–109, Bringing Hope to Youth: Religious Education for Public School Students

Fanton, Jonathan F., 2001–2002, pp28–32, Chicago Council on Foreign Relations

Feinstein, Dianne, 2003–2004, pp25–32, Call for Restructuring of the Intelligence Community

Feldbaum, Carl B., 2001–2002, pp163–170, Keeping the Faith

Gephardt, Richard A., 2000–2001, pp90–97, Educating America: A National Challenge for the 21st Century

Giles, Bob, 2002–2003, pp109–116, Preserving an Open Democracy in a Time of Crisis

Ginsburg, Ruth Bader, 2000–2001, pp3–20, Remarks on Judicial Independence: The Situation of the U.S. Federal Judiciary

Girand, Laurie, and Janet Abrams, 2001–2002, pp135–138, S.T.O.P.'s Position on FDA's Efforts Toward BSE to Date

Giuliani, Rudolph W., 2001–2002, pp19–25, United Nations General Assembly Special Session on Terrorism

Guengerich, Galen J., 2001–2002, pp6–10, The Shaking of the Foundations

Hamilton, Lee H., and Thomas H. Kean, 2003–2004, pp47–53, Release of 9/11 Commission Report

Hamilton, Mark R., 2002–2003, pp91–95, Academic Freedom Award

Harman, Jane, 2003–2004, pp13–19, The Intelligence on Iraq's WMD: Looking Back to Look Forward

Harris, Gwendolyn L., 2002–2003, pp159–164, Meeting of the African American Heritage Parade Committee

Harshbarger, Scott, 2000–2001, pp58–67, Regarding Election Reform

Hart, Gary, 2003–2004, pp57–67, Principled Engagement: America's Role in the 21st-Century World

Henderson, Wade, 2001–2002, pp97–98, Statement at SEIU Immigration Press Conference

Hogan, Kathleen B., 2000–2001, pp161–165, Remarks at the Fifth Annual Green Power Marketing Conference

Hopper, John D., Jr., 2003–2004, pp127–132, Tuskegee Airmen Dinner

Hutchings, Robert, 2003–2004, pp3–12, Strategic Choices, Intelligence Challenges

Hutchison, Kay Bailey, 2002–2003, pp180–183, Commemorating the *Columbia* Astronauts

Jefferson-Jenkins, Carolyn, 2000–2001, pp49–57, Making Democracy Work

Jones, Julia Hughes, 2000–2001, pp43–48, Vote Theft 2000: Selecting Our Leaders Fairly and Honestly

Kabbani, Shaykh Muhammad Hisham, 2001–2002, pp33–40, Muslims Within the Democratic Framework

Kaptur, Marcy, 2002–2003, pp19–23, Allies Working Toward a Secure Future

Kay, David, 2003–2004, pp20–24, Testimony Before the Senate Armed Services Committee About WMD in Iraq

Kean, Thomas H., and Lee H. Hamilton, 2003–2004, pp47–53, Release of 9/11 Commission Report

Kennedy, Edward M., 2002–2003, pp10–18, Eliminating the Threat: The Right Course of Action for Disarming Iraq, Combating Terrorism, Protecting the Homeland, and Stabilizing the Middle East

Kerry, John, 2003–2004, pp93–99, Security and Strength for a New World

Kohn, Alfie, 2000–2001, pp110–116, Standardized Testing and Its Victims

Krikorian, Mark, 2001–2002, pp90–96, Immigration and Civil Rights in the Wake of September 11

Langevin, James, 2001–2002, pp171–173, Testimony at the Hearing on Stem Cell Research

Lebow, Steven J., 2000–2001, pp151–158, There Are Giants in Our Midst

Lee, Bill Lann, 2000–2001, pp33–40, Remarks to the National Consortium of Task Forces and Commissions on Racial and Ethnic Bias in the Courts

Levin, Richard C., 2002–2003, pp184–188, Confronting Uncertainty

Lieberman, Joseph, 2002–2003, pp71–79, Safe and Sound: Strengthening American Security Today

Loria, Christopher J. "Gus," 2001–2002, pp43–49, In Defense of Liberty

Lynch, Timothy, 2002–2003, pp122–128, Combating Terrorism, Preserving Freedom

McCain, John, 2000–2001, pp68–73, Opening Statement on Campaign Finance Reform

McConnell, Mitch, 2000–2001, pp74–76, Proposing an Amendment to the Constitution of the United States

McGee, Liam E., 2000–2001, pp79–89, Education Is Everybody's Business

McMasters, Paul K., 2002–2003, pp96–103, The State of Freedom Post 9/11

Merrifield, Jeffrey S., 2000–2001, pp182–194, A Vision of Tomorrow, a Plan for Today

Mineta, Norman Y., 2002–2003, pp47–55, Senate Appropriations Committee

Moyer, Thomas J., 2000–2001, pp27–32, Cleveland City Club

Mullarkey, Mary J., 2000–2001, pp21–26, The Recent Presidential Election: The Residual Effects on the Courts

Murano, Elsa, 2001–2002, pp155–160, Taking Food Safety to the Next Level

Murkowski, Frank H., 2000–2001, pp170–175, A National Energy Crisis Is upon Us

Nelson, Douglas W., 2002–2003, pp131–136, Children's Behavioral Health Conference on "What Works"

Nelson, Gaylord, 2003–2004, pp163–167, National Press Club Luncheon

Newman, Stuart A., 2001–2002, pp174–177, Testimony at the Hearing on Human Cloning

Norton, Gale, 2003–2004, pp121–126, Women During the War

Paige, Rod, 2002–2003, pp144–148, Before the States Institute on International Education in the Schools

Pataki, George E., 2001–2002, pp3–5, Joint Session of the New York State Legislature

Pavitt, James L., 2003–2004, pp33–46, Foreign Policy Association

Pertman, Adam, 2002–2003, pp137–143, Understanding Adoption: A View for Psychiatrists

Pitt, Harvey L., 2001–2002, pp123–127, Remarks Before the Economic Club of New York

Powell, Colin L., 2001–2002, pp59–65, Acceptance of the 14th Annual Philadelphia Liberty Medal; 2002–2003, pp3–9, Testimony Before the House Committee on International Relations; 2003–2004, pp81–92, 2004 Annual Kennan Institute Dinner

Reed, Lawrence W., 2000–2001, pp117–129, A New Direction for Education Reform

Rice, Condoleezza, 2002–2003, pp32–37, Terrorism Grows in the Absence of Progress

Richardson, Bill, 2000–2001, pp166–169, Remarks on California's Electricity Event

Ridge, Tom, 2002–2003, pp84–88, Remarks at Department of Homeland Security Employees Event

Rumsfeld, Donald H., 2001–2002, pp68–70, Arlington National Cemetery Funeral Service for the Unidentified Victims of the Attack on the Pentagon

Sacconaghi, Michele Cavataio, 2000–2001, pp98–104, The Future Is Now: Education in the Internet Age

Schweiker, Mark S., 2001–2002, pp66–67, Flight 93: Our Heroes, Our Family

Seifert, Harold J. "Bud," 2003–2004, pp109–114, Veterans Day 2003

Spanier, Graham B., 2003–2004, pp153–157, The Digital Piracy Dilemma

Sposato, Janis, 2002–2003, pp56–62, Homeland Security: Tracking International Students in Higher Education—Progress and Issues Since 9/11

Stein, Dan, 2001–2002, pp73–85, U.S. Asylum Policy: Reforms Needed in Current System

Sweeney, John J., 2001–2002, pp128–132, Remarks on the Wall Street Rally

Valenti, Jack, 2003–2004, pp135–139, The Moral Imperative

Walters, Lawrence G., 2002–2003, pp117–121, Lou Frey Symposium

Webb, Nicole, 2003–2004, pp115–116, Hope and Freedom

Whitman, Christine Todd, 2002–2003, pp80–83, American Water Works Association's National Water Security Conference

Yasin, Zayed Muhammed, 2001–2002, pp57–58, Of Faith and Citizenship: My American Jihad

Yates, Albert C., 2000–2001, pp146–150, Diversity: A Spirit of Community

Index

Abraham, Spence, 100
Abu Zubaydah, 41
Acheson, Dean, 86
Afghanistan
    9/11 Commission Report, 50
    Bush on, 103, 106
    change in focus and, 8
    Intelligence Community and, 36, 37, 40
    Kerry on, 95
    nation building in, 70, 72
    NATO and, 90
    Pakistan and, 64
    Powell on, 85, 88
    terrorists and, 110
African Americans, 127–132
Agricultural Research Organization (ARO), 177
Al Qaeda
    9/11 Commission Report, 49, 50
    attacks planned, 96
    Bush on, 103
    Intelligence Community and, 15, 36, 39, 41
    Kerry on, 95
    Powell on, 14
    September 11 and, 45
    in Yemen, 61
Alabama, 151
Albright, Madeleine, 82, 83, 91
Alexander, Lamar, 100
alliances
    difficulty maintaining, 6
    Kerry on, 94, 95
    Powell on, 89, 90
    principled engagement and, 60
American dream, 136
American Prospect, The, 74
American Women's Voluntary Services, 125

Amnesty International, 72
Anderson, Charles "Chief", 128, 130, 131
Anderson, Jim, 130
Andrews Sisters, 122
Angelou, Maya, 123
anti-Americanism, 6, 69
Arlington National Cemetery, 111
Armistice Day, 112
Ashcroft, John, 150, 153
Asia Society, 68
Australia, 172

Balkans, 70–72, 110
al Baluchi, Abu Musab, 41
Barnes, Jerry, 117–120
Ben-Veniste, Richard, 47
Bierce, Ambrose, 137
bin Attash, Khalid, 41
bin Laden, Osama
    9/11 Commission Report, 49, 50
    Intelligence Community and, 15, 40, 41
    Kerry on, 95
biological weapons enforcement protocol, 75
Bishop, Hazel, 125
Blair, Tony, 88
blue star, 123
Bosworth, Dale, 177–183
BP, 175
Bradshaw, David, 101
Broader Middle East Initiative, 106
Bronson, Rachel, 68–73
Brown v. Board of Education, 131
Bullard, Jacques, 128
Burns, Bill, 88
Bush, George H. W., 79
Bush, George W.
    9/11 Commission and, 47–48
    foreign policy of, 92
    Hart on, 57
    on Iraq, 78, 86
    Kerry on, 93, 95, 98
    Kyoto Protocol and, 171

on nation building, 70
National Energy Policy Plan, 187
on natural resources, 167
on terrorism, 82, 105
transparency and, 77
undermining democracy, 75
unilateralism and, 6
War on Terror, 100–106
on WMD, 13–14, 20, 28, 29
Business Environmental Leadership
    Council, 174
Business Software Alliance, 148
Byrd-Hagel resolution, 170

California, 179
Carnegie Endowment for International
    Peace, 14
Castro, Fidel, 91
cemeteries, 111, 112, 113, 119
Center for American Progress, 74
Central Intelligence Agency (CIA)
    Bush on, 105
    Director of Central Intelligence and,
        18
    Directorate of Operations, 33
    increasing size, 39
    as pathfinder, 42
    recommendations for, 30
    shrinking size of, 38
Century Foundation, 74
Cheney, Dick, 77
Chicago, 181
China
    as U.S. ally, 91
    changes and, 5, 12
    democratic evolution in, 64, 65
    greenhouse gas emissions and, 172
    military power of, 63
    oil demand of, 185
    Vietnam War and, 119
Chirac, Jacques, 21, 82
Christensen, Tom, 6
Churchill, Winston, 84
Civil Air Patrol, 125
Civil Rights Act (1964), 132
Claussen, Eileen, 168–176
Clean Air Act, 186
climate change, 168–176
Clinton administration

Iraq and, 15
Kyoto Protocol, 75, 170
natural resources and, 167
Strategic Petroleum Reserve, 186
on terrorism, 82
unilateralism and, 6
Clinton, Hillary Rodham, 74–80
Coalition of Entertainment Retail Trade
    Associations (CERTA), 158–160
Coast Guard, 126
Code of Conduct, 110, 138
Cohen, Stuart, 9
Cold War
    Corona program and, 44
    end of, 4
    intelligence and, 6–7
    NATO and, 89
    Tolkachev and, 37–38
Coleman, Bessie, 128
Colombia, 36
Comey, James B., Jr., 148–152
communism, containment of, 58, 67
Comprehensive Test Ban Treaty, 75
Computer and Telecommunications
    Coordinators (CTCs), 150
Computer Crime and Intellectual Prop-
    erty Section (CCIPS), 150
Computer Hacking and Intellectual
    Property (CHIP) Units, 150
Congo, 64
Congress
    Armistice Day, 112
    on digital piracy, 155
    on integration, 131
    Intelligence Community and, 43
    9/11 Commission Report, 52
    oil demand and, 185
    on property rights, 146–147
    recommendations for, 30, 79
    on sustainability, 166
    on terrorism, 104
    war making and, 28
Corona program, 44
Costello, Elvis, 155
Council on Foreign Relations, 57, 69
counterfeiting, 148–152
Counterterrorist Center, 39
Cuba, 110
Cuban missile crisis, 6, 23, 38, 91

Davis, Benjamin O., Jr., 129
Declaration of Independence, 76
Defense Department, 19
DeLong, James V., 140–147
democracy
    America as, 58
    applying rules of, 75
    doctrine of preemption and, 77
    Powell on, 85
    principled engagement and, 60
    tensions in, 76
denial and deception (D&D), 7, 9
Department of Energy, 165
Department of Veterans Affairs, 110, 111
Digital Millennium Copyright Act, 154,
    155, 156
digital rights movement (DRM), 144–145
digital technology
    DeLong on, 140–147
    intellectual property rights and, 149
    piracy and, 153–157
    Valenti on, 135–139
diplomacy, 84, 88, 91, 94
Dole, Robert, 79
Domenici, Pete V., 184–188
Donio, Jim, 158–160
Duelfer, Charles, 23
Dulles, Allen, 45
DuPont, 174, 175

Earth Day, 163, 177, 178
Earth Summit, 169
East Asia, 5
Economic Espionage Act, 151
ecosystem management, 179
Eisenhower, Dwight D., 112
Eldred v. Ashcroft, 146
energy, renewable, 174, 187
England. *See* Great Britain
Europe, 5, 45, 73
European Union, 172

Faulkner, William, 135
Federal Bureau of Investigation (FBI),
    18, 39, 52, 101
Feinstein, Dianne, 25–32
Fielding, Fred F., 47
file sharing. *See* peer-to-peer
Financial Times, 81
Finley, Mike, 167

foreign policy
    Kerry on, 93–99
    nation building, 68–73
    new strategies, 74–80
    Powell on, 81–92
    principled engagement, 57–67
Forest Service, 177–183
Fox, Vincente, 76
France, 71, 111
Fricke, Lisa, 117

GAO, audits by, 78
Gardner, Jay, 72
Gates, Robert, 16
Gellman, Barton, 14
General Robert M. Shoemaker High
    School (Texas), 113
geological sequestration, 174
Germany
    cooperation with, 105
    nation building in, 70
    NATO and, 90
    Powell in, 83
    on WMD, 21
Gettysburg (PA), 113
Ginsburg, Ruth Bader, 146
global warming, 168–176
globalization, 66, 67
Gnutella, 137
gold star, 123
Goldwater-Nichols Act (1986), 19, 51
Gore, Al, 170
Gorelick, Jamie S., 48
Gorton, Slade, 48
Goss, Porter, 17
"government girls", 124
Graham, Bob, 16, 31
Gray Lady Corps, 126
Great Britain, 63, 101, 111, 154
Greatest Generation, 93, 94, 99, 123
greenhouse gas emissions, 169–173
Grokster, 137, 157
Gross Domestic Product (GDP), 148, 171

Hagel, Chuck, 79
Haiti, 70, 88
Hambali, 41
Hamilton, Lee H., 26, 48–53, 81, 82, 87
Hamre, John, 16
Harkin, Tom, 78
Harman, Jane, 13–19

Hart, Gary, 57–67, 93
Hazlitt, William, 139
Al Hazmi, Salem, 48
Healthy Forests Initiative, 181
Healthy Forests Restoration Act, 181
Heartland Military Museum, 120
Helms, Richard, 44
homeland security, 18, 101
Hopper, John D., Jr., 127–132
Hunnicutt, Doris, 115
Hussein, Qusay, 36
Hussein, Saddam
    biological weapons and, 14, 16, 28, 29
    Bush on, 103, 104
    diplomacy and, 91
    intelligence assessments about, 27
    Iraq under, 41
    meeting threat of, 32
    support of, 61
Hussein, Uday, 36
Hutchings, Robert, 3–12
hydrogen, 174, 187

Ikenberry, John, 6
India, 64, 65, 88, 172
informed consent, 75
intellectual property
    CERTA and, 158–160
    DeLong on, 140–147
    digital piracy and, 153–157
    mitigating theft of, 148–152
    Valenti on, 135–139
Intellectual Property Task Force, 153
Intelligence Authorization Act, 31
Intelligence Community
    imperative of reform, 18–19
    increased authority for, 24
    Kerry on, 97
    9/11 Commission Report, 51
    Pavitt on, 33–46
    restructuring, 3–12, 25–32
    skepticism about, 17
    WMD and, 15
international alignments
    IP crime and, 152
    Iraq and, 5
    Middle East and, 5
    nation building and, 71

    peace-making and, 66
International Atomic Energy Agency,
    102
Internet, 137, 144, 152
Iran
    Bush on, 106
    foreign policy and, 62
    nuclear program and, 21, 42, 105
    support of regime in, 60
Iraq
    Bush on, 103, 106
    CIA and, 42
    Clinton on, 78, 79
    foreign policy and, 61, 69
    General Robert M. Shoemaker High
        School and, 114
    intelligence community and, 27, 36,
        37
    international alignments and, 5
    Kerry on, 95
    nation building in, 72–73
    NATO and, 90
    Pavitt on, 41
    Powell on, 85, 88
    Resolution 1441 and, 21
    restructuring of, 64
    terrorists and, 110
    332nd air expeditionary wing and,
        132
    Vietnam War and, 119
    WMD program, 7, 9–10, 104
    See also weapons of mass destruction
Iraqi Survey Group
    Kay and, 10, 20
    on Resolution 1441, 21
    WMD and, 8
Israel, 62, 177, 182–183
Italy, 71, 105

James, Harold, 11
Japan, 91, 185
"jaw-jaw", 84
Al-Jazeera, 40
Jewish National Fund, 178, 179, 182–
    183
John Paul II, Pope, 165
Johnson, Lyndon B., 24, 132
Jollie, Susan, 126